SPEAK TRUTH TO POWER

SPEAK TRUTH TO POWER

BLACK PROFESSIONAL CLASS IN UNITED STATES HISTORY

Darlene Clark Hine

Foreword by Joe W. Trotter

Carlson Publishing, Inc.
Brooklyn, New York 1996

Copyright © 1996 by Darlene Clark Hine

Library of Congress Cataloging-in-Publication Data

Hine, Darlene Clark.
    Speak truth to power : Black professional class in United States history / Darlene Clark Hine ; preface by Joe W. Trotter.
        p.   cm.
    Includes bibliographical references and index.
    ISBN 0-926019-91-0
    1. Afro-Americans—History.   2. Afro-Americans in the professions—History.   3. Afro-American women in the professions—History.
I. Title.
E185.H535 1995
305.896'073073—dc20   95-47307

Typographic design: Ann Harakawa

Text typeface: Adobe Caslon

Composition: Joseph E. L. Fortt

Jacket and case design: Ann Harakawa

Printed on acid-free, 250-year-life paper.

Manufactured in the United States of America.

First printing, January 1996

To the memory of

Willie Leon Thompson, uncle, musician.

And to

Murry N. DePillars, friend, artist.

Contents

Preface by Joe W. Trotter   vii
Introduction   xvii
Interview with Darlene Clark Hine   xxxv

PART 1   Becoming a Black Woman Historian
The Greater Kent State Era, 1968–1970: Personal
   Transformations and Legacies of Student Rebellions
   and State Repression   3
Ivory-Tower Reflections: A Black Woman in the Academy   13

PART 2   History, Gender, and Culture
"In the Kingdom of Culture": Black Women and the Intersection
   of Race, Gender, and Class in Black History   33
Quilts and African-American Women's Cultural History   47
Culture, Consciousness, and Community: The Making
   of an African-American Women's History   53
The Making of *Black Women in America: An Historical
   Encyclopedia*   65

PART 3   Speak Truth to Power
For Pleasure, Profit, and Power: The Sexual Exploitation
   of Black Women, or Anita Hill and Clarence Thomas
   in Historical Perspective   83
Booker T. Washington and Madam C. J. Walker   95
Paul Robeson: Truth and Punishment   105
Divine Obsessions: History and Culture of Miles Davis   115

PART 4   Race, Gender, and Change
An Angle of Vision: Black Women and the Constitution,
   1787–1987   129
Black Lawyers and the Twentieth-Century Struggle
   for Constitutional Change   147
The Intersection of Race, Class, and Gender
   in the Nursing Profession   169
To Heal the Race: African-American Health Care Professionals
   in Historical Perspective   181

Notes   193
Acknowledgments   209
Permission Credits   211
Index   213

Preface

It is an honor to offer a preface to Darlene Clark Hine's collection of essays on the black professional class. When she allowed me to read the volume, I was moved by the power of her appeal to historians to craft a fuller and more inclusive history of African Americans and the nation. I was also struck by the very fruitful discussions between Professor Hine and her sister Barbara Clark, a case worker in the Department of Public Services in Chicago. Their interchange reminded me of conversations with my sister, Isalene Jackson, a public services case worker in the Canton-Massillon, Ohio, area. Indeed, I soon wrote to Darlene expressing my enthusiasm for the book and how I had shared her story with my sister.

    Shortly thereafter, I received a letter from editor Ralph Carlson inviting me to write a preface to the volume. He suggested that it might be interesting for a scholar of the black working class to comment on a volume on the black professional class. I agreed, but only after a phone conversation with Darlene did I fully grasp the broader significance of this offer. As she put it, research and writing on different aspects of the black class structure proceed apace, but we need ways to brings these insights together. In short, Darlene Clark Hine and Ralph Carlson conceptualized the preface as an opportunity for a historian of the African-American working class—building upon his own research as well as the essays in this volume—to speak comparatively about the experiences of black workers and the black middle class.[1]

Speak Truth to Power explores the lives of black educators, physicians, nurses, attorneys, and artists. It illuminates the development of the black professional class from slavery through the late twentieth century.[2] As such, a comparison with recent scholarship on African-American working-class formation is particularly instructive. Studies of the black working class emphasize the rise of a free rural proletariat during the emancipation era; the emergence of a new urban-industrial labor force during the early to mid-twentieth century; and, most recently, in the emerging postindustrial economy, the growth of an increasingly unemployed/underemployed poor working class. More specifically, black working-class formation (and reformation) involved interactions of black workers with white employers, labor, and the state; the transformation, though not in a linear way, of the socioeconomic and political status of African-American workers and their communities; and the reorientation of black culture and consciousness, including the shifting worldviews of black elites and the black middle class.[3]

Professor Hine's collection allows us to build upon prevailing conceptualizations of the black working class and analyze the emergence and growth of the black professional class in historiographical, theoretical, and substantive terms. Like many civil rights–era historians of the black experience, Professor Hine began her career by emphasizing the primacy of race in the development of black and U.S. history. By the late 1970s and early 1980s, however, along with other women's historians and the escalation of the women's movement, she started to accent the significance of black women and gender issues in shaping African-American and American history (see especially her interview with Roger Adelson and "Ivory-Tower Reflections: A Black Woman in the Academy"). At about the same time, along with labor historians and the onset of deindustrialization, scholars of the black experience like myself shifted the focus from race to the impact of "class and race." In *Black Milwaukee: The Making of an Industrial Proletariat, 1915–45* (1985), for example, I emphasized the interplay of racial and class consciousness in the development of the black working class.[4]

Over the past decade, gender, class, and race treatments of the African-American experience increasingly converged. In growing numbers, scholars of class and race incorporated gender issues and vice versa. In *Coal, Class, and Color: Blacks in Southern West Virginia, 1915–32* (1990), I retained the focus on class formation or proletarianization while seeking to integrate more fully the history of black women. Studies by historians Earl Lewis, Robin D. G. Kelley, and others advance the same agenda. From a different direction, Professor Hine undertakes a similar project in the current volume. As she puts it, "With this book the larger intent is to underscore the importance of a class analysis, in addition to that of race and gender, to achieve a more comprehensive understanding of both the new African-American past and the old United States history" (Introduction, p. xviii–xix).

Speak Truth to Power also invites substantive comparisons between proletarianization and professionalization. Black population movement, institutional racism, and residential segregation all figure prominently in the growth of both the black proletariat and the black professional class. As in the rise of the black working class, migration represents a recurring theme in the development of the black professional class. This is apparent in Hine's narration of her own family's movement from a small Missouri town to southern Illinois and finally to Chicago. It is also clear in her discussion of African-American health care professionals and the rise of Madam C. J. Walker's million-dollar cosmetics business. In other essays too, whether implicit or explicit, the role of migration is key.

Compared to studies of the black working class, however, *Speak Truth to Power* suggests important differences in the migration experiences of black professional people. The often hostile reactions that confronted working-class black migrants are largely absent from this account. Working-class migrants faced repeated injunctions to dress, speak, and behave "properly." Indeed, according to some studies of the black working class, Southern black professionals found greater acceptance among the old residents than from their working-class counterparts. As migration historian James Grossman notes, "Middle-class migrants sought acceptance into Chicago's black bourgeoisie and shared its attitudes toward street life, boisterous behavior, and the trappings of lower-class life. They no more wished to be associated with southern rural culture than did the Old Settlers."[5]

Black professional people, like their working-class kinsmen, faced exclusion from employment and training opportunities. The essays in this volume document the ways that white professional organizations, particularly Southern medical and legal professionals, used their power over state legislative, licensing, and regulatory agencies to exclude and limit the practices of their black counterparts. Unlike white professional people, white workers were less successful in gaining the state's support to bar blacks from employment in a variety of jobs. African-American workers found employment in the lower ranks of numerous companies that otherwise excluded blacks from the professional and managerial ranks. Nonetheless, black workers faced the blunt hand of the state and local governments, particularly during economic downturns, when they were no longer needed. State and local officials often joined hands to remove unemployed black workers as vagrants without visible means of support. Although such responses were especially prominent in the South, they were not limited by region. Following World War I, for example, when war production ended and jobs disappeared, three squads of detectives entered Milwaukee's black community and arrested nearly forty black men for vagrancy. A local judge sentenced nearly thirty men to ninety days' labor on county work gangs and warned them to leave the city after serving their time.[6]

Recent scholarship also documents the interplay between workers' access to economic opportunity and the nature of their lives at home and in the larger community. Emphases on segregated and dilapidated houses, poor health care, crime, and inadequate leisure, business, and professional services are prominent in treatments of the black working class. Such conditions affected the entire black community but were quite different for black professional and working people. The middle class occupied the most suitable quarters in the increasingly segregated black community. In his study of Norfolk, Virginia, historian Earl Lewis revealed a common pattern: "Whereas middle-class blacks found living conditions a discomfort, working-class blacks found them deadly. . . . Whereas one in every twenty white babies died before the age of one in 1920, one in every six black babies died. Some speculated that the rate for blacks was even higher, because not all black midwives reported deaths to the city. It was clear that poor housing conditions and stagnant water in low-lying areas aggravated the problem."[7]

Restrictions on residential, business, and professional services created conditions for the growth of the black middle class. This collection illuminates the ways that the black professional class, unlike its white counterpart, was called into being to serve a people "perceived to be marginal and peripheral" by virtue of their race and class. Still, Hine concludes that this class was also brought into being by its own "multifaceted and relentless" individual and collective struggle to acquire the educational and material resources to ensure its own survival, as well as the development of the group. Kin, friendship, and organizational networks played important roles in this process. Studies of black workers also stress how they helped to make themselves, using their kin and communal networks not only to organize their own migration to the major urban centers but to secure jobs and housing as well.[8]

As suggested from the outset of this essay, studies of the black working class document the transition over time from one type of working class to another. Several studies focus on the transition of African Americans from agricultural, domestic, personal service, and common laborers to a new urban industrial working class between the two world wars.[9] Others are beginning to address the conditions leading to the spread of unemployment and poverty in the aftermath of the modern civil rights movement.[10] Similarly, this volume illuminates roughly a parallel process. It shows how a modern college-educated (in predominantly black institutions of higher learning) black professional class emerged during the early to mid-twentieth century. It also suggests how this class declined in the wake of the modern civil rights movement, as a new professional class gained ascendancy. The new class received training in predominantly white institutions and pursued careers serving a predominantly white clientele (see especially "The Intersection of Race, Class, and Gender in the Nursing Profession" and "To Heal the Race: African-American Health Care Professionals in Historical Perspective").

In neither this collection nor in proletarian studies are these processes treated in a linear fashion. Both acknowledge the impact of adverse socioeconomic and political changes on the dynamics of class formation within the black community. Specifically, recent studies of black workers and their communities emphasize not only the impact of the two world wars, the Great Depression, and the long-run trend toward deindustrialization. They also accent the significance of regional differences, showing how the composition of the black working class varied significantly from region to region and from city to city. African Americans worked almost exclusively in the steel industry in western Pennsylvania, in the coal industry in West Virginia, in a variety of mass-production industries in Chicago, and in a more diversified range of mass-production, transportation, and trade positions in cities like Philadelphia and New York after World War I.[11] Both implicitly and explicitly, the current volume confirms a similarly complex process for black professional people.

Although black professional and working people helped to transform themselves under diverse conditions, dependence on each other in a segregated environment had important implications for intraracial political and social relations. As the black working class increased, some business and professional people appealed to them to support their programs for empowerment in the larger urban political economy. Studies of black workers and their communities repeatedly document the emergence of solidarity across class lines. Likewise, Darlene Clark Hine suggests that race-based class oppression helped to mediate intraracial class relationships, foment the rise of a collective culture of struggle, and prevent internal fissions from splintering and immobilizing the black community.

According to Hine, only during the late civil rights and post–civil rights era would the black community lose its earlier cohesiveness and split into many conflicting and often destructive parts. This is a fine point that challenges existing historiography on the black middle class during the twentieth century. Professor Hine's argument suggests that the real change in the nature of the black middle class, aside from greater dependence on black patronage in the wake of the segregationist system and the later onset of the Great Migration, came much later, during the era of the civil rights movement. Despite this persuasive argument, however, early to mid-twentieth-century studies of black workers suggest that internal conflicts often fragmented the black community and split the black professional class itself. At various moments, different segments of the black professional class appealed to the perceived class as well as racial interests of black workers. During the 1920s, for example, in numerous communities across the nation, some black professional people allied with the predominantly working-class Garvey Movement, while others shunned it as inimical to the interests of all African Americans.

A close comparison of the proletariat and the professional class suggests that the social dynamics of multiclass black institutions and the problems and prospects of inter- and intraracial alliances require further investigation and research. This volume links multiclass black institutions—particularly churches, schools, and hospitals—to the professional class's service ethic, which emphasized extraordinary work for the community far beyond the narrow scope of their training and occupations.[12] Essays by Hine show how black professional people not only played a key role in the struggles of the black community but also addressed "publicly key issues of inequalities" and helped to transform U.S. society itself. This is especially apparent in the way that segregated black institutions gave rise to the modern civil rights movement, which ended legal impediments to political and economic rights and ushered in new opportunities for Americans of various class, ethnic, nationality, and gender backgrounds, particularly white women. Such insights into the ideology and worldview of the black professional class encourage us to probe deeper and ask if such an ethic existed within the black working class, and, if so, how did it differ between the two groups?

Existing studies of black workers stress their collectivist orientation compared to the individualist orientation of black professional and business people. Moreover, scholarship on black workers emphasizes the distinction between the middle class and the black elite, who represent the most prominent members of the black business and professional class. Such studies suggest that the elite took a disproportionate number of leadership positions in multiclass black organizations and sought to harness the resources of the black middle and working classes to its own agenda. While all black professional people gained considerable prestige and honor as a result of their education, skills, and training, a few black elites took the lion's share of such perquisites. As a group, black workers had to wage the most determined inter- and intraracial fight to win recognition for their skills and the value of their manual labor.[13]

Black workers developed perhaps a more complicated class and racial consciousness than did their professional-class counterparts. Their worldview stressed the compatibility of goals with the black middle class while at the same time acknowledging the ways that the interests of the two diverged. Thus, black workers could sometimes develop short-lived alliances with white workers in important struggles to change the conditions of labor for all. This happened, for example, in the coal industry, among longshoremen, and among meatpackers in the era of World War I. Indeed, African Americans were sometimes admitted into the unions on an equal footing with white workers. Labor organizations and various informal modes of cultural expression—music, dance, and folklore—came to characterize much of black workers' reactions to their status and gave them an awareness of themselves as workers who had to negotiate a complicated set of obstacles—between white workers, employers, the state, and the black middle class as well.[14]

This volume will play a key role in future research on the black class structure. By focusing mainly, though not exclusively, on black professionals rather than businesspeople, it sharpens our perspective on the social composition of the black middle class. This approach also implies that it is time to think carefully about distinctions between black professionalization and its larger ethnic white and nonwhite counterparts. As I have written elsewhere, unlike their white counterparts, black professionals tended to merge their professional services with business enterprises. As C. Wright Mills suggested in another context: "Out of this merging, professions have become more like businesses, and businesses have become more like professions. The line between them has in many places become obscured."[15]

Finally, this book highlights the limitations of several prevailing conceptualizations of the African-American urban experience. Scholarship on African-American urban history has unfolded within the distinct but overlapping frameworks of race relations, ghettoization, and, more recently, proletarianization. Together, such studies increase our understanding of the complicated patterns of black-white social interactions, residential segregation, and the rise of new class relations within the black community. Yet these perspectives neglect key aspects of African-American history, politics, and culture, especially the role of gender.

Professor Hine convincingly integrates cultural and gender dynamics into her analysis of professional-class formation. Essays on professional black women, including her own experiences as an historian, reveal myriad dimensions of continuity and discontinuity in black feminist consciousness—from the pre-emancipation era through the testimony of Anita Hill at the congressional hearings on Judge Clarence Thomas's nomination to the Supreme Court. She also merges her interest in black feminism with nascent investigations of black masculinity. In her essay on Miles Davis, for example, she suggests that gender constructions are historical processes involving both black men and women within the context of often hostile class and race relations.

In short, *Speak Truth to Power* challenges us to rethink the larger processes of class, racial, gender, and community formation in American society. After reading these essays, it will be difficult, indeed impossible, to treat African-American and U.S. history in the same old way.

Joe W. Trotter
October 1995

Introduction

I

One of the distinguishing characteristics of the black professional class is its service to people whom the larger American society perceived to be marginal and peripheral by virtue of their race and subordinate in socioeconomic and political status. Since the end of slavery, black Americans have struggled to win essential rights as citizens and to achieve recognition and acceptance of their intrinsic humanity. Dimensions of this multifaceted and relentless struggle involved the acquisition of educational and material resources necessary for survival. Critical material resources sought went beyond employment opportunities to include the acquisition of land, health care, and businesses such as banks, newspapers, funeral homes, insurance companies, and control over a plethora of religious and secular agencies. Another dominant feature of the black culture of struggle involved the possession and protection of the ballot and the exercise of commensurate political power as guaranteed by the Fourteenth and Fifteenth amendments to the United States Constitution. The first postemancipation generation sought political rights and power to demonstrate autonomy and determine their destiny, but also as essential weapons against the white response to black independence.

  Deeply angered and humiliated by the loss of the Civil War and determined to maintain a social, political, and economic hierarchy grounded on black subordination and white supremacy, the vanquished Confederacy set out to retain hegemony. Thus, the collapse of Reconstruction in 1877 signaled the restoration of the antebellum social order, except in two significant ways—black people were no longer property and there existed a group of professional black politicians that had exercised a measure of power. Throughout the latter half of the nineteenth century, the forces of white Southern nationalism (unlike black nationalism, which sought autonomous control of black destiny) created a Jim Crow society, inherently separate and unequal. Actually, the entire country endorsed the Jim Crow regime and discrimination against African Americans was the prevailing white ethos. Within the framework of Social Darwinism, black Americans were to be separated and subordinated because of their alleged genetic inferiority, bestial natures, and rampant immorality. In a national climate of pseudoscientific Social Darwinism mixed with naked imperialism, the idea of white supremacy gave license to lynching, rape, sadism, and anti-black aggression.

The emergence of the early members of the black professional class is therefore a consequence of the ostracism, separatism, and subordination of African Americans. Black professional men and women nurtured the institutional foundations that facilitated general black survival and progress during the twentieth century. Much like the blues and other artifacts of the cultural productions of an oppressed but resourceful people, subsequent generations of black professionals gazed simultaneously outward and inward. The wisdom and commitment of black leaders of previous struggles taught them how to assess more accurately the contemporary needs of their people. With the advantage of hindsight, the third generation of black professionals—especially in the 1930s, 40s, and 50s—fashioned appropriate resistance strategies and an oppositional consciousness required to launch the social transformations that generated the educational, medical, legal, cultural, and sexual rights movements of our age.

This book concentrates on the experiences, successes, and shortcomings of four generations of black professionals in education, law, medicine, nursing, and culture. In my earlier volume, *Hine Sight: Black Women and the Re-Construction of American History* (1994), I was concerned with the need to include gender as a fundamental category of analysis in the writing and teaching of American history. With this book the larger intent is to underscore the importance of a class analysis, in addition to that of race and gender, to achieve a more comprehensive understanding of both the new African-American past and the old United States history.

The new black past is characterized by a deepening concern with questions of class formation, privilege, and stratification. In a recent review of *The Bell Curve: Intelligence and Class Structure in American Life*, historian Carl Degler referred to class as America's dirty little secret.[1] To be sure, many black historians and scholars such as Joe Trotter, William Julius Wilson, Robin D. G. Kelley, and Earl Lewis have increasingly made class analysis central to their work.[2] Yet, in spite of the more sophisticated approaches and perspectives exemplified in the burgeoning new scholarship, class remains a slippery and ambiguous concept. The wariness surrounding class, within the African American context, is probably due, in part, to the absence of a theoretical model nuanced and complex enough to encompass the myriad ways class operates within black communities. Most extended black families are comprised of poor, working-class, professional, underclass, and middle-class members. They range in skin color from ebony to ivory. Economic status, education, and occupation along with skin color have all affected class stratification. During the 1960s some nationalist writers considered middle-class blacks to be the "house Negroes" and thus less heroic than the more authentic "field Negroes," to paraphrase Malcolm X's famous dichotomy. Today, the worsening conditions of "black underclass" men and women mandate a closer examination of class differences as prelude to a new black unity in the ongoing struggle against oppressive inequalities in the distribution of opportunities and resources.

This is a collection of, for the most part, unpublished or revised essays, reflections, and lectures. They embody a variety of methodological approaches and styles. The essay format complements, but does not replace, the traditional historical monograph. Yet the diversity of this format provides multiple (and experimental) advantages in history writing and permits attention to a larger number of theses, issues, events, and personalities. In any event, the essay format may facilitate making historical knowledge and thought more accessible to a wider public audience.

The collection is divided into four sections. In the first section, consisting of autobiographical essays, I situate myself as a professional middle-class black woman within a predominantly and historically white elite academy. My life and career experiences form a text from which to explore past and present black professional class consciousness, race and gender concerns and identities. Part 2 focuses on assessments of the history and culture of black women and represents a measure of the work on gender that has commanded so much of my attention over the past decade. In Part 3 I employ a biographical strategy to delve into the lives and careers of black professional men and women who have profoundly shaped African-American culture. The essays are individual- and event-specific. The final section is more traditional in that the articles are historical narratives on the ways black professionals have used their status and power to transform United States society, or at least to address publicly key issues of inequalities.

II

The thread that unites this collection of essays and lectures is the theory of class-based resistance born of racial oppression and exploitation. Black professionals lived and worked in a peculiar social context and environment shaped by the negative views, customs, and practices of the larger white society. Furthermore, there were quite a few black men and women who internalized these negative perceptions and consequently derided and doubted black professional competency. After all, they reasoned that the black professionals had received inferior training at segregated institutions that often lacked the quality of resources and facilities available at the white schools. Former Morehouse College president Benjamin Mays in an aptly title autobiography, *Born to Rebel*, recalled a perhaps apocryphal story of a conversation between two black women in which one confided to the other that a mutual friend was so sick that she was "sick enough to have a white doctor."[3]

Resistance to internal reservations and external hostility became woven into the fabric of black professional identity. The professionals had continuously to prove themselves worthy of black community patronage in spite of the fact that black men and women often received inadequate and disrespectful treatment at the hands of white professionals. The struggle to win internal allegiance and acceptance involved doing considerable race work, or performing service. To be sure they could charge fees for the professional service rendered, but even more was expected of them. Whether real or symbolic, service combined with certain intangibles ranging from simply the appearance of resolve to outright evidence of courage and self-respect mattered greatly.

Given the complex and deeply nuanced position of the black professional confined to the community, any misstep spelled disaster. The forces of white opposition scrutinized the behavior and demeanor, as well as the activities of black professionals, especially in the South. Although it is commonly agreed that black professionals could be effective leaders within their communities, because their economic lives depended on black patronage it would be wrong to conclude that whites could not affect or even destroy them.

The experiences of attorney Fred D. Gray provide some illumination of the difficulties of balancing career and race service on the Jim Crow tightrope. Some white authority figures in Alabama abhorred the very existence of the committed young civil rights attorney who during the height of the Montgomery bus boycott kept getting protesters out of jail. Their attempts to stop his activities with threats, arrests, and through the military draft were to no avail. They then used economic reprisals against members of his family.[4] It was not easy being a black professional providing critical service to the black community within a racially segregated and economically stratified society.

While Gray continued on course, other black professionals demonstrated similar courage. English professor Jo Ann Gibson Robinson described her contribution to the civil rights movement in a moving memoir, *The Montgomery Bus Boycott and the Women Who Started It*. She surreptitiously used Alabama State facilities to print thirty thousand fliers and with the aid of students distributed them under cover of darkness. The fliers enjoined black citizens to stay off the buses in the wake of the arrest of Rosa Parks who had refused to abide an unjust law requiring her to vacate her bus seat for a white male passenger.[5]

Gray and Robinson with their own resources operated out of a black professional class consciousness that had coalesced during the first half of the twentieth century. The embryonic phase of this culture took shape in the race-segregated graduate and professional schools in the South. Meharry Medical College in Nashville, Tennessee, and

Howard University School of Medicine in Washington, D.C., trained over 80 percent of all black physicians. A similar percentage of black women nurses received their training in segregated black hospitals and nursing schools. The Howard University Law School was the dominant site for black legal education, especially for the study of civil rights law, during the 1930s and 1940s.

One of the characteristics of professionalization is exclusion. Black professionals, denied membership in such organizations as the American Medical Association, the American Nurses' Association, and the American Bar Association, and unwelcomed at the American Historical Association, had no alternative than to pursue a separate but parallel course of professionalization. Thus physicians formed the National Medical Association in 1895, nurses organized in 1908 the National Association of Colored Graduate Nurses, while lawyers organized the National Bar Association in 1925. Black academicians and intellectuals founded and supported a plethora of associations, such as the Association for the Study of Negro Life and History in 1915. Each group arranged and hosted conferences, launched journals, and engaged in various protest activities to win access to and membership in the mainstream professional bodies. These protest activities may well have been the forerunner of resistance strategies pursued in subsequent years to dismantle the entire edifice of racial subordination throughout American society. More significantly, the black organizations provided safe space and place to nurture a special brand of class unity and consciousness among black professionals.

One of the paradoxes of black professional class history is that these race-segregated institutions depended on the skill and knowledge and service of a small but powerful group of black men and women who had been educated and trained at elite institutions. Both Charles Houston and William Hastie were graduates of Harvard University Law School. W.E.B. Du Bois, Carter G. Woodson, and John Hope Franklin received their degrees in history at Harvard University. Their credentials carried little cachet when searching for employment in white-controlled institutions. Again, while some may have preferred to work in black institutions, they did not have the right to choose in light of the illogic, customs, and practices of Jim Crow.

Through training, work, marriage and friendships, fraternities and sororities, religious engagement, professional conventions and conferences the black professional class coalesced and built a community grounded in a race-service consciousness. Individual accomplishment, in order to render service, became the guiding credo of the black professional class and the meaning of a worthwhile life. It is important to avoid creating new myths of transcendent professional heroes and heroines while ignoring lapses. Thus, it is germane to note that some members of the black professional class faltered and actually ill-served their community. Such may have been the case of nurse Eunice Rivers of the infamous Tuskegee syphilis experiment. Nurse Rivers, as she was known, became caught up in a vortex of forces beyond her understanding. In persuading the hundreds of poor black Alabama sharecroppers to remain connected to the deadly experiment, she actually thought she was making a positive contribution. Well intentioned, though flawed, Rivers is emblematic of the many casualties in the war against institutional racism.[6]

To this discussion of black professional class history must be added a layer of complexity. Aside from the economic advantages, large when compared to the life conditions of the majority of black Americans but barely adequate when contrasted to their white counterparts, black professionals derived intangible as well as tangible rewards for their service and, indeed, sacrifices. The black community conferred reverence, admiration, and respect and sometimes envy. Some black professionals, such as Carter G. Woodson, Charles Drew, and Mary McLeod Bethune, achieved iconic status, their names appearing on schools, libraries, and community centers and their images entombed in statuary, their birthdays celebrated, their exploits and accomplishments recorded in song, myths, and stories, preserved in film and biographical studies.

Indeed, an examination of black professional class history leads almost inexorably to a study of black culture and biography, and that is precisely the direction of my future work. A potent characteristic of new black history is its obsession with the lives and deeds of individual black men and women which provides a much more textured account of the African-American past than the history which focuses primarily on race or group categorizations. Within the past several years scores of biographies (E. E. Just, Langston Hughes, W. E. B. Du Bois, Ralph Bunche, Billie Holiday), many of them prize winning, have appeared as scholars in a variety of disciplines have grappled with the challenge of deepening understanding and transforming the broader contours of American history by placing the individual black man and woman at the center of the stage. The rediscovery and reclamation of history through biography is on the one hand a positive development. On the other hand, it is well to caution that an in-depth study of every tree risks obscuring the forest. The systemic range of institutional racism and class and gender inequalities and injustice still begs closer analysis if social transformation is to occur. Thus, the importance of the study of black professional class history. It permits simultaneous examination of larger racial, sexual, and class systems of oppression and the lives of individual black men and women who dared to dissent and to resist overt and covert manifestations of privileged, white, and male power in the United States.

Black professional class history permits even greater opportunity to analyze the dissent of black women to the sexism of black men, and the divisions between gay and lesbian and the heterosexual populations. In short, while we probe issues of class we must be mindful of complexional distinctions and manifestations of privileged "black" and male power.

III

How does one explain a passion for history and bookmaking that goes beyond facile ego satisfaction and pride? When I announced to friends, family, and colleagues that I was preparing another collection of essays for publication only about a year after the first collection, the universal response was, Why? The question gave me pause and requires a thoughtful response. A quick rationale is that I wanted to produce a work with multiple points of entry for a diverse audience of scholars and general readers.

Each essay in this volume was written initially in response to an invitation from a friend or colleague to participate in a symposium or conference or to contribute to an anthology. Given the disparate origins of these essays, the challenge became one of selecting and ordering them so that they make a coherent statement, not only about the process of, and motivation for, history writing but also about the nature of, audience for, and content of history. What is history? Why does it have to be done again and again by each successive generation?

One way of getting at the "why" or the purpose of these essays is to describe how they came into existence and what I learned in the process of research, thinking, and writing about the responsibilities and expectations of a black scholar to various components of the black community. Another way is to explain how contemporary events affected the questions I formulated about the past and the resources I used to unravel connections between the here and now and the then and there.

The essay on sexual harassment began as a series of notes written during and following the Clarence Thomas Supreme Court confirmation hearing and the testimony of Anita Hill. I was, as noted in the essay, profoundly unnerved by the treatment law professor Anita Hill received from the members of the United States Senate Judiciary Committee. Here was a professional black woman who in her own way attempted to speak truth to power, but the humiliating questioning and innuendos reflected a disregard and disrespect of her that reminded me of the way most black women have been treated throughout the course of American history.[7]

The hearings compelled me to look anew at classic instances when black women's efforts to speak truth were dismissed and denied. The experiences of a number of black women such as Harriet Jacobs, Celia, and Joan Little came immediately to mind. The disparate notes, however, assumed essay form only after my colleague, Professor of English, Geneva Smitherman, invited me to contribute to an anthology that she was editing comprised of academic black women's reflections on the hearings. Thus, what began as a personal revisitation of the history of private pain exposed to public ridicule and disbelief evolved into an analysis of the relations among the pleasure, profit, and power derived from sexual oppression and appropriation of black women's bodies, labors, and achievements, and their often futile and disastrous efforts to resist.

The essay on the struggles of twentieth-century African-American lawyers to create a constitutional jurisprudence that would dismantle the edifice of racial segregation and discrimination was written in response to an invitation to participate in the bicentennial celebration of the United States Constitution sponsored by the Smithsonian Institution. This essay focused on the work of Charles H. Houston, William H. Hastie, and Thurgood Marshall, along with a number of local black attorneys who, through the NAACP and the National Bar Association, developed and successfully argued a series of precedent-setting cases before the U.S. Supreme Court during the 1930s and 1940s. This essay is part of a long-standing project concerning the history of blacks in the legal profession.

One of the interesting consequences of preparing and presenting the earlier, and abbreviated, version of this essay at the Smithsonian Institution was meeting attorney Fred D. Gray. Also a participant, Gray had complimented my first book, *Black Victory: The Rise and Fall of the White Primary in Texas* (1979). He expressed interest in the project on black lawyers and spoke of his desire to write his life story. My confession that I had never heard of him elicited an invitation to come to Tuskegee, Alabama, to examine the records he had concerning his work with Rosa Parks, the Montgomery Improvement Association, Martin Luther King Jr., school desegregation, and the Tuskegee syphilis experiment. Intrigued and embarrassed that here was a black lawyer whose impressive work had escaped my notice, I agreed to examine his files. The first visit piqued my interest to the extent that for the next several years I did assist Fred Gray in preparing his autobiography, *Bus Ride to Justice,* which was published in 1995. If there was ever a black professional who spoke truth to power, it was Fred D. Gray, who represents the complexities of those who achieve that status and influence.

The essay on professional black women and the Constitution also was a response to an invitation to participate in a bicentennial celebration of the Constitution. There was, however, a significant difference. Nicholas Canny, whom I met while a fellow at the National Humanities Center, invited me to come to the University of Galway in Ireland to a conference organized by American studies scholars to celebrate the Constitution from the perspectives of minorities excluded. Obviously no group was more ignored by the Constitution framers than black women. Canny confessed that they had initially invited Justice Sandra Day O'Connor and author Alice Walker, but both women had declined. Having no shame as third choice, I readily accepted and then agonized over what to say, given that black women were indeed invisible in the Constitution. I was reminded as I prepared this essay of how important it is to look at the work, experiences, and struggles of those who inhabit the marginal and the peripheral, for their angle of vision reflects, more often than not, the true meaning of power and the importance of resistance and dissent.

I wrote the essay on the "Making of *Black Women in America: An Historical Encyclopedia*" (1993) at the invitation of historians Linda Kerber, Alice Kessler Harris, and Kathryn Kish Sklar, who edited a volume in honor of the life and work of historian Gerda Lerner. I had benefited greatly from Lerner's pioneering work in collecting documents on black women's history. Twenty-five years after its publication, Lerner's *Black Women in White America* remains a classic in the field of women's history. There is a rich historiography of black encyclopedias and biographical dictionaries of black women. In other words, the *Encyclopedia* does not stand alone but emerges from a long tradition of black consciousness and determination to document lives and contributions of professional men and women too often ignored and marginalized by the larger society. The biographical dictionary and black reference books edited by Fisk University librarian Jessie Carney Smith are especially deserving of commendation.

The Director of black studies at Emory University in Atlanta, Georgia, Rudolph Byrd, wanted to acknowledge the centennial of the Atlanta Compromise of 1895 by inviting me to lecture on Booker T. Washington. Now, I confess to having misgivings about Washington and was not easily persuaded that this was an event I should commemorate. Byrd, however, believed that not all had been said about Washington, and as we discussed a possible lecture I told him of my interest in and work on a short biographical study of entrepreneur millionairess Madam C. J. Walker, a Washington contemporary. We agreed that perhaps a comparative analysis of these two self-made black professionals could raise interesting questions and provide useful insights into ways gender affected voice along the spectrum of accommodation and resistance to power.

Finally, two essays in this collection were written in response to invitations from Gerald Early, director of African American Studies at Washington University in St. Louis, Missouri. In many ways they were the most challenging essays to prepare because they required that I confront questions of class, culture, and periodization in black history. The first essay, "In the Kingdom of Culture," was included in an anthology entitled *Lure and Loathing: Essays on Race, Identity, and the Ambivalence of Assimilation* (1993) that consisted of an array of reflections on W.E.B. Du Bois's often-quoted passage about double consciousness. In a direct charge, Early asked that I, along with a score of writers and academicians, use the passage as a point of departure. As I mulled over the passage, all I could think about was how inadequate the metaphor of double consciousness was to the multiple, overlapping, and often contradictory identities black women created in order to transcend the intersection of race, gender, and class oppressions and exploitation. The essay is problematic and too short to do justice to Du Bois's passage. It will take years before I revisit and revise it to my satisfaction.

The second Early-inspired essay deals with jazz trumpeter Miles Dewey Davis. For thirteen months I listened to Davis albums and read biographies, autobiographies, and histories of jazz in preparation for the Miles Davis and American Culture conference in St. Louis in April 1995. Considering the dozens of years I have been researching, thinking, and writing about the history of black professionals in education, nursing, medicine, and law, this was a short time indeed. Of course, as was the case with the Booker T. Washington lecture, I was confronted with the need to say something interesting and thoughtful about one of the most written about professional musicians in black life and culture.

I interviewed and talked to a score of black men, including several uncles and male members of my extended family whose appreciation of Miles Davis's music and of his legendary refusal to bow to white authority made him, in their estimation, one of the great black male cultural icons of the late twentieth century. Like Fred D. Gray, Thurgood Marshall, and Paul Robeson, Davis in his own inimical fashion spoke truth to power. But to understand Davis, I found it necessary, as the essay reveals, to construct an altered periodization of black United States history. I divided the period since 1865 into four eras: the First Era of the Black Man, 1865–1890; the First Era of the Black Woman, 1890–1930; the Second Era of the Black Man, 1930–1970; the Second Era of the Black Woman, 1970–1990. Miles Davis was a product of and a major player in the black culture of the Second

Era of the Black Man. The essay is, at best, exploratory and begs for more contemplation of his genius.

The first essay in this volume, which is also the last one written, was presented at the twenty-fifth commemoration of the killing by National Guardsmen of four students at Kent State University, May 4, 1970.[8] The process of reflecting on the killing during my graduate school experience forced me also to think about and to connect the massacres of black students at South Carolina State College in Orangeburg (1968), Jackson State University in Jackson, Mississippi (1970), and Southern University in Baton Rouge, Louisiana (1972) to questions about power's oftentimes deadly response to truth. The student killings by power, state and local, of the late 1960s and early 1970s had a profound effect on my sense of self and on my political consciousness. Their deaths symbolized at least one kind of consequence of speaking truth to power. But continued silence, and failure to speak in the face of injustice, evil, and oppression, means death more than once.

IV

I feel compelled to address the issue of using my life in my work and the question of audience. Generally speaking, historians are reluctant to insert themselves into the histories they write. There are justifiable reasons for this reticence that pivot on concern for objectivity and the search for truth. Audiences and consumers of historical work must be persuaded that what is being written is the unvarnished truth, to the extent the historian can recover and reconstruct it, of what happened back then. Credibility is compromised when readers perceive that these histories are merely the personal opinions of the authors or their cavalier manipulation of facts.

Truth, objectivity, and a measure of inaccessibility are some of the hallmarks of good history, or so we learn in graduate school. Yet some of us increasingly use our lives, as short as they may be considering the whole sweep of human endeavor, as points of departure for probing the origins or backgrounds of contemporary questions and themes and issues. Some of us also devise this strategy as a means of engaging audiences beyond the historical profession. The quest for a broader audience leads to unavoidable tensions. Nevertheless, I choose to reconcile, or to live with, the irresolution and to write both for historians and for those individuals who I hope will be empowered by knowledge of the lives and struggles of outstanding and obscure black men and women who helped in innumerable ways to create this society. In fact, history is not simply a chronicle of what happened.

Consciousness grows, in part, out of the culture that makes up contemporary American life. Susceptible to public forces, in addition to the scholarly articles and monographs that I consume weekly, my leisure reading most assuredly affects my scholarship, or more precisely, the sensibility brought to that scholarship. Similarly, conversations with family members and friends and my day-to-day responsibilities and obligations effect how I construct arguments, identify the important facts from the mountain of research, and narrate findings and conclusions.

I read mystery novels, science fiction, and race and gender literature. Among my favorite female mystery writers are Amanda Cross, Sue Grafton, Linda Barnes, Patricia Cornwell, Sara Paretsky, Lia Matera, Mary Higgins Clark, and Barbara Neeley. Of the male writers, I read Elmore Leonard, James Lee Burke, John Sanford, John Grisham, Scott Turow, James Patterson, Robert B. Parker, and Walter Mosley. Science fiction favorites are Stephen King, Samuel Delaney, and Octavia Butler. I devour black literature written by both men and women. They include all of the works by Alice Walker, Toni Morrison, Paule Marshall, Gloria Naylor, Terry McMillan, Ishmael Reed, Chester Himes, James Baldwin, Richard Wright, Ralph Ellison, John A. Williams, Cecil Brown, Charles Johnson, Ernest Gaines, and a host of others too numerous to list. Now, given the reading tastes of the general American public, as shaped by the publishing industry, it is exceedingly unlikely that the histories I write will ever match in number the audiences that these authors reach, nor perhaps should that be the case. Am I writing and publishing books, therefore, only for use in graduate student seminars and to fill the shelves of libraries? I think not. Then what is the point?

Given the power of the publishing industry, the politics of publishing, the structures of distribution and dissemination, and escalating production costs, the black public audience I seek will often find my works, and those of many other professional historians, all but inaccessible, out of reach. This has little to do with inherent intellectual readiness and ability to comprehend the materials. Yet I do not despair. Rather, I have internalized and personalized a small segment of the general public to, and for, whom I must write. Thus, I publish these collections of essays and lectures and work closely with Ralph Carlson and Carlson Publishing for a reason. Permit me to elaborate.

First, Carlson Publishing specializes in publishing reference works, and institutional or library sales represent its major business. Second, Carlson Publishing made a strong commitment to publishing reference works in black women's history at a time when few publishers were interested in this subject. Of course, this has changed dramatically within the last half-dozen years. *Black Women in America: An Historical Encyclopedia* (1993), which I edited along with Elsa Barkley Brown and Rosalyn Terborg-Penn, is its flagship reference volume. It won the 1994 Dartmouth Medal of the American Library Association. Beyond this, Carlson Publishing has developed an impressive list of names of ordinary, everyday black readers who order directly from the company, in part because the books are not available in bookstores and also because of his persistent mailings to their homes. In other words, Ralph Carlson has helped to cultivate and continues to nurture an audience for black history in general and for black women's history in particular.

I have been fortunate in my career to have a sister, Barbara Clark, who throughout the past two decades has worked as a case worker in the Department of Public Services in the Illinois Department of Public Aid in Chicago. Over the years Barbara has, like Ralph Carlson, cultivated and nurtured an interest in black history in her coworkers. This group has become akin to an informal study group, reading and critiquing my essays, articles, and books. The women depend for the most part on my sister to order the books and encyclopedias. Accordingly, many of her coworkers have their own Darlene Clark Hine collections. They have taken to giving copies of the books as gifts to relatives and friends for every occasion and holiday. To be sure, total sales amount to relatively small numbers, but the enthusiasm and excitement are unmatched. Moreover, the women have begun to diversify their reading. My sister, for one, now reads many more autobiographies.

There are two things that are fascinating and relevant about this relationship that I enjoy with my sister and her coworkers, most of whom I have never met. Over the years I have come to know their names and the circumstances of their day-to-day lives. Barbara has, during holiday visits home, kept me abreast of all the triumphs and tribulations of this group of largely black women workers and a few of their clients. I have heard stories of the divorces, the health problems, the children and their experiences with abuse, drugs, police brutality, mental breakdowns, unwanted and unplanned pregnancies, and job losses. I have also heard about the good times, including high school and college graduations of children, promotions, remarriages, births, and lottery winnings. On occasion I have also attended birthday parties and celebrated purchases of new homes, jewelry, and cars and reveled in their trips to Las Vegas. I know, probably more than I should, about their love lives, debts, feuds, and fears.

Initially I listened to these recountings only out of a reciprocal politeness. After all, Barbara listened to me talk incessantly about the work and the lives of my colleagues, the politics of the historical profession, and my numerous projects. Gradually, however, my interest deepened. I became intrigued by the high degree of similarities in our stories. There are major differences, to be sure, but the everydayness of life in the academy and in the public aid office seemed remarkably uniform. Yet the lives of the women in the public aid office are not considered important or worthy of study.

As my sister began taking my books to work and encouraging her friends and fellow workers to buy, read, and to discuss them, I found myself eager to know their reactions and thoughts. Their compliments and criticisms were helpful and mattered to me. Although I do not feel circumscribed by their responses, I confess that their opinions are, in some respects, as important as those of my colleagues in the historical profession. It had not been my intention to write for Barbara's coworkers, but gradually they became my internal critics or private public audience. Thus, to a certain extent, this collection of essays, as was the earlier volume, is a recognition of their contributions to my intellectual development, and by extension the lives of countless other working- and professional-class women who labor and serve their communities in various venues in cities across the country. I offer these works to them, to their families and friends, and to all the people who have power over their lives, and importantly, to those over whose lives they too may exercise a measure of power.

A distinct feature of United States black culture is a moral ethic of race service as critical to a fully evolved consciousness. The successes of the modern civil rights movement were partly fueled by the rise of an expanded black professional class. There were significant differences between the older and the younger generation of black professionals. The post–civil rights professionals appeared to be only nominally connected to black communities and institutions. Many of them have secured employment within previously segregated white companies, institutions, and agencies. Inarguably, thirty years of affirmative action policy abetted the infiltration of black middle-class professionals throughout the U.S. economy. The wide-ranging consequences of this integration raise important questions and beg deep analysis. No longer were black Americans of means forced to live in close proximity to the black working poor. No longer were the children of black professionals restricted to attending black colleges and universities. From Main Street to Wall Street, many black men and women earned positions and distinctions in nontraditional occupations and professions. Black professional women especially made significant strides at the same time that changing gender roles unveiled deep-seated tensions within black America.

In spite of these troubling concerns and questions, and the unbridled assault on affirmative action policy, there is still reason for optimism. Each day I hear undergraduate and graduate students in my classes speak of their desire to return to their communities, to give something back, after they achieve their professional goals. Of course, a lot of this talk is a romantic longing for a largely mythical past where, they imagine, all black people lived in harmony and unity in the same neighborhood: a time when class, gender, sexual orientation, and color distinctions did not matter. The intransigence of racism, homophobia, sexism, and classism may be broken yet. New waves of black professionals are leaving the ivory towers, determined to rid America of at least these most ancient and tragic "isms." Meanwhile, they and I will continue to serve the people and speak truth to power.

Interview with Darlene Clark Hine

Roger Adelson

Born in Missouri in 1947, reared and educated in Illinois, Hine earned her bachelor's degree in history at Roosevelt University, Chicago, and her master's and doctoral degrees from Kent State University, in Kent, Ohio. She has written about African-American women by focusing on the intersections of race, gender, and class. In the past fifteen years, Hine has edited forty volumes (including a two-volume historical encyclopedia, Black Women in America), published three award-winning books, and produced over forty articles and essays (some just collected for the book Hine Sight: Black Women and the Re-Construction of American History). As John A. Hannah Professor of History at Michigan State University since 1987, she has developed a new doctoral field in comparative black history. Hine has one daughter, Robbie Davine. This interview was conducted at the Southern Historical Association meeting in Louisville, Kentucky, in November 1994.

ADELSON: Having become one of this country's foremost historians while still in your forties, how do you feel about your career at this time?
HINE: I see it as a privilege to be in a position where I can go in virtually any direction and do what I think needs to be done in African-American history as we enter the twenty-first century. I hope that I can continue to give voice to people who otherwise would be ignored and forgotten or rendered invisible and dismissed as unimportant. If I can use my skills and contacts to impress upon the historical profession

how important it is to talk to those people who do not leave written records but who have remembrances and have influenced generations and people all over the globe, then I feel that my career is worthwhile. To me, the historical profession is still too caught up with the wealthy and influential in political, social, and cultural arenas, who actually number only a very small minority of the human population. History mostly ignores the vast majority of the people who have lived sometimes desperate and at moments transcendent lives. Because so few of the new social historians included black women, who remained at the very bottom of the ladder in the United States, we continue to lose much understanding and wisdom. Don't misunderstand, I still enjoy researching and writing elite history, but I am now more preoccupied with listening to women and paying attention to children. In other words, I feel compelled to attend to the silent and the silences in the historical record.

ADELSON: You chose your family well.

HINE: I'm delighted that my family chose me. Instead of my family castigating me or trying to mold me in a certain prescribed way, I was allowed to develop on my own with my family's encouragement. In some families, when a young girl is studious, relatives can dissuade her by saying she will never find a boyfriend or a husband or that she will ruin her eyes by reading too much. Such signals coming from within the family have discouraged many girls from becoming intellectually minded. Just the opposite happened in my family, because my maternal grandmother early observed that I was "smart," and she saw to it that the rest of the family neither discouraged my reading nor dampened my curiosity.

Fannie Venerable Thompson, now in her early nineties, and I remain very, very close. Besides teaching me the Lord's Prayer and the Twenty-third Psalm, Grandmother Thompson taught me my manners and by example the dignity and value of hard work. One of the earliest memories I have is of her reading from the same black book virtually every night for an hour or so, when she paid little attention to me sitting by her side. I wondered what was in that book that she read, month after month, year after year, but never finished. I wanted to learn how to read so I could find out what was in the Bible.

Shortly after I was born, the eldest of my parents' four children, in a little Missouri town, my mother and father, Lottie Mae and

Levester Clark, along with the rest of the Thompsons, migrated to southern Illinois. There they bought land and became independent farmers not too far from Cairo, called "Little Egypt." When I was three, I stayed with my grandparents on their farm after my father, and eventually my mother, migrated to Chicago to make more money as a truck driver to buy more land. Eleven of my mother's fifteen sisters and brothers reached majority, so there were always lots of aunts and uncles and a few cousins around my grandparents' dinner table.

You might say that I became obsessed with my grandmother. Every Sunday she made sure that the family attended the Baptist church in Villa Ridge. My grandfather and older uncles rarely attended church, although they took us there, first in the wagon and later in the pick-up truck. A powerful figure and a stickler for discipline, Granddaddy Thompson commanded respect for himself and my Grandmother and saw that we all did our share of work on the farm. He talked so much about President Eisenhower when I was a child that I thought all presidents changed their name to Eisenhower when they took office. I was so talkative that Grandfather Thompson often reminded me to stop talking by telling me to "turn off the radio," which the men in the family congregated around every night. He would tell my parents when they came to visit, "Lottie Mae, that child talks like a radio!"

My grandmother's biggest legacy to her family was the importance she attached to doing well in school and getting a good education. Several of my aunts and uncles and cousins earned college degrees, and many are now schoolteachers, physicians, and college professors. From the first through third grades, I attended an all-black two-room school with two black teachers, Mrs. Buckley and Mrs. Harrold. It was important that I had black teachers early on, because I would not have another one until junior high school and one more in high school. We passed from one grade to the next by simply moving across the aisle. When we were bused from the farm to the schoolhouse, we passed by a big brick school for white children, whom I saw only on the playground. My life at home, church, and school was segregated by race but not by age. Since I was so closely associated with my elders in my childhood, I suspect that I became oriented toward history from an early age.

ADELSON: How old were you when you left your grandparents' farm in southern Illinois to join your parents in Chicago?

HINE: I was nine years old when I moved in with them and some members of our extended family. In the late 1950s, the west side of Chicago had a smaller black community than South Chicago, where my mother and father had initially lived. One of my mother's brothers, Robert, a taxicab driver whom we called Tip, had saved enough money so that, along with that of some other family members, he was able to buy a two-story house with four apartments that the family rented in a kind of family cooperative.

From the fourth grade until I graduated from high school, my weekly routine was the same: Sundays to church, Mondays through Fridays to school, and Saturdays to the public library. Family, church, school, and the library were the institutions that most influenced me in my youth. My family's expectations reinforced the lessons of diligence that I had already learned from my grandparents, including working hard, being thrifty, and taking responsibility. Every summer I went back to Villa Ridge to be with grandmother, until I graduated from high school. The nuclear family was my anchor, but I was also steadied by my extended family. My aunts and uncles, as well as my mother and father, believed that daughters were not supposed to leave home until they were married.

Sunday was the day my mother slept in, so my father took my sisters, brother, and me to the Metropolitan Missionary Baptist Church, an imposing neocolonial structure where the Reverend E. F. Leadbetter was pastor. I couldn't do anything else on Sunday unless I had first gone to church. I identified with Mrs. Lillie Rose, a wonderful Sunday school teacher. When I graduated from Crane High School as valedictorian, the congregation took up a collection and gave me $100 to buy books; the only requirement was that I come back to see them and never let college turn me into a godless creature. I was grateful for the money but did not go back to Metropolitan Missionary Baptist Church. I am, however, still trying to finish reading the Bible.

The students in my elementary and secondary schools were predominantly African American, with the white minorities being mostly Italian, Mexican, and Puerto Rican. I remember Mr. Weis, my sixth-grade homeroom teacher who looked like a Shakespearean actor. If we students behaved, he would read Homer's *Iliad* and *Odyssey* to us for the last 30 or 45 minutes of the day, which thrilled me. In high school, I was very close to my uncle Dennis Perry, a microbiologist who was a professor at Northwestern University Medical School and a resident along with my Aunt Fannie in the family home. Uncle Dennis helped me with science projects and fairs. To please him, I planned to become a microbiologist, but my favorite subjects during secondary school were history and English literature.

I really enjoyed reading all the history books and novels I borrowed from the local public library, located within easy walking distance of the house. Every Saturday I checked out five or six books to take me through the week. My weekly ritual remained the same from the late 1950s to the early 1960s, although I became somewhat addicted to television. Whenever a black person appeared, I'd yell that a "Negro" or a "colored" man or woman was on TV, and everyone would hurry into the living room. Although I recall the coverage of the civil rights movement, none of my family was very involved in the civil rights movement until later in the 1960s.

ADELSON: Why did you go to Roosevelt University in Chicago?

HINE: I had wanted to go away to school, but my mother, father, aunts, and uncles did not believe that their daughters should leave home to go to college unless absolutely necessary. The matter was settled when Roosevelt University offered me a complete scholarship package so that I could continue to live at home. Roosevelt is located downtown on Michigan Avenue, and it was an exciting new world for me since it was surrounded by the Art Institute, Field Museum of Natural History, Shedd Aquarium, and the Planetarium, where I spent many afternoons, when I was not working in the library. A private university founded after World War II, Roosevelt had mostly older students who worked full-time while taking classes. In the mid-1960s, most of the students were Jewish or African American.

When I started university in the fall of 1964, I was planning to become a microbiologist. In the summer between my freshman and sophomore years, my daughter, Robbie Davine, was born. When I decided not to marry Robbie's father, my parents, aunts, and uncles were very upset, since nobody in our family had had a child without getting married. My mother said it would crush her mother if I did not marry, but Grandmother Thompson came to my rescue. She advised everyone to stop pressuring me to marry and told my mother to take care of the baby and to let me finish my education. I stayed with my aunt Maplean King and her family until Robbie was born. My father visited me every other day after work to keep my spirits up. My parents embraced Robbie, who became not only the most important person in my life, but the center of my mother and father's lives. With my baby daughter to support and educate, I became more determined than ever to be a success, even though her father contributed to her care.

ADELSON: You were at Roosevelt during the upheavals of the late 1960s, which were particularly explosive in Chicago?

HINE: Most of Roosevelt's students ranged from slightly radical to very radical, or so it seemed. This was very unsettling. Roosevelt was the first place where I met people who were enraged about racism. I did not know what to make of racism, since I had been insulated from its overt ravages by my family and the black community on the west side of Chicago. Naive about whites hating blacks and blacks hating whites, I was initially too perplexed to be radical. Hearing black activists refer so often to history, seeing the black culture of the past and present celebrated by Chicago artists such as Murry N. DePillars, and reading many new works penned by black authors helped convince me that I should major in history. I made this decision at the moment when black consciousness was being raised not only in Chicago but throughout much of the United States and was covered so extensively by the media, especially television.

Chicago was in turmoil throughout the summer of 1968, after the assassinations of Martin Luther King Jr. and Bobby Kennedy earlier that year and especially during the Democratic National Convention that convened in downtown Chicago to nominate a presidential candidate. If I had been in my right mind in 1968, I never would have walked by myself along the streets of Chicago, many of which were then filled with policemen and National Guardsmen, weapons and tanks in position, amid burning buildings, shattered glass storefronts, smoke, and rubble. I was a wanna-be historian so I observed these things with my own eyes.

During my four years at Roosevelt, I worked in the library and met lots of people there. We had an underground reading list that circulated among our friends, including *The Autobiography of Malcolm X*, Frantz Fanon's *Wretched of the Earth*, John A. Williams's *The Man*

Who Cried I Am, Ralph Ellison's *Invisible Man,* Richard Wright's works, especially his *Native Son,* and Amiri Baraka's plays, poetry, and essays, *The Dutchman* and *The Slave.* Lerone Bennett, the editor at *Ebony,* gave lectures that I attended, as did John Hope Franklin, Charles V. Hamilton, and St. Clair Drake. And Professor John Henrik Clarke came from New York to speak. I learned lots of things on the street, at parties, in gatherings of Black Panthers and at Nation of Islam meetings, at poetry recitals and art fairs, and from books published by independent black presses, especially the Third World Press. Picking up all of this stuff transformed me more than the course work I did each semester.

By 1968 I had begun to read more about race relations. Several of Roosevelt's regular and visiting faculty have since gone on to make significant contributions to black history and studies. My adviser, Hollis Lynch, encouraged me to pursue a doctorate in history at Kent State University with August Meier, a leading scholar of African-American history. When I visited Ohio, Meier treated me very cordially and supported my application for a graduate fellowship at Kent State.

Convincing my family to let me leave home proved rather difficult. My mother simply could not understand why I had to leave Chicago for graduate school. She wasn't impressed when I told her that I was going away in order to study black history: "There are obviously more black people in Chicago and in all the universities here." After talking on and making no headway, I'll never forget the moment she suddenly smiled and said that I could go away to graduate school. When I asked her why she had changed her mind, she answered: "It just occurred to me that you'll be back very soon because there can't be that much black history to study." I have been away twenty-five years now and I'm still trying to find my way back to Chicago.

ADELSON: After you took your qualifying exams for your Ph.D. at Kent State University, but before you finished your dissertation, you taught for a couple of years at a black college in South Carolina. Was this your first trip to the South?

HINE: Yes, and it was the biggest cultural shock. But I was glad to leave Kent State, as I had not been happy there after the Ohio National Guard killed students protesting the Vietnam War in May

1970. In 1972, I accompanied my then-husband, William C. Hine, to South Carolina. I accepted a position teaching black history and U.S. history at South Carolina State College in Orangeburg. In my mid-twenties, I had a romantic image of the black people in the South struggling heroically against the white demons who had enslaved them and still oppressed them. After all, the February 1968 Orangeburg Massacre, which resulted in the deaths of three black students shot in the back by white state troopers, was still in my memory. I had read about the massacre in the Nation of Islam's newspaper, *Muhammad Speaks*.

At South Carolina State College I discovered class differences in the black community itself. Skin color mattered. Upper-middle-class African Americans controlled the college and, since they had already found ways to order their own lives, they were wary of outsiders. Some black class consciousness in the South also related to how far back you could trace your ancestry. So there I was—a dark-skinned, mildly radical, black graduate student from the Midwest who could trace her people back only to pre–Civil War Mississippi and Arkansas—teaching at a tense little campus where some of the students were very excited by my courses and some of my colleagues were very pleased that I was there. However, I had to make some adjustments. I remember the president of the college making statements about the importance of the faculty dressing appropriately. Once a colleague advised me to go home and take the braids out of my hair. But the hardest thing about the position was the heavy teaching load—fifteen hours per semester.

ADELSON: During the two years you were in South Carolina, you researched the white primary in Texas for your dissertation?

HINE: The topic had been suggested to me by my supervisor, August Meier, who was working on a history of the National Association for the Advancement of Colored People. It made sense for me to work on something that he knew a lot about, so he suggested that I work on the white primary in Texas and the NAACP's struggle against it. Initially, I concentrated on the constitutional issues, the legal strategies and the court's arguments from *Plessy v. Ferguson* (1896) through *Nixon v. Herndon* (1927), *Nixon v. Condon* (1932), *Grovey v. Townsend* (1935), to *Smith v. Allwright* (1944), when the Supreme Court finally concluded that the Democratic white primary had disfranchised black citizens in violation of the fourteenth and fifteenth amendments to the U.S. Constitution. Eventually, I went off in a different direction from that which Meier and I had originally intended, after I discovered how important black Texans were in this struggle. I became increasingly impressed by the mobilization of local communities and the pressure they exerted on the leadership of the NAACP. Because I was so intrigued by the story that I wanted to be able to present it in greater detail, I spent a lot of time traveling around Texas and interviewing people rather than confining myself to the NAACP archives in Washington, D.C.

ADELSON: You turned your dissertation into a book, *Black Victory: The Rise and Fall of the White Primary in Texas*, after you joined the faculty at Purdue University, in West Lafayette, Indiana?

HINE: My first book was published in 1979, five years after I had left South Carolina to take an entry position at Purdue, where I found a number of congenial colleagues, such as Harold Woodman and Donald J. Berthrong, and a much lighter teaching load with more emphasis on research and writing. At Purdue I was promoted from assistant to associate to full professor and even took on some administrative positions, as I served for one year as interim director of the Africana Studies and Research Center and for five years as vice provost.

ADELSON: When did you become interested in the history of black women?

HINE: My interest in gender and history began late in the summer of 1980, when I received a telephone call from Shirley Herd, then president of the Indianapolis section of the National Council of Negro Women. Herd asked me to write a history of Indiana's black women. After hearing me tell her that she could not simply call up a historian and order a book the way you drive up and order a Wendy's hamburger, and after listening to a long list of my protestations, Herd explained that her group had already raised money from the Indiana National Bank and the Church Federation of Indianapolis and had spent the previous two years collecting papers and records of black women throughout Indiana. I agreed at least to look at the papers. That next weekend, Herd and Virtea Downey, another primary school teacher, drove up to my house in a station wagon loaded with boxes and carried them all into my living room. For the next six months I went through letters, diaries, obituaries, club minutes, church bulletins, newspaper clippings, receipts, and legal papers, which revealed how black nurses, teachers, social workers, librarians, domestic servants, laundresses, beauticians, and others had raised money to keep many churches in operation, founded schools and settlement houses, provided funds for scholarships, welfare for orphans, homes for the aged, and clinics for the sick. Within a year, I published a short book, *When the Truth Is Told: Black Women's Community and Culture in Indiana, 1875–1950,* and Herd and Downey returned the papers to their donors. This history demonstrated black women's activism and agency operating in Indiana, the kind of local mobilization that I had been impressed by in my study about the opposition of Texas black leaders to the Democratic white primary.

ADELSON: What about the project on black women in the Middle West?

HINE: After finishing the Indiana book, I felt so guilty about all the documents being put back in closets, basements, and attics and lost to history that I initiated the Black Women in the Middle West Project, secured a $150,000 grant from the National Endowment for the Humanities, and developed a network of over 1,500 Midwestern women and men, black and white, academics and community-based individuals, all of whom helped amass and identify records pertaining to the lives of black women in Illinois, Indiana, Michigan, Ohio, and Wisconsin. The NEH eventually required us to limit the project to Illinois and Indiana. In only eighteen months, we had managed to establish an archive of three hundred different record collections on black women in the Middle West housed at the Indiana Historical Society and the Chicago Historical Society. The Indiana Historical Bureau published *Black Women in the Middle West: A Comprehensive Research Guide, Illinois and Indiana,* which historian Patrick Bidelman and I edited.

ADELSON: You also pursued research that led to *Black Women in White: Racial Conflict and Cooperation in the Nursing Profession, 1890–1950*?

HINE: In the 1980s, my research shifted to nursing as my interest in gender questions and issues increased. *Black Women in White* describes the small number of black nursing schools and how their graduates could find employment only in private homes or in public health since hospitals and medical schools were segregated. I also was able to demonstrate how hard the National Association of Colored Graduate Nurses fought against racism to achieve full professional status in nursing, the breakthrough coming during World War II as black nurses were integrated into the Armed Forces Nurse Corps even before black troops began to be integrated into the U.S. armed forces.

ADELSON: Some of your many articles and essays are reprinted in a new volume cleverly titled *Hine Sight*?

HINE: This collection brings together fourteen of my most significant articles and essays from various journals and books so as to make my work on black women's history more accessible but also to trace the evolution of my thinking about black women as historical subjects. The first part, historiographical and theoretical in nature, concerns such questions as black women in slavery and freedom; black women being raped and the development of a culture of dissemblance; the stereotyping of all black women as promiscuous; and the efforts black women made to resist by migration from the South and by membership in various women's clubs that helped them to achieve greater respectability and power. The second part provides case studies of the kinds of community work that black women did in the urban Midwest from the late nineteenth century to the mid-twentieth century, such as the Housewives' League of Detroit, whose economic nationalism anticipates post–World War II efforts. The third part of *Hine Sight* examines black women in the medical and nursing professions, while the last part analyzes African-American studies, reprinting rather controversial reports and essays. I hope the book stimulates more historical exploration of black women in U.S. history.

ADELSON: At the end of *Hine Sight*, you published a plea to "Stop the Global Holocaust." What prompted this statement?

HINE: In September 1992, two of my teenage nephews were shot and injured, but not killed, while they were standing in the doorway of a friend's house right across the street from where they lived with their extraordinarily good mother, my sister, on the south side of Chicago. In August 1994, the older brother of these two boys wrote to me about what it felt like to be a twenty-one-year-old black male in Chicago: He was hurting and needed direction but could see no escape.

His letter broke my heart, so I called him and told him that his brothers had been living with their Aunt Darlene for two years, holding down jobs and going to school, and that there was room for him as well. He's now staying with me, has a job paying $7.10 an hour, and is saving money to enter Lansing Community College in 1995. Although my nephews have also had the family support that I had when growing up in Chicago in the early 1960s, today there are no shields thick enough to protect them from the bullets and beatings and terrorism in the city. All this happening to me, in-the-face, so to speak, has really hit me, yet I do not exaggerate when I write of a generation of our young people wiped out by being subjected to forces more threatening and potentially more genocidal than anything else we've encountered in our history. The economic transformations that have occurred since World War II have led us to a moment where some people are considered obsolete and have no claim to existence. If you don't have a job, if you're not in school, if you don't have credit, then you're not needed. Too many of these kids hear their country saying in words and in actions that it doesn't want or need them anymore.

ADELSON: You recently witnessed some urban horrors in Brazil?

HINE: Early in 1992, when I gave a paper on African studies in the U.S. at an international conference on black studies and race relations held at a university in Rio de Janeiro, I walked once again where I probably shouldn't have been, but I saw enough street children, I saw enough poverty, and I saw enough wildness to believe the reports of murderers being hired to shoot children in the streets. How can I be a member of the human race and not be affected by such terrible sights? How can I consider myself a family member if I do not help my nephews who refused to join a gang and were hit by bullets with their names on them?

ADELSON: But how do you get this across to others, particularly historians?

HINE: Early in 1993 I was invited to Germany to speak about black history and black women's history to Americans teaching at Department of Defense schools for the children of U.S. service personnel. In my tours of schools and discussions with the teachers, I was again rudely awakened. One man wondered if we should teach about racism in the schools, because it upset students. "Since slavery is so depressing," he asked, "why should we teach it when it makes the black kids feel bad and the white kids feel guilty?" Another teacher asked me, "Don't you think it's best not to bring up these depressing subjects to students?"

Sometimes I believe that in order to teach, you have to preach, and I am rarely reluctant to do either. I stated that if teachers do not address racism in the curriculum of our schools, then we utterly ignore racism as a global phenomenon. I complicated the discussion by talking about sexism and class differences as well as the consequences of deprivation and humiliation. By the end of the afternoon, all but one of those American teachers in Germany had at least begun to understand some of the things I was saying about racism. One teacher refused to believe that women were suffering because of the patriarchal institutions of American society, which have clearly made it even more difficult for black women to upset the myths and stereotypes about them. The latest example of a popular myth is that welfare recipients have no interest in improving their lives and that they alone are responsible for bringing "obsolete" children into the world. Finally, even after most of the teachers were starting to grasp the problem, they still remained very reluctant even to discuss racism in their classrooms. They preferred to show some nice films and use some nice books that entertained their students rather than educating them about race. I am afraid that out of reluctance to pass hurt on to their students, some teachers promote ignorance of racism.

ADELSON: Who said the truth has to be entertaining? Have you found the attitude of these American teachers in Germany replicated in the United States?

HINE: No. Unfortunately I have not spoken with as many teachers on this side of the Atlantic. I would like to believe that they at least understand that racism is widespread. Perhaps the most distressing thing about the conversations that I have with school teachers on this side of the ocean is that they want to know what I can do to help them. I'm just one person, and I can't visit every high school.

ADELSON: You can't visit many schools, but some of the forty volumes of readers, anthologies, encyclopedias, and collections that you have edited or coedited in the past few years help those teachers, students, and scholars who are involved with studying African-American history.

HINE: Exactly. During the past couple of years I have served as a general consulting editor with Chelsea House to produce a series of books called *Milestones in Black American History*, geared to the primary schools, but especially to middle- and high-school students. For this sixteen-volume series, I just finished a book of synthesis, written in a more lively fashion than usual, that takes African-American history from 1931 to 1948, from the notorious Scottsboro rape case to Jackie Robinson's breaking baseball's color barrier. I wrote this particular book with my nephews in mind.

ADELSON: How have you managed to edit so much quality work in such a short time?

HINE: I agree to work only with people who are determined and committed that the highest level of quality will be invested in the editorial project. First, the book has to look good. If I talk to publishing people who are less committed than I to aesthetics, then I refuse to work with them. Secondly, I always request a timetable. If the publisher cannot assure a beginning and a reasonable end, then I don't do it since these projects must be brought to a close. Finally, I am very careful about the people with whom I choose to work. I have a lot of contacts with other scholars and graduate students around the country who advise me and on occasion undertake specific projects. Very often the people who help me are otherwise rarely approached by senior scholars or academic publishers since a certain amount of invisibility operates in our profession—as, for example, with those who teach at small schools and get little or no funding to go to professional meetings. I believe that these things have made it possible for me to complete my editorial projects.

ADELSON: Could you talk about the Comparative Black History field that you've developed for Ph.D.s in history at Michigan State? You have received $186,000 from the Ford Foundation for this program, which might make East Lansing the leading center in the United States for studying comparative black history.

HINE: Well, I hope that we will be successful, since this is one of the most exciting things that I'm doing within the larger field of African-American history at present. The idea occurred to me when I assumed a John A. Hannah chair. There are six others, all occupied by scientists or social scientists, and I am the first woman. Hannah, the president for twenty-six years, not only transformed Michigan State from a "cow" college to a major university but also chaired the U.S. Commission on Civil Rights under President Eisenhower and took a leading role in helping the starving children of Africa before he died in 1992.

When I got to East Lansing, I found all of these people in the History Department who worked individually on the black diaspora, including Africanists, African Americanists, Latin Americanists, a historian of the U.S. South, and a couple of other people in the History Department who were interested in black topics. I wondered why we couldn't bring all this talent together and create a program so that students could acquire a Ph.D. in comparative black history. It took a while to create because faculty members, like others, have their own agendas and because the History Department, like others, has its own divisions. After six years of talking and meetings, we have now structured a comparative black history field and succeeded in getting a generous grant from the Ford Foundation to add Caribbean history to our departmental offerings. With our four African Americanists, three Africanists, two Latin Americanists, one U.S. southern historian, and a visiting professor in Caribbean history, I know of no department that can offer more extensive coverage of the black diaspora.

Our idea is very simple. We developed two foundation seminars that focus on comparative methods and comparative perspectives, with each of us teaching one of the seminars during the course of a semester. Students take those seminars plus course work in two to three different specific areas. Their dissertation topic remains focused, because it's very difficult for graduate students to do comparative dissertations. Our intention is that our history Ph.D.s will have been so impressed by the methods and perspectives of comparative history that their mature work will place black history in global contexts that transcend narrow geographical, temporal, disciplinary, and ideological boundaries. I believe the students are responding well as we ask the "big" questions.

ADELSON: Students of history can visualize the planet Earth as a tiny dot in space and can think more than earlier generations about ecology and the environment, problems that have to be solved internationally and regionally, not nationally.

HINE: As historians on the eve of the next century, I think we need to do a better job than our predecessors have done since the nineteenth century in transcending the boundaries of the nation-state. We need to denationalize history just as we need to deracialize history. "Wait a minute," some people will ask, "weren't you just talking about the impact of racism?" What I am saying is that nationalism and racism can be seen as stages in a larger historical process. I think that one of the ultimate objectives for humanity is for everyone on this globe to feel appreciated, to know he or she is important, and to be able to contribute to the betterment of people all over the world. Historians should offer perspectives that go beyond the notion that people live simply to accumulate as much of Earth's resources as they can appropriate, steal, or lobby for in order to serve their own personal ends or to aggrandize themselves. Historians should help students become less indifferent to people besides their neighbors next door. In other words, I believe that historians must play a larger role in shaping the way people identify themselves with the human race and in their relations with the rest of the world. That's a tall challenge, but I hope that more historians will rise to it in the twenty-first century than have in the nineteenth and twentieth centuries.

ADELSON: Your publications use the word "womanism" as well as "feminism." Could you define these terms and how you use them?

HINE: I use "womanism" and "feminism" sometimes interchangeably, but I prefer the latter term because feminism has such a powerful history. Black women have contributed to that history, even when they did not call themselves feminists or when they have not regarded their movements as feminism.

I think it is important for the historian to communicate with people as you find them. Many black women use the word only "womanism" because it speaks to their double legacy of oppression and their resistance to discrimination because they, as black people and as women, are members of two subordinate groups in the United States. Womanism specifically addresses those combined oppressions. Feminism focuses more on the gender questions and perhaps pays too little attention to the racism that black women encounter. Feminism also can sometimes obscure the racism that some white women direct against black women.

I prefer the term "feminism" because I think that differences in gender are as fundamental in importance as are those of race and class. We need to understand the differences of race, just as we need to understand the differences of class, the differences of culture, the differences of religion, along with other differences. In this way historians will arrive at an understanding of the similar forces that bind us together, specifically those experiences that we share because we are women. We need to understand the power that women possess and how it can be used to change oppressive conditions and systems wherever they exist in the world. For me, politically as well as intellectually, feminism is important because it not only seeks to understand the oppression but also establishes an agenda for the transformation of societies.

ADELSON: What are the main themes that you teach about African-American history since the Civil War?

HINE: There are four broad themes and periods that I emphasize. I begin by talking to my students about freedom, not just what freedom means for black folks, but freedom in the legal, cultural, and social sense, because citizens cannot function in American society unless they understand freedom. Only when they know the meanings of freedom can citizens grasp deviations from freedom and wage strategic struggle to attain it. The second historical theme involves urbanization and migration. After slavery, the two most significant changes in black America were the urban transformation and the massive migration of black people out of the South. To get up and leave is important, because that has been the ultimate expression of freedom for black people. Historians have yet to appreciate fully how black migration transformed the United States. In a personalizing moment I may tell students of how my grandparents, parents, aunts, uncles, and I have migrated and how my nephews are still migrating. The third theme I emphasize is the great struggle for civil rights. Despite all that happened in the 1960s and the repetition of the television series *Eyes on the Prize*, I think that we still only dimly appreciate it. The struggle for civil rights has a long history that relates back at least to the democratic struggles for human rights in the late eighteenth century and extends all over the world. Besides jazz, I think the greatest contribution that black people in the United States have made to the world in this century has been their struggle for civil rights and human dignity. This theme allows me to lecture about history on the community level and to emphasize the empowerment of local leaders, without whom nothing happens. To understand warfare, historians can't just look at the generals, but have to grasp the soldiers in the field; to understand politics, historians can't just look at Washington, but have to look at local competition. Similarly, African-American historians need to understand what the Depression meant for neighborhoods. The final theme I deem essential for understanding not only black America but the entire world since the Civil War is the changing status of black people, particularly that of black women. The new social history told us to write history from the bottom up, but not many of the new social historians realized how far down the bottom went. As far as I'm concerned, we really investigate the bottom in this country when we explore the complex and exciting history of African-American women.

ADELSON: Thousands of honors students are initiated into Phi Alpha Theta each year and receive a year's subscription to this journal. Do you have any advice for them?

HINE: The best advice I can give, growing out of my own experience, is to read and study widely. Never limit yourself to a single specialization, attractive as it may seem to be an authority on a particular topic. I think historians best prepare themselves by studying the histories of people all over the world; the more you know about how other people have handled some of the same problems, the sharper you can develop your analytical skills for understanding those human activities or inactivities that interest you most deeply. Also, I'd advise students not to be afraid of their own impulses and hunches. Go with them even if you don't know where they're leading you.

PART 1

Becoming a
Black Woman Historian

The Greater Kent State Era, 1968–1970
Personal Transformations and Legacies of Student Rebellions and State Repression

It is important to situate the Kent State/May 4 killings of Allison Krause, Jeff Miller, Sandy Scheuer, and Bill Schroeder between two other, equally significant but often ignored, deadly confrontations between students and state police authorities in 1968 and 1970. The deaths of three unarmed students at South Carolina State College, in Orangeburg, on February 8, 1968, and of two students at Jackson State College, Jackson, Mississippi, ten days after Kent, comprise a trilogy of tragedies I refer to as "The Greater Kent State Era." Kent State's tragedy is rightly remembered with vigils and symposia, but seldom do we attend gatherings at the other campus killings. As a graduate student at Kent State in May 1970, this lived history exploded my parochial political consciousness. The events shaped the nature of my scholarship and the strategies of resistance I have employed this past quarter of a century. Indeed, it has taken me twenty-five years to break a self-imposed silence about what I experienced, and an equally long period of ivory-tower reflection to articulate the personal, professional, and systemic legacies of Greater Kent State.

On February 8, 1968, South Carolina highway patrolmen killed Delano Middleton, Henry Smith, and Samuel Hammond Jr. following a series of demonstrations to protest racial exclusion and to desegregate the local, white-owned bowling ally. Jack Bass and Jack Nelson in the only book-length account, *The Orangeburg Massacre* (1984), astutely observed, "The real tragedy is that there were lessons to be learned from the Orangeburg incident: lessons in how not to exacerbate a situation of mounting student tension and frustration and in how not to handle student demonstrations. Ohio officials learned nothing from the South Carolina experience."[1] As a consequence of not having learned the lessons of history, administrators at a larger institution in the Midwest repeated the mistakes of their South Carolina counterparts. And ten days later the unthinkable happened again, this time at Jackson State College, where city police shot and killed James Earl Green and Phillip L. Gibbs.[2]

A score and five years have passed. Still, it is necessary that we keep alive the memory of these struggles and rebellions and of the sacrifices of all nine students and the scores of wounded. I am persuaded that these tragedies could happen again. There are even more of us who will forever bear psychological scars, invisible and buried. Our healing comes through repeated public affirmations that students are human beings, and as citizens they have a right as guaranteed by the First Amendment to the United States Constitution to speak truth to power and to assemble in dissent, without fear that the awesome power of the state will take their lives.[3]

On May 4, 1970, I stood on the perimeter of the Commons, near Bowman Hall, home of the History Department. Surrounded by other history graduate students and faculty I anxiously observed the line of armed Ohio National Guardsmen at one end of the grassy expanse and the scores of defiant, unarmed students exercising their right to assemble in dissent. To be sure, I had read about the Orangeburg Massacre in the Nation of Islam's *Muhammad Speaks*. The white media deemed the matter too insignificant to cover. Perhaps black deaths were too common an occurrence to be considered news. Little did I know that four years following the Orangeburg shootings I would be a faculty member at South Carolina State College and that each day for two years I would walk past the markers that commemorated the dead students. Given the intractable racism that permeates American society and afflicts us all in one way or another, it is telling that I could never have imagined, on that bright sunny May 4 morning, as I looked back and forth from the armed guards to the milling students, that the killings that took place on a black college campus in the Deep South could occur at a large, predominantly white institution in Northeastern Ohio.

Perhaps a class analysis combined with my racial one would have had greater predictive accuracy as to which whites had the more expendable lives. After all, students at the University of California at Berkeley and at Columbia University, New York, had dissented, rallied, trespassed, and transgressed for years, but no state police authority had dared to shoot the sons and daughters of the white elite.

A veteran observer of two previous confrontations between citizens and state police authority, I was reminded of the explosions on the west side of Chicago in April 1968 in the wake of the assassination of Martin Luther King Jr. There, armed Illinois National Guardsmen sought to stop friends, neighbors, and others from venting their rage. My mind flashed forward to scenes viewed from the windows of Roosevelt University later in August, of Chicago police bashing the heads of antiwar demonstrators in downtown streets during the Democratic Party's National Convention.[4] Still, these previous conflagrations little prepared me for what I witnessed at Kent State. And when, ten days later, police would kill two students on the campus of Jackson State, nothing made sense.

With a hope and idealism born of the civil rights movement, I had believed that America could be made into an open, tolerant society that welcomed different points of view and encouraged dissent. By the end of May 1970, I knew how quickly and with what ease America could become a police state ready to stamp out dissent with force when property was threatened. More chilling still, I now knew that vast numbers of Americans actually sanctioned official violence.[5] The demonstrations at Kent State were in no sense a prelude to the revolutionary overthrow of the U.S. government. But the overreaction of elected state officials and military officers revealed an eagerness to use lethal force. What further bruised an already shattered psyche were the statements I overheard from some white citizens, parents, and even fellow students declaring that the guardsmen should have shot more protestors. Any fantasies I may have entertained about the efficacy of social activism and overt challenges to authority abruptly evaporated, to be replaced by a silent commitment to engage in day-to-day long-term resistance that would transform scholarship, curriculum, and classrooms, and yes, maybe even minds. I vowed to stay away from grassy knolls and street protests, armed guardsmen, and inflammatory rhetoric. Figuratively and literally, I, and thousands of others, quietly withdrew into university libraries where we studied, thought, and practiced silence.

Much the same as I had migrated from Chicago's west side to pastoral Kent to escape civil rights strife, I now settled, at least metaphorically, into the library. I studied the U.S. Constitution and researched the strategies and tactics pursued by other generations of resisters. The first result of my "library exile" was *Black Victory: The Rise and Fall of the White Primary in Texas* (1979). In the ensuing years I would concentrate on reclaiming the history of "the silent and silences" and would develop a "dissemblance as resistance" motif, all of which are especially pronounced in my writings on black women's history. After Kent State, my courses and publications aimed to teach students that America's unity is tested but not destroyed by dissent and diversity. It is through an understanding of our differences that we map the road to unity. My work over these past two decades makes entirely unacceptable *Newsweek*'s prophesy that "By the time the history of the 20th century is written, the shootings at Kent State University might not merit more than a footnote."[6]

Powerful historical forces created the political, cultural, racial, and sexual preconditions for the emergence of a host of challenges to the American academy in the wake of Greater Kent State. For the remainder of this essay, I will focus on the legacy of South Carolina/Kent/Jackson State in the realm of black studies, women's studies, and ethnic studies.[7] I am particularly interested in the agency of excluded and marginalized groups in American society and the strategies they employed to overcome intolerance.

The student and women's movements of the 1970s were remarkably intertwined. The students' call for the development of new areas of study, the hiring of more black, female, and ethnic professors, and the subsequent creation of new knowledge produced by these scholars refuted long-held stereotypes, biases, and assumptions of power and privilege that revolutionized American higher education more effectively than an armed uprising. The culture war that today pivots at the intersections of race, class, and gender had its origins in this era. Allow me to elaborate. Immediately after the Kent State killings, approximately 400 colleges and universities closed. The American educational enterprise experienced the greatest student and faculty strike in its history. The significance of this strike cannot be overemphasized, yet it is seldom analyzed. The strike punctuated the end of one era and shaped the new one. Some students desired to show solidarity and sympathy with those fallen. Some university administrators, perhaps fearful of possible student rage and potential demonstrations, and even more wary of the violence of unchecked state police power, sent students packing. Photographs in *The New York Times* showed angst-ridden university presidents meeting with President Richard Nixon. Either way you approach or interpret this shutdown, the results were the same—the education industry confronted its weaknesses and admitted vulnerability.

When classes commenced in the fall of 1970, students, faculty, and administrators entered a decade-long negotiation over structures, nature, and content of the curriculum. All parties seemed willing, for diverse reasons, to create an array of new programs and units. The 1970s witnessed a proliferation of black studies, women's studies, and ethnic studies programs, departments, and centers.[8] Many were short-lived, but the more resilient found powerful allies and much-needed external funds in the philanthropic community, especially from the Ford and Rockefeller foundations.

Black studies and women's studies experienced a phenomenal growth. By the 1973-74 academic year, there were an estimated 2,000 courses offered concerning the roles, contributions, and treatment of women on campuses across the nation.[9] There were soon more than 500 black studies programs. What is to be underscored, however, is the rapidity with which demands would shift. Historian John Bracey, director of Afro-American studies at the University of Massachusetts at Amherst, declared in 1975, "Our impact right now should be to infuse the entire arts and sciences curriculum with a black influence." Margaret Walker Alexander of Jackson State believed that the promise of black studies was "to bring a new humanism to American education, to infuse our system with a black perspective."[10] By the end of the decade black students and faculty and academic feminists were abandoning the inclusionary model of integration of black people or women into traditional disciplines. Now they embraced a model of curriculum transformation. In the early 1990s black students recognized that struggles for freedom and full humanity required concomitant radical transformation of political and economic institutions and changes in cultural and personal values. To elaborate the changes in student consciousness, some black scholars developed and popularized the concept of Afrocentricity as a potent challenge to, and critique of, Eurocentrism's intellectual dominance in the academy.[11]

The fiscal crises of the 1980s triggered the demise of many of the new programs. While some black battle fatigued faculty and students protested, many administrators resolutely cut funding. Within traditional departments mounting allegations of erosions of standards led to the denial of tenure and promotion to many black, women, and minority faculty. The tensions on campus grew more heated, and today issues of affirmative action and political correctness spark endless debate. In one arena, however, there was simply no way that the clock could be stopped or reversed. By the 1990s, the scholarship that the Greater Kent State generation had created focused on themes and theories revolving around the social and political constructions of race, class, gender, and sexual orientation as important variables in virtually every traditional field of study. I need only speak of the work of one group of scholars to illustrate this point.

The pioneering generation of black studies and black history scholars who entered the academy in the post–civil rights period amassed an impressive record of scholarship in the area of slavery studies. Because of the path-breaking and imaginative work of John Blassingame, Leslie Owens, Albert Raboteau, Barbara Fields, and Deborah Gray White, and of such white scholars as Eugene Genovese, Ira Berlin, Herbert Gutman, Peter Wood, Todd Savitt, James Roark, and Michael Johnson, we now know a great deal more about slavery as an institution and about the inner lives of slaves. This scholarship on slave communities, slave religion, slave health, and slave families not only provided more factual information but also deepened our appreciation of nontraditional source materials. We know, thanks to the new social history methodologies, that even the most oppressed and downtrodden people (who do not leave manuscript collections, write diaries, or build monuments) nevertheless created and sustained significant institutions and fashioned a remarkably resilient culture reflected in song, folktales, dance, and decorative crafts. Their essentially humanistic values and belief in the sanctity of life and their worldviews grounded largely upon a theology of hope helped to foster an oppositional consciousness that ensured the survival of African Americans in slavery and in freedom.

Universities have historically served a legitimizing function in the larger society. This is most graphically illustrated in the development and establishment of new professions, or the transformations of certain occupations into professions. But universities legitimize also by exclusion. In 1979, I launched a research project on the history of black men in the learned professions, specifically medicine, law, theology, education, and science. At this time, the notion of women as agents and subjects of history was not a significant part of my consciousness and vision.[12] This soon changed as my political, social, and economic thought expanded to incorporate gender as a conceptual category of analysis. Black women became the major focus of my scholarly work, and my study of the nursing profession illustrated the legitimizing power of university.

In the late nineteenth century, nursing was a low-status occupation performed by poor women who acquired training by working long apprenticeships in hospitals and clinics before receiving a diploma. By the early 1900s, nurse activists determined that greater status and respect, higher wages, and increased opportunities were dependent upon moving nursing education from the hospitals into college and university curriculums. They met with massive opposition from the male-dominated medical profession and the doctors and hospital administrators who feared women's autonomy and the loss of women's cheap labor. Nurses persevered, and by following their own parallel course, or duplicating medicine's professionalization process, nursing eventually acquired the legitimacy conferred by the higher education institution.[13]

Those of us who study blacks and women likewise fought for legitimacy within the academy. The results of this long struggle have been mixed. On the one hand, the impact of feminist scholarship in the academy has been substantial although uneven, across disciplines. History, English, and psychology departments initially proved more willing than others to develop and offer courses focusing on women.[14] By the 1990s the combined impact of feminist and black scholarship on history was especially pronounced. Today history pays considerable attention not only to women but also to social relationships and the construction of gender systems, to issues of race, to the concerns of the poor, to the structures and experiences of daily life, and to the construction of popular culture. The late historian Nathan Huggins maintained that "The object is not merely to mention and discuss African American, women, Hispanic Americans, Asian Americans, white ethnics, and Native Americans—those who have been marginalized in the standard history. Rather, it is to understand the past through them, to see history through their eyes, making them essential witnesses to the events historians discussed."[15]

Today, it is safe to say that feminist paradigms have provided frameworks for understanding what had seemed like anomalous data, offered aid in reinterpreting traditional texts, and facilitated the expansion of canons in virtually all fields to include previously unknown materials.[16] What has been most challenging for women's studies scholars was the need to expose the ideological groundings inherent in "neutral" or "traditional" scholarship while simultaneously demonstrating that to recognize the presence of ideology does not necessarily "leave scholars with only a mindless relativism that disregards evidence and logic."[17] Scholars in both black history and women's history are now developing diasporic, global, and comparative methods and approaches. As a harbinger of where scholars in these areas are headed, Michigan State University established in 1993 the first comparative black history Ph.D. program in the country. Pushing against and beyond the boundaries of the nation-state is the next frontier in this revolutionary scholarship.

Without the grants from the foundations, from the National Endowments for Arts and Humanities, much of the progressive, boundary-crossing scholarship produced by the generation emerging out of the Greater Kent State Era would not exist. But even more important than the myriad books produced by those who, like me, retreated to the libraries, is the unshakable conviction that there is tremendous variation in human experiences and that both diversity and unity should be central to historical and, in fact, all educational endeavors. In the current culture war those who call for the dismantling of the arts and humanities endowments despair of this reality. Gary Nash, president of the Organization of American Historians and director of the National History Standards project, recently wrote:

> The controversy over the standards is part and parcel of a larger, profoundly political, culture war.... We see it now in attempts to abolish or cut back the National Endowment for the Humanities, the National Endowment for the Arts, and the Corporation for Public Broadcasting. All of these controversies involve an assault on curators, artists, and historians who have sought more than a single perspective on the past, have tried to open their work to new voices and different experiences.... Some critics believe that young Americans should not learn that life is bittersweet and that every society's history is full of paradox, ambiguity, and irresolution.[18]

Over two decades ago, the demands of the first generation of idealistic women, minority, and black students on predominantly white campuses calling for the creation of black, women's, and ethnic studies programs, departments, and cultural centers sent shockwaves through the academy. Implicit in the demands of these marginalized and excluded groups was a fundamental critique of the underlying assumptions and ideologies of American education. A history of American society—or a canon of great literary works written by privileged elite white males, that depicted an American society as being a land of equality, freedom, and opportunity for all—was inaccurate and unacceptable.

The events of the Greater Kent State Era merely underscored the distance between the mythical America and the reality. With the traditional curriculum unmediated by race, gender, or class analysis, previously excluded students failed to derive a sense of self-esteem, an understanding of how they came to be—or the roles they could rightly aspire to occupy in the present and future America. As Carole Merritt, a specialist in black material culture, put it, "To know that one's people were present when the nation first developed and that their work and culture have been distinctive, yet integral, elements of American life is to be able to assert one's rights with dignity."[19] And I shall remain silent no longer, for evil triumphs when good women and men do and say nothing.

Ivory-Tower Reflections
A Black Woman in the Academy

The surest way to a productive and fulfilling future for black women in any profession is paved with understanding of the experiences of those who went before. It is within this spirit of illuminating the road for those to come that I offer this meditation on my work as a black women's historian during my first few years as John A. Hannah Professor of American History at Michigan State University. Although today several black women historians, including Nell Irvin Painter at Princeton University and Mary Frances Berry at the University of Pennsylvania, hold endowed professorships, this is a recent phenomenon. The professorship that I hold was created to honor Hannah's unique contributions to the institution's development while simultaneously facilitating the research agenda and interests of the faculty member selected to hold the position. I anticipate that the future, given the large number of black women now engaged in history graduate study, will witness increased numbers of endowed professorships held by black women academicians. Still, there remains considerable mystery surrounding these illustrious appointments.

As I lecture and travel around the country, I am frequently asked three questions: What is an endowed chair? Who was John A. Hannah? and How did I become a Hannah Professor? My answers vary depending on the circumstances and the time available to respond. Usually I explain that John A. Hannah was president of Michigan State from 1941 to 1969 and that upon his retirement six Hannah Professorships were established to recruit outstanding research scientists to the university. John A. Hannah served a twelve-year stint as the first chairman of the United States Commission on Civil Rights during the Eisenhower and Kennedy presidencies. He served one term as assistant secretary of the Department of Defense for Manpower in the Pentagon.[1]

In spring 1987 key members of the History Department—Fred Williams, Harold Marcus, Leslie Rout, and Gordon Stewart, to name only a few—nominated me for the Hannah Professorship. Within months after my initial conversation with Harold Marcus, whom I met while a fellow at the National Humanities Center in Research Triangle, North Carolina, I was invited to campus. I sat in the office of Provost David Scott (himself a physicist and former Hannah Distinguished Professor and now chancellor of the University of Massachusetts at Amherst) and questioned him about the John A. Hannah Professorship. Although it had been in existence for almost two decades, no woman, black, or humanist had ever been appointed to a Hannah Professorship. Specifically, I wanted to know what would be expected of me were I to accept this honor. As I listened to Scott's response, I imagined that I had died and gone to academic heaven. "Your acceptance of the John A. Hannah endowed Chair in American History means," he said, "that it is up to you to decide how best you will serve Michigan State University." I remember thinking, Wow! so this is what it's all about! Words fail adequately to express my delight to have an opportunity to work on big research projects, but most important, to exist in the academy on my own terms.

An endowed professorship facilitated work in black women's history and on the multivolume project concerning the history of blacks in law, medicine, nursing, science, theology, and education that I had launched while at Purdue University. I was cognizant of how rare it was for a black woman scholar, especially one who worked at the intersections of black and women's history, to be accorded such a prestigious position within the academy. After leaving Scott's office, I had had a brief conversation with John Eadie, dean of the College of Arts and Letters, about the powerful symbol of the receipt of the Hannah chair as an acknowledgment that the research and writing on black women had become a valued and legitimate part of the academy.

Even as I savored my good fortune, I was never so sanguine as to believe that if I had written only about black women in the early stages of my career I would have been accorded a chaired professorship at the relatively young age of forty. I had proven that I could produce more traditional male biased/race relations/social problems oriented history. By 1987 black women's history was still in its infancy and had not acquired widespread acceptance and legitimacy. Many in the profession considered it to be just a fad. My early work crossed fields and boundaries in political, constitutional, and legal history. Undoubtedly, race and gender worked to my advantage. Moreover, for six of my thirteen years at Purdue University, I had served in a variety of administrative capacities including interim director of the Africana Studies and Research Center and vice provost. By the time I was offered the Hannah Professorship I had written over thirty refereed articles and two monographs, had edited three volumes, and had served as a distinguished visiting professor at Arizona State University (where my former student, Professor Wanda Hendricks, is now on the faculty).

The other items on my curriculum vitae that may have favorably impressed the Hannah Professorship selection committee included grants and fellowships from the Rockefeller and Ford foundations, the American Council of Learned Societies, and the National Humanities Center. I had served on committees in all of the major professional organizations, including the Advisory Board of the *Journal of Negro History* published by the Association for the Study of Afro-American Life and History. Luckily, while the negotiations were underway for the Hannah Chair, *The New York Times* published a long story about the Black Women in the Middle West archive creation project. Nor did my involvement in the *Eyes on the Prize* film project hurt. I had worked as a senior academic adviser to Henry Hampton's television documentary series and coedited with Vincent Harding, Clayborne Carson, and David Garrow a documentary history under the same title. Moreover, I had consulted with the producers and appeared in a recently released Florentine Films production, *Sentimental Women Need Not Apply: A History of American Nursing*. These activities, along with a few good words from the historian John Hope Franklin among others, surely influenced the decision to grant me the Hannah Chair.

This record notwithstanding, I anticipated adjustment difficulties as I settled into the department. In other words, I refused to let my joy over the appointment blind me to the problematics of being a black woman in the academy. Jealousy and envy are human characteristics. In this day and age, it is still a challenge for some male colleagues to transcend their own bitterness about the lack of similar recognition of their work. This bitterness is often veiled behind attacks on affirmative action or windows of opportunity hires and laments about the so-called lowering of standards. I expected that a couple of my new colleagues would find my presence disconcerting. I did not have long to wait. As I lunched with one colleague in the fall of my first term, he cautioned me not to let the Hannah Chair go to my head. He declared that although I had joined the department as the Hannah Distinguished Professor, there were at least five others who were equally, if not more, deserving. I smiled at this unsolicited advice and thinly veiled admonition that I should stay in my place. Humor is an effective technique to defuse unpleasant encounters. I responded "Goodness! I thought I had met everyone in the department." It caught him off guard. We laughed to ease the tension and turned to other more important concerns, such as the name of a good dentist and automobile mechanic. On the whole I have been well received in the department.

Given that one of my many aims is to help black women faculty and graduate students survive and flourish in the academy, it may be helpful to comment more fully on the first-year transition from Purdue University to MSU. I arrived at MSU ready to hit the ground running. There were the requisite receptions and an inaugural address to be delivered, but the most pressing task was to learn who the other black faculty and staff people were. Black faculty and administrators and women's studies faculty offered warm words of welcome, and many treated me to lunches. For an inaugural address I decided to lecture on black women's relationship to, and perspectives on, the United States Constitution. It seemed a fitting topic given the fact that everyone was celebrating the bicentennial of the Constitution, a document that had paved the way for the institutionalization of race and gender inequities while simultaneously providing an intellectual and political rationale for relentless resistance against injustice.

After the protocol obligations were fulfilled I immediately went to work to establish a Ph.D. program in comparative black history. The idea for this field, which has now been approved by the department, took shape when I noticed the large number of colleagues in the department who were concerned with black subjects in their research and teaching: The department numbered four African

Americanists, three Africanists, one historian of the U.S. South, one who taught Latin American history, and one who taught Mexican history, all of them willing to become the core faculty of the new field. Throughout the seven years of endless meetings and mediation of personality conflicts and long-standing grievances, I derived enormous benefit from the insightful suggestions, advice, and comments of David Barry Gaspar of Duke University. Gaspar's expertise in Atlantic world history and his friendship and collaboration proved critical to the success of the new comparative black history program. Receipt of a Ford Foundation grant in 1991 made it possible for Professor Gaspar to serve as a visiting professor and to teach a seminar in Caribbean history.[2]

Throughout the 1980s, and even more so since arriving at MSU, the bulk of my scholarly attention has focused on black women's history. It is ironic to note that when I first entered graduate school at Kent State University in 1968, the history of black women was the furthest topic on my mind. Accordingly, my entry into black women's history was somewhat serendipitous. In the preface to *Black Women in America: An Historical Encyclopedia* (1993) edited with Elsa Barkley Brown and Rosalyn Terborg-Penn, I recount how in 1980 primary school teacher Shirley Herd, who was also president of the local chapter of the National Council of Negro Women, successfully provoked me to abandon a research project on blacks in the medical profession in order to write a history of black women in Indiana. I am still embarrassed at my initial response to Herd. It is ironic that I had attended graduate school with the intention of becoming a historian in order to contribute to the black struggle for social justice, yet I met Herd's request to write a history of black women in Indiana with condescension. Specifically, I had given little thought to black women as historical subjects with their own relations to the state's history. I thought Herd's request an extraordinary intrusion and so informed her. I assured her that no one could write such a book. I was both arrogant and wrong.

History is more than an accumulation of facts, names, dates, and events, yet no one could write a worthwhile book without access to adequate primary sources. The historian's task is to make sense, to give order and coherence to disparate bits of data, to fashion a resonant narrative full of explanatory power. Only later did I concede how straightforward and reasonable had been Herd's request and invitation to redress a historical omission. Indeed, black women were conspicuous by their absence from the history of Indiana. None of the social studies texts or state histories that Herd had used to teach her students made mention of the contributions of black women. Since historians had left them out, she had reasoned, only a "real" historian could put them in, and since I was the only tenured black woman historian in the state of Indiana at that time, the task was mine. Herd rejected my reservations, completely ignored my admonitions, and dismissed assertions of personal ignorance about the history of black women in Indiana. My confession of having never studied the subject in any history course, or examined any sources pertaining to their lives did not daunt her. Black women as historical subjects and agents were as invisible to me as they had been to school textbook writers.

A less determined black woman would have relented, but not Shirley Herd. She demanded that I connect my biology and autobiography, my race and gender, my being a black woman, to my skill as a historian and write for her and the local chapter members of the National Council a history of black women in Indiana. In the face of such determination, I gave in and wrote the modest volume as requested, *When the Truth Is Told: Black Women's Culture and Community in Indiana, 1875-1950* (1981). The process of writing the book humbled and astounded me. The array of rich primary source materials Herd, her best friend and fellow schoolteacher, Virtea Downey, and the other members of the Indianapolis club had spent two years collecting included diaries, club notes, church souvenir booklets, photographs, club minutes, birth, death, and marriage certificates, letters, and handwritten county and local histories. Collectively this material revealed a universe I never knew existed in spite of having lived with black women all of my life . . . and being one myself. Or more accurately, black women had not penetrated my historical consciousness. Now, looking back over the past decade it is clear that I traveled along two paths, that of black history and that of women's history.

I am struck by how consuming were questions of race and race relations throughout my college education and the early years of my career as a professional historian. Questions of race dominated virtually every academic conversation. The historian Evelyn Brooks

Higginbotham persuasively argues that the metalanguage of race silences all other discourses.[3] This was certainly reflective of my own intellectual migrations. Rarely, if ever, were questions of the relationship between sex and class raised. I distinctly remember engaging in misguided and ill-informed discussions with fellow students at Roosevelt University, about the absence of a class structure within black America. To me and my undergraduate friends, black women stood "outside" of history and were not subjects of study.

The primary source materials Herd and the Council members had so painstakingly collected launched my transformation into a historian of black women, a true historian of the margin. In 1982, following the completion of *When the Truth Is Told*, Herd, Downey, and I, with the help of white male historian Patrick Bidelman, launched the Black Women in the Middle West project (BWMW) for the sole purpose of making a black women's history archive. With funds from a National Endowment for the Humanities grant and the help of some 1,200 black women from all walks of life, we collected primary source materials from black women and their families throughout Indiana and Illinois and deposited the bulk of them at the Chicago Historical Society and the Indiana Historical Society.[4]

An unforeseen but invaluable benefit of the BWMW project was the rare opportunity afforded to talk with hundreds of ordinary community black women about their experiences, deeds, beliefs, and values. As I studied the dusty records, frayed diaries, yellowed club minutes, faded photographs, brittle newspaper clippings, and scores of obituaries, as I listened to oral interviews, and as I engaged in countless discussions with longtime residents of Middle West communities, the sheer force of these everyday narratives and the urgency with which their authors spoke shocked me and left me questioning the very nature of history.

Imperceptibly at first, I began to reconsider a great many of the cherished values and beliefs that I had internalized in graduate school concerning the nature of the historical enterprise, and reevaluated the profession's notions of historical merit and worthiness. As a black historian I knew that the construction of history reflected the existing system of power relations. As long as privileged white men held the authority and power to define the nature and content of history, blacks would never secure more than a token hearing or representation before the academic canon. But I had never extended that analysis specifically to include black women. I had not asked questions about, or even considered interrogating, the processes that rendered them invisible to historians. Two things converged to force my awakening: Herd's call and the call from the American Historical Association.

By the 1980s the field of African-American history had acquired legitimacy and respect. In 1983 the American Historical Association sponsored a major conference at Purdue University on the research and teaching of black history. I chaired the committee that organized the conference and edited the resultant volume, *The State of Afro-American History: Past, Present, and Future* (1986). After the conference the committee recommended that I write an essay to cover the one major theme that had been omitted or that remained inadequately addressed in the other essays. More to the point, as we assessed the state of black history it became patently clear that the history of black women was its least-developed area and had the least amount of scholarship. If black history was to be fully representative and accurate then it was essential that black women be included. These are the thoughts and commitments that I brought to fruition during my tenure at Michigan State University.

While in hindsight it is easy to explain why black women were omitted from both black and women's history, the issues and difficulties that challenge contemporary black women in the academy still beg excavation and analysis. As members of two subordinate groups in American society, black women fell between the cracks of black history and women's history. Historians assumed that whatever was said about black men applied with equal validity to black women and that the history of white women covered black women as well. Thus, it was left to the small number of black women scholars to insist that black women's experiences, precisely because of their race, gender, and class, were different and distinct in fundamental ways from those of black men and white women and deserved to be studied in their own right. Black women historians argued that simply to add black women and stir was an unacceptable and inadequate response and that all of American history must be rewritten and reinterpreted from multiple perspectives. In 1989, two years after arriving at MSU, I joined forces with Ralph Carlson who had founded his own publishing company. This collaboration generated two major reference works in black women's history. The first was a sixteen-volume series consisting of 248 previously published articles, five unpublished dissertations, and a proceedings volume of papers delivered at a conference on the role of black women in the civil rights movement. The second project that I helped to edit, with Elsa Barkley Brown and Rosalyn Terborg-Penn, was the two-volume *Black Women in America: An Historical Encyclopedia* (1993). Shortly before publication of these reference works I published *Black Women in White*, a monograph on the history of black women in the nursing profession.

Today, black women professors comprise a small but emerging force in the academy. In many ways they are the most recent immigrants in an increasingly diverse professorate. Two thousand black women attended the January 1994 Massachusetts Institute of Technology conference on Black Women in the Academy that historians Robin Kilson and Evelynn Hammonds convened. However, only approximately 100 black women possess Ph.D. degrees in history. A significant number of these individuals hold faculty positions at historically black colleges or in black studies programs and departments. Too few traditional departments in predominantly white colleges and universities, regardless of discipline, boast more than one black woman professor at any given time. Clearly there exists a need for many more black women academics, especially if black women's history is to have a secure place and space within American history and in black studies curricula.

Becoming a member of the academy does not automatically translate into a successful and stress-free life full of honors and lots of free time. The problems and frustrations of many black women academicians can be grouped into three clusters. First, there is geographical isolation. Most of the predominantly white colleges and universities that provide career opportunities for a significant percentage of black women historians are located in small predominantly white towns. These towns and cities, places such as Bloomington, Ann Arbor, and Evanston, are not known for their large racially and culturally diverse populations. The options for developing a viable social life outside of the academy remain limited, especially for the single black woman academician. Black women faculty often must travel to secure intellectual stimulation, rest, and spiritual renewal, or simply to find communities of other black scholars and like-minded people. There is very little that can be done about geography.

Limited social options promote a related set of problems for the black woman professor. While a number of white female colleagues rightly bemoan the need to balance demands of their families with the obligations of their careers, a significant percentage of black women will never have to confront that particular dilemma. Demographics and geographical isolation conspire to produce a sex-ratio imbalance among black academicians. Therefore, few single black women professors of my generation have had the opportunity to encounter suitable partners, to marry, and to bear children. The latter is exacerbated by the relentlessly ticking biological clock. This is not to say that it is impossible to enjoy a productive, self-fulfilling, and rewarding career without the benefit of matrimony. It is to suggest that those who desire to develop a mutually supportive relationship with a significant other may have scant opportunity to do so. In short, too many first-generation black women academicians never have the luxury of making a choice of whether to live alone.

While many unmarried black women academicians do not have to juggle the demands of family with those of career, that does not mean they have complete control over unlimited time. Rather, the demands of community, church, and social organizations are added to committee assignments and expectations within the academy. It is precisely the isolation, the aloneness, the uniqueness of her position in the departments of institutions located in small white towns that give rise to the third set of problems and frustrations. All too frequently, the black woman professor is called upon to serve on every committee that needs the representation of a minority, a woman, or a black. She is stretched to the limits of physical and emotional endurance with these endless professional service demands.

In addition to the service demands, the black woman professor is expected to be a role model and mentor for the black undergraduate and graduate students who seek her out for knowledge, advice, sympathy, and friendship. Of course, these students are often themselves feeling the adverse affects and consequences of living in isolated small white towns. Moreover, for the black woman academician, the role model obligations extend far beyond the physical boundaries of the campus. Local churches, women's groups, civic and rights organizations, cultural and social service agencies, and the media frequently appeal to her to speak and lecture on a variety of topics. Usually, the requests peak during Black History and Women's History months and are issued all too frequently without mention of any remuneration.

While most black women professors willingly accommodate many of the service demands made upon their time within the academy, they are often frustrated by the knowledge that service counts for very little when it comes to achieving tenure, promotion, or higher wages. Black women professors earn less than white men and women, and black male professors. Nor is there the supportive understanding evidenced by administrators and colleagues that community and student service obligations are often performed at the expense of research and writing time. The future survival and success of black women in the academy depend on the extent to which institutions will provide them with course release time and greater financial support for their research.

It often requires an iron will and a strong constitution to do all the service, mentoring, and friendship work while continuing to produce scholarship. After I completed the Black Women in the Middle West project and before producing the Carlson Publishing reference series, I turned to blacks in the medical profession. By then my focus had shifted from medicine to nursing. In 1989 I published *Black Women in White: Racial Conflict and Cooperation in the Nursing Profession, 1890-1950.* The history of black women health care professionals proved to be the ideal vehicle to study gender relations and the problems growing out of the intersections of race and sex. Moreover, the study of this group of black women professionals has helped me to understand better the experiences of black women in the academy. There are, in other words, significant parallels, even though a century separates us.

My study focused on the earliest generation of activist black women who were also providers of nursing services—Harriet Tubman, Sojourner Truth, and Susie King Taylor nursed wounded black soldiers during the Civil War. By the end of the 1890s, in countless farm and small city communities, black women helped to found training schools for nurses and operated local well-baby clinics.[5] This activism and institution-building work of the first generation of black nursing professionals was necessary in order to overcome the racial exclusion and discrimination rampant in the larger society and within the profession itself. In 1908 the black nurses organized the National Association of Colored Graduate Nurses. In 1980 black women historians founded the Association of Black Women Historians. Both groups used their organizations to forge professional identities and to help their members combat racial and sexual discrimination and exclusion.

The work on black health care concentrates on the institutional apparatus for training practitioners while highlighting the accomplishments of several representative members of the twentieth-century health care profession. Black nurses' battles against racism and sexism prefigure the struggles that awaited my own generation of black women professors. A few women nurses and physicians best illustrate this point. Affectionately referred to by her patients as "Dr. Susan," Susan McKinney Steward was born of mixed European, African, and Shinecock Indian stock in 1847, the seventh of ten children. She entered the New York Medical College for Women in 1867 and graduated three years later as class valedictorian. She was the first black woman to practice medicine in New York and the third in the nation. In addition to a full medical practice, Steward found time for other causes: She was active in missionary work, a devout supporter of female suffrage, and president of the Women's Christian Temperance Union Number 6 in Brooklyn, New York.

The first trained black nurse in America, Mary Eliza Mahoney completed the nursing program at Boston's New England Hospital for Women and Children in 1879, a time when the institution's charter stipulated that each class include only one black student and one Jewish student. Like most new nurses, she first practiced private-duty nursing. (It wasn't until after World War II that any appreciable number of white nurses were hired by hospitals; black nurses were denied hospital staff positions for even longer.) Mahoney was one of the few black nurses accepted for membership in the Nurses Associated Alumnae of the United States and Canada, which was later renamed the American Nurses' Association (ANA). The majority of black nurses were denied membership into the ANA and accordingly in 1908 organized the National Association of Colored Graduate Nurses (NACGN). In 1936, the NACGN established an award in Mahoney's name to honor her distinguished service and the outstanding work of other black nurses. And forty years later, the ANA named Mahoney to its Hall of Fame.

Before she died, Anna DeCosta Banks, an early graduate of Dixie Hospital and Nursing Training School at Hampton Institute in Virginia, had hoped that it would be said of her, "She did what she could." And it has been said. As head nurse for the Hospital and School for Nurses in Charleston, South Carolina, Banks saw to it that the black community in Charleston received much-needed health care and that all interested black women (who were denied admission to the City Hospital Training School) received training in nursing from the Hospital and School for Nurses. At the same time, she encouraged the white community to employ black nurses by supplying the Ladies Benevolent Society with black nurses who would work flexible hours for cheap wages. It is impossible to find a woman who had a more critical influence on her community than Banks.

Born in Barbados in 1890 and raised in Harlem, Mabel Keaton Staupers fought racism in nursing through every stage of her career. As a young graduate of Freedmen's Hospital and Nursing Training School at Howard University in Washington, D.C., she helped to organize Booker T. Washington Sanitarium, the first in-patient center in Harlem for blacks with tuberculosis and one of the few city facilities that hired black physicians. As executive secretary of the NACGN during World War II, Staupers fought the government—and won. She seized the opportunity created by a shortage of nurses during the war to improve the lot of black nurses in the military. Thanks in part to her efforts, segregation of black nurses in the Armed Forces Nurse Corps ended shortly before the war itself. In 1951, the NAACP awarded Staupers the Spingarn Medal for breaking down barriers against black women in the nursing profession.

Finally, born in 1901 in Palestine, Texas, Estelle Massey Osborne and her ten brothers and sisters were not allowed to work for white people because their mother didn't want them exposed to racism—and the message stuck. Osborne went on to do her best to obliterate racism. Her goal was to improve the quality of education for black nurses nationwide. Working through the National Association of Colored Graduate Nurses as well as on her own, Osborne organized conferences, gave seminars, and conducted workshops across the country. She was the first black consultant to the National Nursing Council for War Service and served in executive positions with most of the important nursing organizations in the country. In one remarkable two-year period, she helped to increase the number of white nurses' training schools that admitted black students from fourteen to thirty-eight.

It is true that almost a century of racial exclusion, class oppression, and sexual discrimination thwarted even the most ambitious black women as they searched for mainstream educational opportunities in nursing and in medicine. For some black women professors the struggle is to win recognition for their scholarship, especially work that focuses on the historical experiences of black women.

Black women professors must tackle head-on the problems of having their research and scholarship taken seriously. This is precisely the area where they most share the frustrations and problems much discussed among white female colleagues, especially those who, during the early 1970s and 1980s, engaged the study of women. Although women's history has made great strides, and indeed some of the most sophisticated historical scholarship being produced today is in the field of women's history, there persists the slightly raised brow about the legitimacy of black women's history, literature, and studies.

Black women scholars, however, remain sensitive and vigilant to the ways their scholarship is received. Many will privately comment on their almost total exclusion from the key thematic or general interest journals in the field. I am concerned about the lack of institutional and professional organizational interest in black women's development. Others eschew close working relations with white women scholars, expressing suspicion as to the depth of their commitment to actually transforming the academy. But all is not doom and gloom. There are exceptional performers, to be sure. There are black women professors who have effectively demonstrated the possibilities of achieving respect, recognition, and reward for their work and enjoy solid careers within the profession. Still, there are always costs. Some of these star performers would be loathe to reveal inner anguish, doubt, anxiety, or the extent of their battle scars resulting from racist and sexist encounters with privileged or "status threatened" white and black male colleagues.

In many ways the experiences of black women professors serve as a window onto the issues, problems, and frustrations most marginalized groups, and women in general, daily encounter in the academy. There is never enough time to devote to self. Too much of the service performed goes unrewarded and unrecognized. Too often white male professors and administrators lack appreciation for scholarship produced. Black women professors in the academy still have to work twice as hard and be three times better just to be perceived as average and to win tenure and promotion.

Given the difficulties and challenges, the key question is how can black women survive and flourish in institutions that were never created with them in mind? Important weapons that can never be overemphasized are friendship, networks, and mutual support. While a supportive and informed professional community of likeminded colleagues is critical to success within the academy, it is equally important to have friends both within and outside the ivory gates. Throughout my academic career I have invested as much time and energy developing community among black historians and women's studies professors as I have employed in creating a body of black feminist scholarship. Phone calls, notes, letters, occasional visits, meeting at conferences, and attending sessions where black historians are presenting are the essentials tools for building and sustaining personal and professional friendships. It is worth underscoring that black women should make a point of attending and participating in the conferences of the relevant professional associations. This will give them and their work greater visibility. Attending annual meetings of the Association for the Study of Afro-American Life and History and participating as a life member in the Association of Black Women Historians were essential activities in both my professional development and intellectual evolution. These organizations provide a site for the sharing of war stories in the ongoing struggle against racism and sexism in the academy. Moreover, these groups and others are important advocacy agents for the teaching of African-American history and black women's history. They nurture the soul and spirit as well. Difficulties and personality conflicts occasionally surface, but for the most part these organizations and others like them are the garrisons to which weary intellectual warriors retreat for healing, affirmation, renewal, and guidance.

To be even more personal in my illustration of the necessity of friendship, it is impossible to exaggerate the importance of my convention conversations with University of Illinois Professor James D. Anderson. He informed me of all the records pertaining to black hospitals, and medical and nursing training schools located at the Rockefeller Archive Center in Tarrytown, New York. Without this information it would have been impossible for me to have written my book on black nursing. Conversations with Alton Hornsby of Morehouse College led to my being invited to serve on the editorial board of the *Journal of Negro History*. Similarly, it was while attending meetings of the Association of Black Women Historians that my friendship took root and bloomed with black women historians Linda Reed, Sharon Harley, Evelyn Brooks Higginbotham, Nell Irvin Painter, Rosalyn Terborg-Penn, Elsa Barkley Brown, and Mary Frances Berry among others. Their spoken words and writings have made the academy a much more hospitable site for black women's intellectual work.

I participated in other conferences and organizations to develop community with white feminist sisters whose work has influenced my own. The Berkshire Conference of Women Historians and the Southern Association of Women Historians afforded an opportunity to become acquainted with, and to form lasting, mutually supportive, friendships with historians Susan Reverby, Gerda Lerner, Anne Firor Scott, and Betty Brandon among others. Over the years we have read and commented on one another's manuscripts, grant proposals, and editing projects and offered invaluable moral support.

I know that in some circles it is fashionable to bash white males and to blame them for whatever ills and misfortunes befall those on the margins of, or excluded from, the historical mainstream. While some of the laments are inarguably justified and must be aired before healthy relations can be constructed, it is important to acknowledge the value of friendships and essential support that cut across gender and race boundaries. Were it not for the friendship, advice, encouragement, and strategic support of William C. Hine of South Carolina State University, Harold Woodman and Donald Berthrong of Purdue University, Harold Hyman of Rice University, Gordon Stewart, Harold Marcus, and William B. Hixson of Michigan State University, and Steven Lawson of the University of North Carolina at Greensboro I certainly would not be in the position I enjoy today.

Finally, I am especially grateful to my colleague and friend Wilma King who saved me from being the only black woman in the history department at MSU in much the same way that Gwendolyn Keita Robinson, my friend since our undergraduate days at Roosevelt University in Chicago, saved me from a similar fate at Purdue University. The future of black women in the academy is full of promise and exciting possibilities. Today I have under my direction six young black women working toward Ph.D. degrees.[6] Perhaps these reflections will help ease their journey in the academy.

PART 2

History, Gender, and Culture

"In the Kingdom of Culture"

Black Women and the Intersection of Race, Gender, and Class in Black History

Black thinkers have pondered and agonized over questions of race, racism, and racial identity since the times of Phillis Wheatley. And even before Maria Stewart broke with convention and spoke before a mixed audience in 1831, black women wrestled with the complexities of constructing a racial identity that incorporated gender and class. From the outset black women encountered an America that denied their humanity, debased their femininity, and refused them self-possession. The acquisition of a measure of freedom and citizenship privileges would have to await a modern civil rights movement that they profoundly initiated and sustained.

When in 1903, W.E.B. Du Bois, the preeminent black scholar of his generation, wrote about racial identity in terms of "twoness" and "double-consciousness," he gave the term "Negro" a generic meaning: "It is a peculiar sensation, this double-consciousness, this sense of always looking at one's self through the eyes of others, of measuring one's soul by the tape of a world that looks on in amused contempt and pity." Du Bois's compelling prose in *The Souls of Black Folk* (1903) captured well his perception of the dichotomous nature of black identity struggles and the pressure to choose one or the other: "One ever feels his twoness,—an American, a Negro; two souls, two thoughts, two unreconciled strivings; two warring ideals in one dark body, whose dogged strength alone keeps it from being torn asunder."

Had Du Bois specifically included the experiences and lives of black women in his lament he probably would have had to modify his prose. For Du Bois, race was the master key to understanding American reality and the most potent factor shaping identity. Still, I suspect, had he considered the issue of gender, instead of writing "One ever feels his twoness," he would have mused about how one ever feels her "fiveness": Negro, American, woman, poor, black woman. An examination of the separate realities and complex identities of black women offers greater illumination of the power relations that operate along the interlocking grid of race, sex, and class in America. Du Bois's analysis dominated black thought for most of the twentieth century. As African-American men and women of all classes, however, confront the twentieth-first century there is a need for new thinking and more inclusive and varied metaphors about black identity and the process of assimilation. The history of the American Negro is more than a history of efforts, as Du Bois put it, "to attain self-conscious manhood"; it is simultaneously a story of the development and preservation of a dynamic, multiconscious black womanhood.

For the record, no such person as a generic Negro or a generic American exists. Inasmuch as we all experience life along axes of difference, each black or American is a person of some specific sex or sexual orientation. Each person has a certain class or social status, and each belongs to what is called a "race." Here I must underscore that there is only one biological race, and that is the human race. Today, when we use the term "race" we are actually talking about the social construction of differences. Race, class, and gender are not the only factors that shape identity, but they are, even more to the point, potent indicators of an individual's relation to power.

I will use the concepts of race, class, and gender in addition to those of region and profession as analytical tools to describe the process by which black women, too, became, in Du Bois's words, "co-worker[s] in the kingdom of culture." My own academic work focuses on the history of black women in the Middle West and in the nursing profession. I will return to these topics later in this essay, but first I want to focus attention on two crucial developments that formed black women's identity and affected the extent of their assimilation in America—the institution of slavery and the rise of women's clubs.

I

Fully to understand black women's identities requires that we push back the historical curtain to look yet again at the institution of slavery. My thinking about the multiple identities of black women and their adversarial relations with most of American society has led me to conclude that to the extent that assimilation depends upon, and is a reflection of, cultural values and material possession, black women are at once the most and the least assimilated Americans.

Slavery was the dominant economic and social system that shaped the experiences and lives of black women from the early seventeenth through the middle of the nineteenth century. Scholars have scrutinized and dissected this institution more than any other. But until the advent of black women's history, historians focused exclusively on male slaves, and even the new generation of revisionist scholars assumed little difference in the experiences of men and women slaves. The recent authentication of slave narratives written by captive women such as Harriet Jacobs and Elizabeth Keckley, however, as well as the appearance of monographs such as Melton McLaurin's *Celia, A Slave* (1991), and Deborah Gray White's *Ar'n't I A Woman?: Female Slaves in the Plantation South* (1985), point to a more inclusive scholarship in the future.

Slavery was many things, but it was first and foremost concerned with extracting the greatest amount of labor with the least amount of capital investment. While male slaves were highly valued for the work they were capable of doing, the whole institution rested most profoundly upon the backs of black women. Southern slavery developed a rigid political economy and social hierarchy with black women at the core. The very structure and organization of coerced labor depended on the subordination and control of the women. Here I am suggesting that unraveling the interwoven systems of racial and sexual oppression and class exploitation in this society dictates a fundamental reconceptualization of African-American and indeed all of American history, from the perspective of black women. I am neither sanguine about the difficulty of such a project nor am I persuaded that this will be done soon, although important research and writing is underway.

As slavery became deeply entrenched in southern states, and as the prospect of securing fresh Africans disappeared after 1807 with the official end of the slave trade, slave masters knew that control of the reproductive capacities of black women amounted to the only sure way of maintaining a viable slave-labor population. Regardless of the specificities of crop cultivation, or the myriad configurations of work assignments on farms and plantations, the need for new slaves steadily increased. The unending challenge therefore was to make black women envision their reproductive work as part of what it meant to be a woman, while insisting that their productive labor constituted a definition of what it meant to be a black. The master's objective was twofold: to enslave her mind as well as her body and to exploit both in order to maximize his profits.

But economic interests were actually only the most apparent concern. The effective management of slave women also meant appropriation of their sexuality. Slave masters, overseers, and other white men could and did rape slave women at will. Black women suffered direct white male sexual aggression, but the slave community as a whole was indirectly assaulted. No segment of the slave population possessed immunity from the psychological impact occasioned by white male sexual aggression against powerless women. The scholarly consensus is that at least 58 percent of all slave women between the ages of fifteen and thirty were sexually abused by white males. Rape had the added advantage of producing new slaves and thus enriching masters while satisfying white men's carnal desires. Perhaps the most daunting task confronting black women historians is to persuade students of slavery to see it as more than an economic institution. Slavery was also a sexual institution, and it was white male control of black women as sexual beings that shored up the patriarchal dimension of the system. Until gender becomes a central analytical concept in the writing of the history of slavery, our appreciation of the complexities of the American past remains stillborn.

It would be a mistake to see black women solely as victims under slavery. It is equally undesirable, however, to create myths of the superheroic black woman who stoically met every obstacle, endured total debasement, only to rise above her tormentors and captors. Black women in all eras understand the multilayered realities of their oppression and exploitation and develop an array of survival strategies and functional identities. On plantations and farms of all sizes and purposes, black women developed networks with each other, and, where feasible, they embraced their own form of Christianity, crafted a distinct moral code, and fashioned permeable family boundaries that freely made room for blood relatives and fictive kin. The extended, flexible, adaptable black family is as much black women's invention as it is an African retention. In other words, part of the requirements for survival dictated that black women, when necessary, reconfigured and reimagined families, communities, and themselves. Survival mandated that they develop private identities and inner worlds known only to their own.

Because of their separate realities and material conditions, black women created identities that remain ambiguous and are seemingly contradictory. In tandem with their enslavement, the dominant society fostered a host of negative ideas about black women's character, humanity, and sexuality. Ironically, in order to justify the multilayered oppression of black women, slave masters and apologists for slavery promoted distorted images that blamed the victim and assuaged the guilt of white men, creating the stereotypical image of the black woman as sexually wanton, while at the same time maintained the image of the devoted house servant who loved her master's family more than she did her own. Few seemed disturbed by this paradox. Slavery was best served by ignoring or denying the existence of rebellious slave women who disguised their true feelings and deeds and attacked with arson, poison, or weapons when pushed too far.

Actually, most slave women cultivated or adopted a series of personas when appropriate. For the most part, slave women did the work assigned them, cared for their families, fought and resisted when they had to, and bit their tongues in order to minimize their hostility toward and discourse with whites. They practiced their religion and participated in the creation and dissemination of a unique culture that was by necessity woman-centered, because the guiding passion of slave masters intent on maximizing profits and their own security was to control and exploit the women who held the key to slavery's perpetuation. Women, like men, were often rendered submissive through brutal beatings. Although such violent attacks on women could impair their slave-bearing capacities and even destroy their lure as sex objects, virtually every slave narrative recounts an instance of the brutalization of a slave woman. Maintaining an atmosphere of terror, whether through violence or through threats of selling her away from her family, bolstered the master's efforts to defeminize and dehumanize the slave woman, to reduce her identity to property and to break her will to resist.

The lives and experiences of two of the most celebrated black women in antebellum America, the ex-slaves Sojourner Truth and Harriet Tubman, are critical to any discussion of identity formation. Both women used their considerable talents actively to oppose slavery, Truth through her participation in the abolition movement and as a fighter for women's rights, and Tubman as a fearless conductor of the Underground Railroad. Truth posited a new, inclusive definition of womanhood in her many speeches, while Tubman demonstrated what it meant to be a human being when she risked her life on dozens of trips to rescue hundreds of slaves along Maryland's eastern shore and in her work as a spy and scout during the Civil War.

For both Truth and Tubman, the unrelenting quest for freedom was the mainstay of their identities. Their passionate embrace of freedom was born not of some abstract commitment to the Constitution or the noble sentiments embodied in the Declaration of Independence, but out of the reality of their enslavement and oppression. They knew firsthand what it meant to be owned by another, to be considered little more than a cow or a mule. Truth and Tubman also mastered the survival skills slavery and multiple oppression required. Slavery, and resistance to it, was the defining moment of the birth of black women's oppositional consciousness. The experiences of slavery and their acts of active and passive resistance deepened black women's understanding of the dynamics of patriarchy and the operation of racism. Out of these specific historical and material conditions black women developed a pattern of values, beliefs, customs, and behaviors that shaped their identities and comprised the heart of black culture.

The strength of the inner identities that black women forged and nurtured during slavery facilitated the transition to freedom. With dispatch black men and women reunited families, established separate churches, opened schools, and even attempted to exert some control over their economic lives by inventing the sharecropping system. In spite of these manifold efforts to give meaning to hard-won freedom, one thing, their economic subordination, remained fixed.

Notwithstanding the gradual rise of a black middle class, the vast majority of black women worked in domestic service and agriculture. The location of most of their jobs in white women's kitchens meant that at least some black women, even in freedom, remained vulnerable to white male sexual aggression. But the tenuous grip of black males on employment opportunities necessitated that married black women remain in the labor force. The intersection of race and gender constructions, as well as relentless poverty, consigned black women to the least desirable jobs for which they received negligible wages.

Black women's economic woes matched their low political status in a period that historian Rayford Logan called the nadir. Given the patriarchal nature of American society, it is not surprising that with few exceptions black men and women applauded, in 1870, the adoption of the Fifteenth Amendment to the U.S. Constitution. Inauspiciously, this amendment in some ways cemented a gender breach in black culture. While a large degree of sexual equality was manifested between slave men and women, the adoption of the Fifteenth Amendment created a fundamental inequality in their access to power. Once black men gained the right to vote, black women had no alternative but to negotiate with and convince their male relatives to use the ballot to advance group as opposed to individual interests. Black women dealt with questions of black political participation just as they appeared to acquiesce to their lack of visible positions of leadership in black churches. They worked to persuade men that their individual ballots were in reality their collective property.

I suspect that the most disturbing thing about the Fifteenth Amendment from a black woman's perspective was that it allowed black men the latitude to determine the public agenda in the struggle against racism. Black men embraced the ideology of integration. Few representative black leaders, despite advocacy of different tactics and strategies, questioned the rightness of the goal of full, unfettered assimilation. This is by no means intended to ignore the movement of the thousands of African Americans who left the South in the 1880s and established scores of all-black towns on the western frontiers. I am suggesting, however, that male leaders of the millions of blacks who remained in southern states and in some northern communities differed only as to the means by which assimilation and integration were to be achieved and over what time frame. Black men from Booker T. Washington to W.E.B. Du Bois viewed the establishment of autonomous, separate organizations and institutions essentially as a means to an end. Of course Marcus Garvey in the early 1920s and Du Bois by the 1930s denounced integrationism. But when they did so they swam against mainstream black political thought.

As integrationism became the entrenched ideology and goal in the public-sphere debates, black women were increasingly silenced and overshadowed. Their desires for and efforts toward the creation of a network of separate autonomous community institutions as an end unto itself garnered less public regard. This does not mean that black women eschewed the fight for equal representation and full citizenship. Examples of their protest activities, from washerwomen strikes in Atlanta to civil suits against segregated trains throughout the South, readily disprove such notions.

In response to sexual repression within and without the black community, black women developed a two-pronged attack. Some loudly proclaimed their allegiance to black men and insisted that the struggle for rights and opportunities had to be a unified one. Others looked to one another for the power they needed to change their lives. Many of the strategies that had enabled them to survive slavery were revised to meet contemporary exigencies. African-American women combined work to advance the race as a whole with efforts to carve out psychic space for the development of a new collective black women's oppositional consciousness that was appropriate in the era of Jim Crow.

Black women's culture reached a new height of self-awareness in the closing decades of the nineteenth century. As they consolidated and formed national organizations such as the National Association of Colored Women in 1896, black women defined the issues about which they would be concerned and the strategies they would employ. A direct line of activism extends from Harriet Tubman's work on the Underground Railroad to Ida B. Wells's antilynching crusade. Black women never abandoned their belief that the liberation and safety of black men was an inextricable component of the overall struggle, but they were acutely aware of gender concerns.

Within the confines of their separate realities, individual African American-women had to create a patchwork of identities just to get through most days. Because the vast majority of them were poor, and therefore imprisoned in a horizontally segregated labor force, black women urgently yearned for middle-class respectability. Their legendary desire for respectability is reflected in a preoccupation with appearance, hair, dress, and skin color. Considering the singular wealth Madam C. J. Walker of Indianapolis, Indiana, amassed in the opening decades of the twentieth century, one could conclude that ambivalence existed in the American part of black women's identity. Is it possible to measure black women's assimilation in the Progressive Era not by the reform and social-welfare work they engaged in but by the extent to which they straightened their hair, wore socially accepted styles, and endeavored to lighten their complexions with cosmetics?

It is tempting to argue that black women made Madam C. J. Walker America's first self-made millionairess because she gave them the means to approximate whiteness by dispatching tightly curled hair with the straightening comb and miraculous hair tonics. But black women did not purchase beauty products and use skin-bleaching creams to obscure or to camouflage their blackness, their distinctiveness. Rather, they used these technologies and products out of a desire for greater access to economic opportunities in a society that measured worth according to color and gender roles and material possessions. Cosmetics, dress, and hairstyling became essential equipment in the unending work of black women to manipulate workable identities while shielding their inner lives from view. Black women desired the same opportunities as whites. They did not wish to be white, for to do so meant abandoning the culture and institutions they had created to ensure the survival and progress of their people.

Scholars of black women's history have performed an immense amount of research into the history of the rise of black women's clubs beginning in the late nineteenth century. Such concentration is warranted. The myriad organizations founded were more than a response to the insulting declarations of white newspaperman James T.

Jacks that all black women were liars and prostitutes. Moreover, the clubs were not simply reactions to white women's denial of membership in their organizations. Rather, club formation continued the organizing work of antebellum black women in the antislavery movement. Propitiously, coming together in clubs helped black women to accumulate information concerning the tribulations involved in migrating and to establish the networks needed to ease the stress of resettlement in regions such as the Middle West.

Through the vehicle of their clubs and organizations, which provided a measure of individual invisibility and protection, black women collectively addressed urban social problems by (re)creating an array of self-help institutions. This work on behalf of their communities reinforced their own self-constructed identities as respectable, moral race women and thus enabled them to be even more effective workers and leaders in "the kingdom of culture."

II

In examining the culture and experiences of middle western black women as a group or the life of individual blacks nurses, I seek to know what they believed, valued, and accomplished and how they resisted the multiple oppression that are constant forces in black women's existence. Black women are grounded in familial and friendship networks and in larger social units that form communities. How these groups and communities define race, class, and gender roles and develop resistance strategies reflect the often invisible but nevertheless consequential work of black women. It is through their individual and collective work within families, friendship networks, and communities that a clear picture emerges of the contours of black women's identity, consciousness, and interdependence.

Any study of an individual black woman needs to place her in specific regional communities that possess a range of clubs, civic and religious organizations, and institutions. Black women's organizations nurtured and sustained black women and empowered and supported black communities. Through voluntary organizations black women were able to develop by the turn of the century a substantial reform and race-uplift agenda. Specifically, the club movement and the early entry of black women into key female professions, such as nursing, social work, librarianship, and teaching, afforded them the means and latitude to impose their own distinct visions and ideas and to initiate a plethora of programs and projects. Black women's activism within the structure of clubs, organizations, and institutions made possible greater sexual autonomy, encouraged economic development, and promoted racial progress, all without seeming to threaten or challenge male dominance.

In particular, the history of black women nurses provides ample illustration of how black women actually constructed positive identities and achieved greater self-awareness while permitting a glimpse of the abstractions and stereotypes that even now often diminish and caricature their lives and experiences. In the larger society, historically women's quest for personal achievement and self-fulfillment has been possible only through carefully prescribed channels. For black women, the range of roles permitted was even narrower; yet, on occasion, they forced reality to diverge from the so-called idealized construction of women's sphere. Perhaps black women gained valuable breathing space when the larger society denied them membership in "the cult of true womanhood" characterized by piety, purity, submissiveness, and domesticity. It was within this breathing space that they subtly challenged the notions of "woman's sphere" and of a "black's place."

In 1908 black nurses founded the National Association of Colored Graduate Nurses (NACGN). It became, under the dynamic leadership of Mabel Keaton Staupers in the 1940s, a powerful weapon in the struggle against discrimination and segregation in the nursing profession and in the fight to abolish the quotas imposed by the U.S. Armed Forces Nurse Corps during World War II. Staupers boldly attacked the racist policies of top military authorities and demanded that they dismantle Jim Crow quotas. Through the NACGN black women nurses acquired professional identity and the voice to articulate their grievances, and they were able to develop more sophisticated connections with black communities that proved essential to the successful outcome of the overall quest for integration in nursing.

The white nursing profession held black nurses in low regard, frequently judging their skills and aptitude inferior to whites. Prior to the successes of the modern civil rights movement, few white hospitals admitted black women into nurses' training, hired black graduate nurses, or advanced them to supervisory positions in visiting nurse agencies. As private-duty nurses black women received less pay and were often required to perform household chores in addition to nursing service. White nurses and white clients saw black nurses as little more than uniformed domestic servants.

In marked contrast, black communities held these same nurses in high esteem, according them the pride and dignity denied in their dealings with their white professional peers. Acting in their own best interests, black nurses grounded themselves within the communities that created and supported a nationwide network of clinics, hospitals, and training schools. The relationship black nurses enjoyed with black communities therefore served as a powerful antidote to the racism, sexism, and elitism prevalent within the larger profession and throughout American society.

Black nurses were not the only ones who looked to community for a healthy sense of professional and personal identity. Midwestern black women, and I suspect the same is true for black women in all regions, developed an impressive array of clubs and created autonomous organizations and institutions that first ensured racial survival and second facilitated selective adaptation and measured assimilation. Certainly, the schools, hospitals, libraries, community centers, settlement houses, day-care centers, and employment agencies that they erected and sustained had a strong "domestic" cast. But be not misled—they were decidedly public in orientation. Again, these nurturing institutions cloaked black community women's individual and collective intent to erect bulwarks against the internalization of self-damaging norms, against beliefs that difference meant inferiority.

Not all black women successfully resisted assaults on their consciousness. Many succumbed to the forces that denigrated and marginalized their identities and experiences, filling them with self-loathing and self-abnegation. Not surprisingly, then, some black women straddled, trying to adhere to the traditional cultural values and beliefs of the black community while embracing white ways in order to seize new opportunities. Had all abandoned their communities, families, and friends, there would be precious little to talk or to think about in black women's history. Cultural ambivalence notwithstanding, the founding of Provident Hospital and School of Nursing in Chicago united these disparate contexts and thus serves as a potent illustration of the way that race, access to resources, and gender roles forged black women's consciousness and activism.

When Emma Reynolds, the sister of a prominent black minister in Chicago, arrived in 1890 from Kansas City with hopes of attending nurses' training school, she quickly discovered the doors of the existing institutions closed. Denied admission into every nursing school in the city, Reynolds spoke to her brother, who in turn sought advice and assistance from physician Daniel Hale Williams. A group of black ministers, physicians, and businessmen approached white authorities but failed in their attempts to pry open the doors of the white nursing schools. Williams thereupon appealed for aid to the Reverend Jenkins Lloyd Jones, pastor of All Souls' Church, who placed the issue squarely before the members of his congregation. The indefatigable black clubwoman and organizer Fannie Barrier Williams was in the congregation. With her usual verve, Williams, along with other black clubwomen, played a major role in mobilizing community support and raised money for the establishment of Provident Hospital and School of Nursing, thus ensuring that black women would have access to this profession and that black patients would be treated with respect by their own physicians.

It is senseless to discuss the impact of racism on the formation of black identities without concomitant explorations into the ways race, a social construct of tremendous importance, nevertheless intersects with constructs of gender and class. Arguably, the history of black women in the United States provides the best available lens through which to illustrate the intersections of race, gender, and class across time. In other words, the ironies, contradictions, conflicts, and paradoxes of American history and culture are seen most graphically in the enigmatic black woman. An examination of this underside of American history requires an awareness of the relentless struggle black women continue to wage against sexual oppression, economic exploitation, social ridicule, and personal dehumanization.

Quilts and African-American Women's Cultural History

On July 19, 1988, Jesse Jackson addressed the Democratic Party Convention in Atlanta, Georgia, and made poignant remarks about the functional and political dimensions of black women's quilting. He declared:

> When I was a child growing up in Greenville, South Carolina, and Grandmomma could not afford a blanket, she didn't complain, and we didn't freeze. Instead, she took pieces of old cloth—patches—wool, silk, gaberdine, crockersak—only patches, barely good enough to wipe off your shoes with. But they didn't stay that way very long. With sturdy hands and a strong chord, she sewed them together into a quilt, a thing of beauty and power and culture.[1]

In telling this story, Jackson paid tribute to the way a black woman's quilting provided a resourceful solution to an urgent family problem as well as an object they considered beautiful. That he chose to convey this story to a national audience on such a historic occasion suggests the importance that quilt making has played in the lives of black men and women in this country.

Quilts are often the only physical evidence or historical testament revealing aspects of the inner lives and creative spirits of many otherwise obscure and unknown black women. Imbedded in quilts produced through history have been deep reflections on the everyday activities, values, and beliefs of ordinary folk. But the quilt, like any other document, needs to be interpreted and analyzed if we are to appreciate fully its significance in the history of African Americans and, in particular, African-American women's cultural history.

Increasingly scholars are focusing attention on the history of black women's experiences in America. For centuries African-American women existed outside of history. They were neither subjects nor objects of history. Indeed, during my formative years as a young historian, black women were deemed important and worthy of note only as they were related to men, organizations, or institutions. A facile assumption held that whatever was said and written about black men applied to black women, and that the study of white women's history covered black women as well. Scholars rarely granted black women separate and distinct treatment. Indeed, in most school textbooks the only three black women discussed were Phillis Wheatley, Harriet Tubman, and Sojourner Truth. Accordingly, in the late 1960s black women fell through the cracks between emerging black studies and women's studies on most of the nation's campuses. By the 1980s both black history and women's history had become accepted and legitimate areas of scholarly inquiry. Few scholars noticed the absence of black women, let alone their contributions in the realm of material culture.

Two of the important early works that challenged the exclusion of black women from the historical record were *Black Women in White America: A Documentary History*, edited by Gerda Lerner, and *The Afro-American Woman: Struggles and Images*, edited by Rosalyn Terborg-Penn and Sharon Harley.[2] More recently, in part spurred by the black women's cultural renaissance of the late 1970s that witnessed the rise of several writers including Alice Walker, Toni Morrison, and Paule Marshall, modern reclamation scholars have published several important books and articles that chronicle the lives and deeds of individuals and analyze the collective social reform work of thousands of black clubwomen across the nation. One of the benchmarks in the flowering of black women's history was the publication of the two-volume *Black Women in America: An Historical Encyclopedia* (1993) that Elsa Barkley Brown of the University of Michigan, Rosalyn Terborg-Penn of Morgan State University, and I edited.

The appearance of the *Encyclopedia* signaled the existence of a new system of meaning, based on black women's experiences, triumphs, and tribulations in the ongoing struggle against racial intolerance and sexual exploitation. The *Encyclopedia* with its over 600 biographical entries and 150 topical essays not only enhances the visibility of black women but also validates the viability of black women's history. It is within this intellectual and academic context of an emerging body of new knowledge and insights about black women and their culture and community that the book *African-American Quilt Making Traditions in Michigan* makes a unique and significant contribution.

A study of Michigan quilters and their artistic creations enhances our ability to know and to see black women in more complex, less stereotypical ways. Black women acquired subjecthood through their creative works. An examination of this complex creativity of black women as manifested through their quilts opens a window onto their culture and their community. The art of quilt making brought black women together in protected spaces where they could cement friendships, share ideas, acquire information, and find and give to one another essential support and encouragement. As their stories and quilts amply demonstrate, black women's artistic contributions allowed a greater appreciation of the traditional practices and ways they devised to "make community" and to thus ensure the survival of their people and to maintain respect for themselves as women. By "making community" I mean the process of creating social, religious, educational, health-care, philanthropic, political, and familial institutions and organizations that ensured racial survival and progress.[3]

In his *Black Culture and Black Consciousness: Afro-American Folk Thought from Slavery to Freedom*, historian Lawrence Levine described black culture as a dynamic product of interaction between the past and present, characterized by its ability to react creatively and responsibly to the realities of a new situation. He called for the development of a fresh sensitivity "to the ways in which the African world view interacted with that of the Euro-American world into which it was carried and the extent to which an Afro-American perspective was created."[4] Levine is quick to point out that African-American culture is neither "abject surrender of all previous cultural standards in favor of embracing those of the white master" nor inflexible resistance to change.

Quilting is, perhaps, one of the most striking illustrations and embodiments of African-American women's culture. Even though the quilt is one of the most commonplace domestic examples of black American material culture in United States history, few scholars actively engaged in its study until relatively recently. In 1978, a landmark exhibition at the Cleveland Museum of Art entitled The Afro-American Tradition in Decorative Arts presented, for the first time, black material folk culture in a fine arts setting. John Vlach, curator of the exhibit and author of the accompanying catalog, challenged visitors to reexamine previous conceptions and misconceptions about decorative arts and to view this material culture, including quilts, as an essential part of Afro-American art and cultural history.

This exhibition served as a catalyst for examining the ways quilt making embodies Euro-, African-American, and African artistic traditions. Vlach observed that "the Afro-American quilt provides us with an example of how European artifacts may be modified by African canons of design and thus stand as statements of cultural survival rather than surrender."[5] Quilting gave to many enslaved black women, and later to the freedwomen, a mechanism with which to transmit and preserve a "cultural memory."

The techniques of quilt construction, designs, styles, and patterns used by black quilters are derived from both African and Euro-American sources. Much has been published on the work of quilters, particularly in the nineteenth and early twentieth centuries and primarily from Southern states, whose work reflects a distinctly African aesthetic. For instance, in the string or "strip" quilt, women sew together scraps of cloth into strips and then assemble the strips into various patterns. Vlach commented on the "transatlantic continuity of aesthetic preferences" evidenced by this form of quilting:

> When a Sea Islands woman mixes and matches thirteen assorted strips of cloth to make a quilt, she is inspired by the same creative muse that leads the Ashanti weaver to make a priest's robe out of fifteen different strips of Kente Cloth. The African weaver continues to use the techniques of his [her] ancestor while the Afro-American quilter has had to learn new techniques. The ancestral ideas, however, remain the same.[6]

Appliquéd quilts that communicate a story have often been linked to African oral narrative and design traditions. One of the most famous enslaved black women quilters of this style was Harriet Powers (1837–1911) of Athens, Georgia. Her two known extant "Bible Quilts" (c. 1886 and 1898) are owned respectively by the Boston Museum of Fine Arts and the Smithsonian Institution in Washington, D.C. To convey both local history and biblical events and stories, Powers used appliquéd silhouettes of human figures, geometric motifs, and other design combinations that resemble the styles found among the people of ancient Dahomey in West Africa. Vlach asserts that "what may in the end be regarded as the most important feature of Afro-American quilting is the apparent refusal to simply surrender an alternative aesthetic sense to the confines of mainstream expectations. Euro-American forms were converted so that African ideas would not be lost."[7]

African-American women, as slaves and freedwomen, converted the utilitarian quilt into an object of art and transformed quilting into a social and cultural community affair. Ex-slave Mary Wright of Kentucky reminisces about quilting: ". . . den wemns [women] quilt awhile den a big dinner war spread out den after dinner we'd quilt in de evening, den supper and a big dance dat night, wid de banjo a humming 'n us niggers a dancing. . . ."[8] The importance of quilting as a social activity continues today as witnessed in such Michigan groups as the African American Quilting Group in Flint and the Quilting Six group in Detroit. Contemporary black woman artist Samella Lewis reminds us that African art rose above its roots in utility; indeed, the majority of works of African art were made to fulfill the needs of the communities.[9] By studying these groups and their individual members one can learn much about individual African-American women as well as artistic, social, religious, and even political dimensions of community histories.

Although African art served political and social needs, this did not negate the fact that it also represented individual expression. It is especially suggestive that quilting is a creative process whereby black women can give voice and vision, structure and substance, to their personal and spiritual lives. In the introduction to the 1980 museum exhibit catalog, *Forever Free: Art by African American Women, 1862–1980*, the first anthology of the art specifically of African-American women, editors Arna Bontemps and Jacqueline Fonville-Bontemps correctly point out:

> Black women—through the intellectual and aesthetic choices they made and the traditions they helped preserve—played a vital role in developing those meaningful forms of self-expression by which Black people in America have managed to survive two-and-a-half centuries of chattel slavery and nearly half a millennium of racial oppression.[10]

The art and quilts provide eloquent testimony to the existence of a vibrant and vital black women's cultural tradition. May the historical contours and value of their quilts and the stories of their makers continue to excite and enrich us all.

Culture, Consciousness, and Community
The Making of an African-American Women's History

In *Darkwater: Voices from Within the Veil* (1920), W.E.B. Du Bois declared that "after the [Civil] war, the sacrifice of Negro women for freedom and uplift [was] one of the finest chapters in their history." He went on to note that while the men of the race received more press and praise for their accomplishments, women's achievements had been more impressive: "As I look about me today in this veiled world of mine, despite the noisier and more spectacular advance of my brothers, I instinctively feel and know that it is the five million women of my race who really count." Insisting that black women were the foundation of the *public schools, settlement houses, and churches* (emphasis mine) within the black communities and that African Americans possessed more than $1 billion in accumulated property and goods, Du Bois demanded, "Who shall say how much of it has been wrung from the hearts of servant girls and washerwomen and women toilers in the fields?"[1]

With this question Du Bois issued a challenge that has deep resonance for today's community of scholars. In a not unrelated vein, historian John Hope Franklin has issued another challenge. "Every generation has the opportunity to write its own history, and indeed it is obliged to do so. Only in that way can it provide its contemporaries with the materials vital to understanding the present and to planning strategies for coping with the future. Only in that way can it fulfill its obligation to pass on to posterity the accumulated knowledge and wisdom of the past, which, after all, give substance and direction for the continuity of civilization."[2]

Black Women in America: An Historical Encyclopedia is one example of my generation's struggle to reclaim and make accessible the history of black women in order that their lives and stories may inspire and empower us all in the ongoing struggle against race and sex systems of exploitation and oppression. History's power resides in its capacity to explain why things are. Black women have long recognized the importance of telling their stories to the world, yet until very recently only a few, mostly other black women—their daughters, sisters, mothers—heard their voices or were able to make sense out of these lives. For the vast majority of Americans, black women were simply an amalgamation of stereotypes and myths ranging from mammy, Jezebel, Sapphire, to today's castrating matriarch and welfare queen. One of the major objectives of the *Encyclopedia* therefore, is to destroy all negative, dehumanizing stereotypes by presenting an abundance of written and photographic information concerning real black women.

The two-volume *Encyclopedia* spans 1,530 pages and contains 640 biographical entries and 163 topical essays dealing with diverse topics from black sororities to religious orders to protest groups. Essays cover black women in slavery, Civil War and Reconstruction, and their experiences with domestic work and sexual harassment. The biographical entries profile the lives of 116 educators, 101 political activists, 39 physicians, 19 nurses, 17 abolitionists, 5 nuns, 38 actresses, 17 entrepreneurs, 77 writers, and 1 astronaut. The index is 150 pages, the twenty-five-page chronology begins in 1619, when the first three black women landed at Jamestown, Virginia, and ends with the election of Carol Moseley-Braun to the United States Senate.

While a couple of reviewers have questioned the amount of space accorded one black woman versus another, or mused about who was missing, they all conclude that the *Encyclopedia* is an "astounding" achievement. Columbia University black law professor Patricia Williams (in a review in *MS*, May/June 1993) declared that the existence of the *Encyclopedia* rendered all the standard references and histories of America suspect and inadequate. We are now in a position to judge and to assess earlier and future historical scholarship in quite different ways. The *Encyclopedia* has ushered in a new meaning system grounded in an understanding of the intertwined analysis of the historical and social constructions of race, gender, and class. Simply put, the making of an African-American women's history has changed everything and makes it impossible for an enlightened historical profession to rationalize continued exclusion, distortion, and marginalization of black women.

The *Encyclopedia* is part of a virtual revolution that strives to write the lives and voices of ordinary people into the history of this country. It is part of a revolution that will affect black history in particular. Twenty years ago, for example, few people wrote about the role of black women in the civil rights movement. Only now are Ella Baker, Fannie Lou Hamer, and Jo Ann Gibson Robinson receiving biographical treatment. *Women in the Civil Rights Movement: Trailblazers and Torchbearers* (1989) edited by Vicki Crawford, Barbara Woods, and Jacqueline Rouse is the first anthology to explore the myriad roles black women played in the movement. The revolutionary transformation of American history that is still unfolding has already affected women's history.

In a recent article, white feminist historian Linda Gordon observed, "Several historians have recently studied black women's civic contributions, but black women's reform campaigns have not usually been seen as part of welfare history." She goes on to ask rhetorically, "How many discussions of settlement houses include Victoria Earle Matthew's White Rose Mission of New York city, or Margaret Murray Washington's Elizabeth Russell Settlement at Tuskegee, Alabama, or Janie Porter Barrett's Locust Street Social Settlement in Hampton, Virginia, or Lugenia Burns Hope's Neighborhood Union in Atlanta, Georgia?"[3] The answer is, of course, none. But the important thing to note is that because of the work of black women historians such as Cynthia Neverdon-Morton, Jacqueline Rouse, Sharon Harley, Elsa Barkley Brown, Evelyn Higginbotham, Tera Hunter, Paula Giddings, Rosalyn Terborg-Penn, Wilma King, and Lillian S. Williams, American, Southern, women, labor, black, and social historians are forced to ask new questions. They are forced to adopt different methods and to create new paradigms and conceptual categories for analysis. It is ironic that just as the embrace of race as an analytical category enriched and enlivened general American history, the incorporation of a gendered analysis promises to excite and to deepen our study of social history.

History is more than the accumulation of new facts and data. It is not enough to simply add a few black women to the existing story and stir. Rather, the task before us is to reconceptualize Southern, Midwestern, and Northeastern history so that the roles, struggles, and perspectives of black women are integral to an understanding of these disparate regions. As I reviewed the *Encyclopedia* in preparation for the Lawrence F. Brewster Lecture, I was again impressed by the preponderance of Southern black women in particular included in the volumes. Thus I will focus specifically on the four institutions within which black Southern women worked out their lives: family, church, schools, and health care. This is not to say that political and economic institutions were unimportant; clearly they were. I am drawn to these institutions and the role of women within them because they hold the key to understanding how black Southerners survived a series of transitions beginning with the transition from slavery to freedom, and from rural to urban. Moreover, a discussion of a few black Southern women professionals in the first half of the twentieth century best illustrates why black women both require and deserve their own separate and distinct historical treatment.

After slavery, black men and women recognized their reciprocal obligations to reconstitute families. The black family has long been viewed as the strongest institutional survival instrument in African-American culture and society. The fluid, permeable structure of the black family made it possible to incorporate many individuals in addition to blood relatives. The extended family evolved largely because black women provided the nurture and the care while men assumed, within the prescribed limits of a racist society, the provider and protector roles. Black women bore the responsibility for maintaining kinship ties and for transmitting through the generations important cultural values essential to heighten self-esteem and social activism, such as respect for elders and community oversight of children. In other words, they believed that the raising of children was the responsibility of the entire community. Joining the family in providing nurture and hope for a better future was the church.

The church served as the initial organizational base for black women's benevolent, social welfare work. In innumerable church clubs, such as the Daughters of Ham, the Household of Ruth, the Eastern

Star, the Sisters of Zion, black women performed invaluable service. To be sure, with rare exception black women did not preach in the pulpit or occupy visible positions of leadership, especially in Baptist denominations, but they ministered to the sick, impoverished, and bereaved. When disasters of economic depression, bankruptcy, and disease struck the black communities in each decade from the collapse of Reconstruction to the Great Depression in the 1930s, black church women were there to keep communities functioning. They created orphanages and launched philanthropies to help widows and the aged. They taught Sunday schools, did missionary work, and participated in endless fund-raising drives to pay off church mortgages. The church rests most securely upon the backs of black women. Next to the church, the schoolhouse remained the most important institutional agency in black America.

To generations of African Americans, education held the key to freedom and opportunity, and for black women it possessed an even more potent value. Historian Jacqueline Rouse summed it up best when she observed that from the days of Maria Stewart and Frances Ellen Watkins Harper, to those of Ida Wells Barnett and Mary McLeod Bethune, to those of Marion Wright Edelman and Marva Collins of Chicago, African-American females have always given high priority to the education of their youth.[4] Education offered black women a possible escape route from sexual harassment, rape, and even domestic abuse. In the aftermath of the Civil War, black women sought to educate all of their children, and during the first generation after slavery more men than women earned baccalaureate degrees. The demand for literacy was so great that anyone with training could find a job. Black women eagerly pursued education that would open up new job opportunities even in a sex-stratified economy. Still, the vast majority of black women worked in domestic service and in agriculture.

In the early decades of the twentieth century, there was a marked shift in the demographics of education. When confronted with a choice as to which child to educate in the face of limited family resources, most parents chose their daughters. Undoubtedly, they knew from experience the degradation and sexual exploitation that domestic service work meant for black women. Historian Linda Perkins offers an additional explanation for the imbalance between black male and female degree recipients after 1910. "The disfranchisement of black men after Reconstruction and the fact that black men could not obtain employment commensurate with their educational experiences resulted in black families educating daughters disproportionately to men in the twentieth century. Teachers were critically needed in the developing school systems in the South and employment was virtually guaranteed to any minimally trained person." According to Perkins, of the 14,028 black students admitted to the seventeen black land grant colleges in 1928, 64 percent of those admitted by high school certificates were women and 73 admitted by nomination were women.[5]

Education represented a significant community investment, and it was clearly understood that the educated children would return to assist in the uplift of the entire community. Innumerable black women became teachers in one-room schoolhouses or even held classes in homes or churches. Others wrote textbooks and manuals about the importance of manners and good behavior. Always undergirding this commitment to, and faith in, education was the element of resistance. In other words, education held the key to liberation. Parallel in importance to education was the work of black women in health care delivery. This is one of the topics that I have treated at length in *Black Women in White*.

One of the most persistent black needs from slavery to today concerns access to adequate and affordable health care. The high morbidity and mortality rates in black communities may have pleased some white supremacists who desired the annihilation of the black race, but late-nineteenth-century black clubwomen were determined that African Americans would survive—for them survival was resistance. In countless communities they used their clubs to launch and to sustain a wide range of health care institutions. For example, in 1896, the members of the Phillis Wheatley Club established the Phillis Wheatley Sanitarium and Nursing Training School in New Orleans, the precursor to the Flint-Goodridge Hospital and Nurse Training School at Dillard University. Due to Jim Crow segregation practices, it was the only hospital facility for black patients and the only place where black physicians could attend their patients in the city.

The morbidity and mortality rates of New Orleans blacks and whites diverged sharply as thousands more blacks than whites contracted tuberculosis, pneumonia, influenza, typhoid fever, whooping cough, malaria, and pellagra. Among black women, puerperal (or childbirth) fever and complications associated with premature births took a deadly toll. Between 1890 and 1900 the death rate in New Orleans dropped modestly, from 25.4 to 23.8 per thousand, among whites. For blacks, however, the rate increased significantly, from 36.6 to 42.4 per thousand. Infant mortality throughout the South remained high for both races, but blacks registered greater losses. In 1920 in South Carolina, 159 babies out of every 1,000 died before they reached one year of age, as compared to 86 white infants per 1,000.[6]

In Charleston, South Carolina, Anna De Costa Banks, an 1896 graduate of Dixie Hospital and Nurse Training School at Hampton Institute, along with physician Alonzo C. McClennan, helped to found the Charleston Hospital and Nurse Training School. As was true of virtually every black nurse training school in the South, the students were hired out to white and black families and the fees for their labor were collected by the hospital. In addition to being hired out, each group of students at the Charleston institution was encouraged to give to the school a class gift upon graduation. Moreover, all student nurses had to participate in fund-raising fairs, the chief moneymaking activity, sponsored by the hospital association. The first class of student nurses (1898) formed a club named the Gatling Guns and performed at the local fairs. Actually, the Gatling Guns perfected a dance routine that proved so successful that they were able to present to the hospital a class gift of an operating table. Subsequent classes, in addition to maintaining the hospital, caring for patients, cooking, and washing, had also to manage a poultry farm operation and tend the vegetable gardens.[7]

The hired-out student nurse, whether she worked among poor blacks or rich whites, was the hospital's goodwill ambassador and in the front line of attack on morbidity and diseases associated with poverty, unsanitary water and food, and overcrowded living conditions. The comments of a white Charlestonian substantiate the good work of the student nurses and the hospital and the positive regard in which they were held in the community. In 1905 the assistant secretary of Associate Charities wrote about nurse Gussie Davis: "It is with sincere feeling that I speak of the work of Charleston's Colored Hospital, it is sending forth women who are not only capable, but tender and faithful. . . . I particularly mention Gussie Davis who during an epidemic of typhoid fever, at our Episcopal Church Home, fought hard often night as well as day for the lives of those children and through the Master's blessing many were saved."[8]

The work of the black nurse and her position in the community were often an extension of her place in the family. Bessie Hawse, a 1918 graduate of Tuskegee Institute's nurse training program, wrote Hospital Superintendent Dr. John Kenney of her pride and elation after having provided good patient care under impossible circumstances.

> I shall tell you of an experience of which I am very proud. Eight miles from Talladega (Alabama) in the back woods, a colored family of ten were in bed and dying for the want of attention. No one would come near. I was glad of the opportunity. As I entered the little country cabin, I found the mother in bed. Three children were buried the week before. The father and the remainder of the family were running a temperature of 102–104. Some had influenza, others had pneumonia. No relatives or friends would come near. I saw at a glance I had work to do. I rolled up my sleeves and killed chickens and began to cook. I forgot I was not a cook, but I only thought of saving lives. I milked the cow, gave medicine, and did everything I could to help conditions. I worked day and night trying to save them for seven days. I had no place to sleep. In the meantime, the oldest daughter had a miscarriage and I delivered her without the aid of any physicians. I didn't realize how tired I was till I got home. I sat up at night alone, and one night with a corpse in the house. The doctor lived about twenty miles away. He came every other day. He thought I was very brave. I didn't realize till it was over just how brave I was. I did feel happy when they were out of danger. I only wished that I could have reached them earlier and been able to have done something for the poor mother.[9]

These four groups of institutions—family, religious, educational, and health care—became the cornerstones of African-American survival and progress. The basic pattern of their formation was the same everywhere. In virtually every black community in the country, black women and men set up families, schools, churches, and health care institutions. This basic work of community making through formation of institutions, in the face of Jim Crow and the virulence of white terrorist attacks, ensured individual and collective survival. The

1890s witnessed an upsurge in lynchings. During 1892 alone, 241 persons across 26 states were lynched. Of this number 160 were identified as African American. Between 1889 and 1918, 50 African-American women were lynched. Indeed, survival was a very important issue.

Black women transcended the private-public sphere dichotomy to create and to sustain this separate, parallel infrastructure of supportive institutions. For them the twin engines of racial uplift, sexual liberation, and group progress proved to be institution building wedded to a consciousness of struggle and continuous resistance. Yet, for many historians, the question lingers, What is different about black women? What makes them worthy of separate and distinct study? All women, in all times and places, have been concerned with family, education, health, and religious matters. Black women are no exception. However, black women *are* different, and the source of their difference is best discerned by examining their interior lives and by understanding their consciousness of struggle and their culture of resistance.

The lives and work of Lucy Craft Laney (1854–1933) and Charlotte Hawkins Brown (1883–1961) open a window onto interior lives of two professional black Southern women. One of the most important black women educators in the late nineteenth century South, Laney wrote in 1897, "To woman has been committed the responsibility of making the laws of society, making environments for children. She has the privilege and authority, God-given, to help develop into a noble man or woman the young life committed to her care. There is no nobler work entrusted to the hands of mortals."

Born in Macon, Georgia, on April 13, 1854, to parents who had purchased their freedom. Lucy received formal education at the white missionary–operated Lewis School. In 1869 she was among the first group of twenty-seven women out of eighty-nine students admitted to Atlanta University. She received her degree in 1873. For four years she taught school in Milledgeville, Macon, and Savannah before becoming a teacher in Augusta, where she played a major role in the fight for Georgia's first black public high school.

In 1886 Laney opened Haines Normal and Industrial Institute in a rented hall at Christ Presbyterian Church. Haines Institute became one of the best secondary schools in the South. Laney had originally desired it to be a girl's school, but necessity dictated that it become coeducational. Most of the students, however, were girls. Her indomitable will and total commitment earned her the appellation "Mother of the Children of the People." Laney was a member of the National Association of Colored Women, the Southeastern Federation of Woman's Clubs, and the Georgia State Teachers Association, and she chaired the Colored Section of the Interracial Commission of Augusta.

Laney's influence spread far and wide. Indeed, Haines Institute became the model for Mary McLeod Bethune's Daytona Normal and Industrial Institute for Negro Girls before it merged with the all-male Cookman Institute in Jacksonville, Florida, in 1923 (renamed ten years later Bethune-Cookman College). The pattern was the same. Although Bethune-Cookman was coeducational, the majority of the graduates have been women. Throughout World War II the college served as a training center for women to participate in the wartime economy. Bethune, for example, capitalized on her prominence in Washington to attract attention and government contracts to the school.

Lottie Hawkins was born on June 11, 1883, in Henderson, North Carolina. She attended Allston Grammar School, Cambridge English High School, and State Normal School at Salem, Massachusetts, where she renamed herself Charlotte Eugenia. While in the New England area she met Alice Freeman Palmer, second president of Wellesley College. Hawkins returned to the South after only two years at Salem Normal School in order to head a one-room school in Sedalia, North Carolina, with fifty children in the first class. When the American Missionary Association decided to close the school, the then nineteen-year-old Charlotte took over and with the aid of the local community opened a new school. She received operating funds from friends, especially Palmer, for whom she named the school. She would retire as president of Alice Palmer Memorial Institute in 1952, just a decade before financial problems forced it to close.

Palmer was married briefly to Edmund S. Brown. After their divorce in 1915, she constructed a family of seven children—nieces and nephews and cousins. All of the children graduated from Palmer Memorial. Brown was passionate about many things: her family, education for black youths, black women's clubs and organizations, social graces, good manners, and civil rights for her people. She was a founding member of the National Council of Negro Women, president of the North Carolina State Federation of Negro Women's Clubs, and president of the North Carolina Teachers Association. She became known as the "First Lady of Social Graces," when in 1941 she published *The Correct Thing to Do, to Say, and to Wear.*

Brown regularly sacrificed her dignity to challenge segregation in transportation. Actually she took pride in the significant number of times she was thrown out of Pullman berths and ejected from first-class railway seats in the South. Ever the fearless champion of black women, Brown made a bold and courageous speech at a 1920 interracial meeting in Memphis during which she catalogued the everyday racism and sexism that black women experience from Southern white men and women. An avid antilynching crusader, Brown insisted that black women were insulted by white men a thousand times more than the reverse.

Lucy Laney and Charlotte Hawkins Brown abhorred weakness and accommodation to oppression. They effectively resisted all situations and people who demanded of them subordination and deference. There are many unique characteristics common to most southern-community black women. The most readily apparent, even to the untutored observer, are their self-reliance, their female network apparatus, their commitment to their people, and their consciousness of resistance and culture struggle. To say this is not to elevate them to the status of superwomen, for it would ill serve them to substitute one group of stereotypes for another, no matter how positive. Nevertheless, ample examples abound even today. Black women always worked, lived, and negotiated within a patriarchal, white, male-dominated capitalistic society that was intent on destroying their self-esteem and individual autonomy. Black women's survival depended on the creation and maintenance of the key institutions of family, church, education, and health care. In the final analysis they had two choices: either become self-reliant and continually resist, or lay down the burdens and die. If most had chosen the latter course, then certainly there would be little interest in, or need to tell, their stories in an encyclopedia or need to make an African-American women's history.

In conclusion, at no time since our struggle began on the west coast of Africa have we been in greater need of the wisdom, courage, and determination of our black foremothers and of a new black history.

Today, many black communities exist in states of chaos, crisis, and conflict. AIDS, drugs, explosive rates of young black male homicides, poverty, unemployment, and premature pregnancies continue to wreck havoc, threatening to engulf us all with despair and hopelessness. These social evils weaken and destroy our institutions and poison our families with misdirected rage and fury. There is no progress without survival. At the risk of sounding sanguine, I believe there is power in history. To tap those hidden reservoirs of power we must reclaim the voices and learn from the transformative good deeds of the women who, like Rosa Parks, Jo Ann Gibson Robinson, Daisy Bates, Fannie Lou Hamer, and Coretta Scott King, brought us this far—too often without our words of acknowledgment and appreciation. In order to make a new American history include us all, black and white, ethnic and native, young and old, differently abled, hetero- and homosexual, it is imperative that we learn from the old. Let's begin the healing and the knowing by listening to the voices and studying the deeds of African-American women.

The Making of Black Women in America: An Historical Encyclopedia

B*lack Women in America: An Historical Encyclopedia* (1993) that I edited in collaboration with Elsa Barkley Brown and Rosalyn Terborg-Penn is 1,500 pages long. Its two volumes contain 640 biographical entries and 143 topical essays. In creating the *Encyclopedia*, my coeditors and I also brought into existence a wide-ranging body of research and reference materials. These provide the essential elements of our quest for the acceptance of black women's history as a legitimate area of scholarly study. The *Encyclopedia*'s existence challenges contemporary historians of every field and has profound implications for the future research, writing, and analysis of women's history, African-American history, and American history in general. This essay lays out the evolution of my thinking as editor and emphasizes what I believe are some of the broader ramifications of this project. I share the belief Gerda Lerner articulated in her major works on the creation of patriarchy and the rise of feminist consciousness: to wit, when women control their past they will control their future.

To make an encyclopedia is to claim a historiographical moment. An encyclopedia of black women not only exposes the state of black women's history, but also suggests the issues, themes, and individuals still in need of exploration and analysis. Twenty years ago it would have been impossible to write an extended essay on the slavery experience of black women. Today several scholars are working on books on the subject. A virtual revolution had to take place in African-American and in women's history, and in the new social history, before black women historians could claim the voice and space for their subjects who warrant a hearing at the bar of history.

This is the revolution in which the *Encyclopedia* participates. When Ralph Carlson, president of Carlson Publishing, first approached me with the suggestion that I edit an encyclopedia on the history of black women, I turned him down. I had gone down that road before. Back in 1980, Shirley Herd, an Indianapolis public school teacher and then president of the Indianapolis section of the National Council of Negro Women, had called me to ask that I write a history of black women in Indiana for her organization. When I told Herd that I knew nothing about black women's history and had never taken any courses in the subject, she was nonplussed. "You are a black woman? You are a historian?" she rejoined. "You mean to tell me that you can't put those two things together and write us a history of black women in Indiana?"

Herd's questions disconcerted me and eventually prompted me to connect my biography with my profession, to forge an integrated identity that equally emphasized my race, gender, and work. My immediate response to her challenge was to write *When the Truth Is Told: A History of Black Women's Culture and Community in Indiana 1875–1950* (1981). The long-term impact of our relationship and my ensuing work with literally hundreds of community black women was to raise my consciousness and forever transform my scholarship to focus more specifically on issues of the intersection of race, gender, and class.

After completing *When the Truth Is Told*, I suffered pangs of conscience due to the fact that all the letters, diaries, club minutes, institutional records, and photographs that Herd and the members of the NCNW Indianapolis section had so painstakingly collected were returned to their original donors. These primary documents had enabled me to write the book, but now they were dispersed and difficult to retrieve. Many future historians would not have the benefit of this material; the lives, deeds, and contributions of black women in Indiana might never find a way into future constructions of the state's history.

To promote the regional study of black women's history, I launched the Black Women in the Middle West archival creation project, securing a $150,000 grant from the National Endowment for the Humanities. I'll always remember how difficult it was to persuade NEH to fund this effort in the face of reviewers' objections. At least one reviewer asserted that black women had never done anything; if they had they would already be in the history books. Their absence convincingly demonstrated that they had done nothing worthy of historical note. As Shirley Herd, Patrick Bidelman, a white male historian colleague at Purdue University, and I wrestled with these simple-minded reservations, I began to question the meaning of history. Fortunately, a program officer, a black male, James Early, strongly supported the project and eventually prevailed upon NEH officers to grant us a portion of the funds we requested.

Two years of intense work with the 1,200 participants in the Black Women in the Middle West project aggravated my discomfort with American history. The very process of reclaiming the past records and documents of ignored, excluded, distorted, and stereotyped black women in Indiana and Illinois taught me valuable lessons about the power of history and the politics of historical construction. I had asked, for the first time, Who decided what events or individuals are important in history, worthy of consideration and investigation? By the same token, I wondered about the psychological and political damage done to those destined never to see their lives or contributions reflected in official chronicles of America's past. I fretted long and hard over the effects and processes of historical black disfranchisement or disempowerment.

By the time Carlson called, a decade after Herd's call, I had written a book on the history of black women in the nursing profession. I had completed the Black Women in the Middle West project and successfully gathered and created archives. I was catching my breath from editing a sixteen-volume series that contained 248 articles and essays, five previously unpublished dissertations, and a collection of conference papers on black women in the civil rights movement, which Carlson had just published.

Don't get me wrong. I was in no way sanguine about the status and progress of black women's history. It still rankled when some white women and black male historians routinely failed to include discussion of black women in their articles, monographs, and surveys, rationalizing that appropriate and accessible material did not exist to allow them to do so. Although black women historians had published several noteworthy books and biographies, they remain, with a few exceptions, uncited and ignored. I, and other black women historians, still witness too many slightly raised eyebrows in the profession when we admit that we do black women's history. The feeling lingers that black women's experiences and lives scarcely warrant distinct and separate treatment. Many believe that black women's history is more appropriately subsumed either under black history or women's history. Much intellectual and political work remains to be done before this area of study approaches maturity. I share a sense of the urgency that grips all of us who are engaged in its pursuits and who embrace the power of history.

For six months Ralph Carlson kept after me until finally I agreed. I had refused for so long, less because I doubted the importance or value of the project than because the idea of editing an encyclopedia of this magnitude and complexity was downright intimidating. To do an encyclopedia is to create a system of meaning. Having been a veteran of earlier projects in black women's history, I feared that the sheer intellectual scope, physical labor, and endless judgment calls would eventually overwhelm me.

Gradually, through conversations with Carlson, I formed a vision of the *Encyclopedia*. I knew that it had to be as inclusive as possible. We had to pay attention to regionality, class, and individual differences while simultaneously educating the general public as to the culture of struggle and resistance that sustains all black women in America. It would not be enough to underscore the victimization of black women. Such emphasis is indeed warranted: The reality of race, class, and sexual oppression and exploitation daily dogs the lives of too many black women. Yet, this three-hundred-year-long history, full of good solid drama, achievement, and transcendent truths, should also empower those who take the time to study the past and generate appropriate respect for the lives and worth of black women.

Initially, because I was so utterly daunted by the challenge of an encyclopedia on black women, I questioned Ralph Carlson's motivations and persistence. What, beyond profit, could motivate a white male publisher's interest in and willingness to tackle such a monumental project? Whatever the answer, and quite frankly I do not believe it was purely for profit, I doubt that Carlson imagined the magnitude of the financial and personnel resources it would require. He remained convinced that the sixteen-volume series had only heightened the need for a major reference work on black women, a source that would contain accurate, accessible information about the lives and contributions of hundreds of nationally and locally known black women. Carlson also confided that he had always wanted to show his support of the women's movement and now he could do so by publishing this work on black women. When I pressed him, he added, "They deserve it." Perhaps he had undergone his own intellectual odyssey. Of course, I shared Carlson's conviction that a truly comprehensive, compellingly written, accessible historical encyclopedia of black women replete with hundreds of biographical and topical essays and with stunning photographs would energize my colleagues and suggest enough potential dissertation topics to sustain several generations of researchers and scholars. I had drawn considerable inspiration and intellectual sustenance from Gerda Lerner's documentary volume *Black Women in White America* (1972) when I began working in the field.

Before describing the actual process of developing the *Encyclopedia* in detail, I would like to reflect on the problematics of black women's history and open up some of the lessons I had learned from a decade of working in the area. Black women's unique experiences and distinct angle of vision enabled them collectively and individually to fashion a worldview, to create their own meaning systems and estimations of what constituted beauty, culture, and respectability. Over the years, black women had assembled an arsenal of womanist strategies ranging from a "culture of dissemblance" to a deep spiritualism that enabled them to reject at least some of the prevalent self-damaging notions of black inferiority. These internal strengths aided their determination to shatter demeaning stereotypes that limited their access to educational and employment opportunities. The battle to reimagine themselves was serious and unrelenting, and it continues to this day.

Mobility is another critical dimension of black women's lives that warrants much greater attention than it has yet received. Both during and after slavery, black women dared to flee situations that dehumanized them. Many of the early free black women inhabitants of the Middle West, for example, were escaped slaves or daughters of women who had risked their lives to secure freedom for them. After emancipation, black women, in numbers that increased with each passing decades, left their Southern homes with and without families to escape rape, the threat of rape, and domestic violence and to secure better education and jobs. Indeed, it was the plight of poor, single, migrating black women who landed on the inhospitable streets of Detroit, Cleveland, Chicago, Philadelphia, New York, and other Northern and Middle Western cities that motivated settled black matrons to open working girls' homes, training schools in domestic arts, and other agencies to rescue them from sexual exploitation and prostitution. The processes of migration and urbanization required that black women redouble efforts to create and sustain the separate parallel institutional infrastructure that they had established in the South in the decades following emancipation and the entrenchment of segregation. Black women, in sum, brought a whole lot more with them on their trek north than their bodies. They carried with them the knowledge of how to organize and build community.

New knowledge has led black women historians to become increasingly attentive to questions about the inner lives of black women and the ways interior consciousness intersects with and is shaped by external community needs. Three questions guide current research: What is the relationship between black women and the black community? What is the relationship between black women and the institutions in the community that ensure the survival and progress of black people? How have these relationships changed over time as reflected in differing gender roles and expectations?

Apparently to protect their interior lives, to maintain self-esteem and dignity, black women sought refuge in a myriad ways. At pivotal moments in history, they withdrew behind their men, or joined with women relatives, friends, and club members, or submerged themselves into their communities. When forced to encounter whites, most black women, with significant exceptions such as Ida Wells Barnett, adhered to the "culture of dissemblance." By dissemblance I mean the behavior and attitudes of black women that created the appearance of openness and disclosure but actually shielded the truth of their inner lives and selves from their oppressors. In other words, while some black women struggled to acquire and project their voice, the majority converted invisibility into a survival strategy.

Institution building, as well as their interior struggles to reconstruct and redefine self, demanded the development of a distinct consciousness. Thus, consciousness and activism was another kind of refuge. Black women internalized and institutionalized the idea of and commitment to resistance. Their consciousness of struggle transcended participation in the established political order. Struggle for black women pivoted on a Harriet Tubman–like obsession to carry on, regardless. I owe a debt to historian Elsa Barkley Brown's analysis of the connection between theory or consciousness and activism. She warns against assuming that theory "is found only in carefully articulated position statements." Brown posits that the clearest articulation of Maggie Lena Walker's theoretical perspectives on the power of black women lay not in her public statements but in her activities, especially the organization and institution she helped to create. "Her theory and her action are not distinct and separable parts of some whole: they are often synonymous and it is only through her actions that we clearly hear her theory." Brown concludes, and I concur, "The same is true for the lives of many other black women who had limited time and resources and maintained a holistic view of life and struggle."[1]

The *Encyclopedia* shatters black women's self-imposed invisibility and lifts the veil of affected ignorance and indifference in the larger society. Its existence portends transformations in both black and white women historians, and eventually will affect all who write American history. The incremental approach of adding one or two black women to discussions of suffrage, reform, the professions, domesticity, and religious work, for example, is rendered inadequate and unsophisticated in face of the impressive number of women engaged in these activities as chronicled in the *Encyclopedia*. No longer will excuses or complaints of insufficient evidence be persuasive responses to black women's exclusion from scholarly texts. The *Encyclopedia* maps new spaces, directing a glaring spotlight on omissions while turning up the volume on silences. This black women's encyclopedia effectively challenges the claims to capaciousness of general surveys about American history that exclude black women. In seizing the historiographical moment of giving black women the space and place to create a meaning system of their own lives, the *Encyclopedia* helps to shape the future of the history of women and of black people in America.

As I contemplated the logistics of the project, Carlson assured me that there would be an even division of labor and that he would employ whatever staff was necessary to handle most of the production details. The more we talked, the more comfortable I became, until I was completely convinced that it was indeed possible to produce, in a timely fashion, a high-quality, intellectually sound, and aesthetically pleasing reference work on black women's history. Without a doubt a smoothly functioning administrative structure, a host of talented people, and a secure organizational base were key factors. Within a matter of weeks, Carlson and I had hammered out a general blueprint of the project. Like most publishers, Carlson was overly optimistic in estimating that the project would take about a year to complete. It actually took almost three years. Nevertheless, given the comprehensive nature of the finished volumes, three years is an incredibly short time frame.

During the period between summer 1990 and fall 1992, I do not recall a day's passing when I did not think about or work on the *Encyclopedia*. I had anticipated that the project would be all-consuming and therefore was not surprised. Excluding the conceptualization phase, the actual work was neatly divided into at least four stages: inviting associate editors and advisory editors to participate; developing a list of entries; making assignments and editing the manuscript; and fund-raising.

The first stage was definitely the easiest and most delightful, for it entailed persuading some of the most talented scholars in black women's history to join me. I assured them that this would be fun and would not unduly tax their time. I invited University of Michigan historian Elsa Barkley Brown and Morgan State University historian Rosalyn Terborg-Penn to serve as associate editors responsible for general oversight of the project. They readily agreed to do so.

I had worked with Brown on the earlier sixteen-volume series and had acquired enormous respect and admiration for the subtlety and range of her intellect and the depth of her commitment to black women's history. She is meticulous and exacting. Elsa agreed to work with us but made it clear that she intended to avoid the three diseases common to encyclopedias: inaccuracies, datedness, and arcane prose. I knew that Brown, herself a relentless researcher and engaging writer, would hold us up to the highest possible standards.

Similarly, I had enjoyed working on numerous projects with Rosalyn Terborg-Penn, beginning with the founding of the Association of Black Women Historians in 1979. Terborg-Penn and I had collaborated on a program funded by the Fund for the Improvement of Post-Secondary Education that Gerda Lerner initiated during her presidency of the Organization of American Historians. The aim of that project was to increase the participation of black women in the historical profession. Terborg-Penn's own pathbreaking scholarship in black women's history has earned her "founding mother" status. Moreover, her knowledge of who is doing what and where he or she is located is in itself encyclopedic. True to expectations, Elsa and Rosalyn proved essential to the success of the project. Once they were on the board, we developed a list of individuals to invite to serve as members of the advisory editorial board. Meanwhile, Ralph Carlson began interviewing candidates to manage the project from his office and launched a search for free-lance staff editors.

Inviting people to the advisory board was itself a significant gesture. Black women scholars are rarely invited to serve on editorial boards of mainstream publishing or media projects. To this day, not one black woman has ever coauthored a general undergraduate textbook in American history. It is difficult to acquire visibility in the historical profession regardless of what you study or who you are, but it is even more so for young black women historians. Thus, in spite of demonstrated ability to do good work, black women historians still, with a few laudable exceptions, inhabit the periphery of the profession. The production of scholarship is one side of the challenge. The other side is to win recognition for the contribution.

Indeed, one of my unshakable principles is to give credit and recognition for the work that others do on any project that I administer. I remain convinced that black women in particular rarely receive the credit or the salaries that they deserve for the work they do. Nowhere is this more graphically illustrated than in higher education. Undoubtedly, as more of us acquire prominence and greater access, the publishing and editing opportunities in the mainstream will increase.

Meanwhile, we must create our own opportunities. Accordingly, I aimed to involve a large number of black women scholars in the development of the *Encyclopedia* for both intellectual and political reasons. I anticipated that for the junior black women historians, service on the advisory board would be an important item on their curriculum vitae. The experience of advising, editing, writing, and reviewing entries would expand knowledge, enhance careers, and cement networks.

With suggestions from Rosalyn, Elsa, and Ralph, I extended invitations to senior scholars Mary Francis Berry, Nell Irvin Painter, and Nellie McKay. Authors and editors of key monographs, dissertations, essays, anthologies, and works-in-progress in black women's history invited to join also included Paula Giddings, Sharon Harley, Evelyn Brooks Higginbotham, Jacqueline Jones, Wilma King, Cynthia Neverdon-Morton, Tiffany R. L. Patterson, Linda Reed, Gwendolyn Keita Robinson, Jacqueline Rouse, Stephanie Shaw, Janet Sims-Wood, Deborah Gray White, and Lillian S. Williams.

We agreed on the importance of inviting scholars who, like Nellie McKay, possessed expertise in cultural studies. It is impossible to imagine how the *Encyclopedia* would have achieved its "astounding" breadth without the critical advice and contributions of Kariamu Welsh Asante on dance, Elizabeth Brown-Guillory on literature, Daphne Duval Harrison on music, and Kathy Perkins on film. With the exception of Catherine Clinton and Jacqueline Jones, all of the members of the advisory board are black women. To be sure, many of the essays and biographical entries are written by white women and by black and white male scholars. Catherine Clinton engaged an entire seminar at Harvard in the preparation of numerous essays for the *Encyclopedia*. Thus, to a noticeable degree this project reflects the greatest collaboration within the academy across race and gender lines that I have witnessed.

Brown, Terborg-Penn, and I met with Carlson in May 1991 to discuss the preliminary list of topics for the essays and the women to receive biographical treatment. We also nominated people to write the entries. We agreed to circulate a basic topical and biographical list to all members of the advisory board. Gradually, over a few months, we hammered out the final list, all the while soliciting comments and recommendations from select black librarians and archivists. Not surprisingly, the index to the sixteen-volume series served as our major guide for the names of historical black women.

In compiling the lists of topical essays and biographical entries, we were guided by the desire to represent the broadest possible spectrum of black women. Black women's history is different from white women's history in many telling ways. Most glaringly is our lack of knowledge and information about the lives of exemplary women in local communities. We were not satisfied simply to identify the one hundred, or even the five hundred, most outstanding nationally and internationally known black women. This reference research tool was not intended to be merely about the notable black woman, the colored counterparts to the notable American white women, or a *Who's Who* companion. We needed to know the "average" black woman. An exclusive orientation would scarcely capture the rich diversity and complex nuance of black women's lives and experiences on American soil.

For over two years a great part of my direct work on the *Encyclopedia* involved searching for both the average and exemplary black woman and for the people interested in writing about them. I would make mental notes of the various topics or unusual lives I heard discussed or mentioned wherever I was invited to lecture. I amassed names and collected business cards as I traveled across the country attending conferences of every stripe. Religiously, I wrote notes directly to individuals or dispatched brief missives to Carlson or to Christine Lunardini, the project's office editor, urging that he or she send a formal invitation to a particular person. This became a standard operating, procedure allowing me to uncover the scores of locally known representative black women. Their inclusion gives the *Encyclopedia* a truly national flavor.

My earlier experiences with black community women made me acutely sensitive to the imperative to include biographical and topical essays about women and groups of women who devoted their lives to serving others and building community. These are the lives that capture best the millions of black women who contribute and endure, who build human bridges, and whose backs carried many of us over to better lives but who never dreamed of seeing their names in any history book.

The *Encyclopedia* had to include certain individuals. To have left out Phillis Wheatley, Harriet Tubman, and Sojourner Truth, for example, would be unthinkable and inexcusable. Yet this *Encyclopedia* had to make a space and place for St. Louis, Missouri, retired pediatrician Dr. Helen Nash; folk artist Clementine Hunter; nurse Anna De Costa Banks (1869–1930) of Charleston, South Carolina; and Hawaiian schoolteacher Carlotta Stewart-Lai (1881–1952); along with the millions of women who worked as domestic servants earning the meager sums that saved families from starvation. The 140 historical essays reclaim the lives of the obscure and anonymous by focusing on a wide spectrum of subjects such as slavery, civil rights, domestic service, religion, and military service.

It is possible to exaggerate the mechanical nature of the process of encyclopedia construction. In several cases serendipity, or just plain luck, accounts for the inclusion of some of the topical and biographical entries. For example, I attended a reception on my campus and just happened to mention to a colleague in the Department of Communications, Lawrence Redd, that I would love to have someone prepare an entry on black women and radio for the *Encyclopedia*. It turned out that this topic was one of his research interests, and he readily agreed to write the essay. A similar conversation at a conference in Galveston, Texas, with Anne Hudson Jones of the Institute for the Medical Humanities of the University of Texas revealed our mutual admiration of the Creole folk artist Clementine Hunter. Jones subsequently wrote the entry on Hunter.

Even more frequently, individual scholars called or wrote to volunteer to write entries in their areas of expertise. Many of my friends and colleagues at educational institutions in every region insisted that I include their favorite deserving local woman in the *Encyclopedia*. Had not historian Albert S. Broussard sent me a reprint of an article he had written on Carlotta Stewart-Lai it is doubtful that the *Encyclopedia* would contain an entry on this schoolteacher who had migrated to Hawaii around the turn of the century.

Black women historians are active in various professional associations, and this proved invaluable as work on the *Encyclopedia* progressed. Prior to annual meetings of professional historical associations, the project staff would circulate topical and biographical lists to members of the advisory group. We scheduled breakfast gatherings or luncheons at the meetings. The largest collection of black women historians usually meets in the fall in conjunction with the Association for the Study of Afro-American Life and History (ASALH). The Association of Black Women Historians (ABWH) enjoys a mutually respectful affiliation with ASALH and has for the past fourteen years hosted a luncheon during that organization's annual convention. The ASALH convention proved an ideal event at which to meet with advisory editors and to deliver periodic updates as a way of maintaining general interest in the project. Late developments were announced and invitations issued for others to recommend additional entries to the *Encyclopedia*. The ABWH/ASALH conferences had the added advantage of providing a good opportunity to go to panels to find out who was doing research on new topics and to make contacts for further essay assignments.

We continued to circulate lists among advisory board members until each entry had a name assigned to it. After approximately five circulations, if there was simply no one willing or able to write a particular entry, it was dropped from the list. On occasion, I or Elsa or Rosalyn had to prepare essays when the person was someone whom we simply could not omit. Time was a constant goad and foe. The longer the project took, the more expensive it became, and the more worn was the patience of those upon whom we relied to advise, review, and write for free.

The large editorial staff Carlson retained reviewed each entry and reshaped, refocused, or shortened when necessary. Elsa, Rosalyn, and I read entries for historical accuracy and interpretive analysis. Mary Wyer did a superb job of editing for readability and style. At the outset we all agreed that the *Encyclopedia* would be free of jargon and would be accessible to the general reader. Yet it was important that the *Encyclopedia* be a useful reference and research tool. Toward this end all entries are signed, and virtually all include a short bibliography. Actually, the bibliographies varied in length from one or two items to two columns, depending on the topic and the individual authors.

Authors maintained the right to review and to question all changes made on their manuscripts. On occasion, essays were returned several times, and in a couple of instances frustrated authors withdrew their submissions. It required great patience and diplomacy not to offend the host of writers and scholars who contributed to the *Encyclopedia*. But when difficult decisions had to be made about quality and relevance, I simply thought about what was best for the *Encyclopedia*. Regrettably, I am sure that I have incurred the wrath of some whose work was rejected. For the most part, all contributors appear quite pleased with the amount of attention accorded each submission.

I encountered my biggest trauma in the fourth stage, fundraising. Although I maintained close—almost daily and sometimes hourly—contact with Carlson about every major and minor aspect of the project, it was nevertheless a shock to receive a letter from him in June 1992 asking for my help in raising $100,000 to pay the printers. Specifically, we had to find ten people who would put up $10,000 each. In return we promised to acknowledge their sponsorship in the *Encyclopedia,* and, moreover, Carlson would pay 15 percent interest on the loans. It is difficult indeed to ask friends and colleagues to give up their time and forego financial remuneration to serve as associate and advisory editors and then ask them to write essential biographical entries and analytical essays. My nerves threatened to abandon me completely when I had to help raise the money to pay the printers. I was petrified to ask my friends to trust me and invest their hard-earned money in the project. With this project, unlike previous undertakings in black women's history, I placed my good name—and, in the end, my personal savings—on the line.

That I was thankful that some of my friends had discretionary funds and a lot of faith is a gigantic understatement. Once my friends put up their money, however, failure was simply out of the question. In retrospect I shudder at the risk I had invited Delores Aldridge, Carolyn Dorsey, Wilma King, Nell Irvin Painter, and Arvarh Strickland to share. Carlson was able to persuade Randall K. Burkett, David Garrow, Betty Gubert, and Richard Newman to become sponsors of the project. Had Carlson and I been willing to delay the launching of the project, we might well have secured a grant from the National Endowment for the Humanities or some other funding agency. But neither Carlson nor I relished the prospect of becoming mired in bureaucratic paperwork, so we stubbornly decided to go it alone. We also doubted whether NEH would be interested enough or willing to fund a project on black women. Nevertheless, my advice to anyone contemplating an encyclopedia or other research or reference project is to secure adequate funding at the outset. It reduces anxiety.

Clearly, Carlson made the greatest economic investment in the *Encyclopedia*. After his letter informing me of his economic woes, I called to ask him precisely when he had decided to throw financial caution to the wind and to go for broke. He confided that the decision had been made fairly early in the project. Only then did I recall how, when presented with a choice, I had invariably selected expensive type, paper, and cover design. I considered the book's esthetics to be of paramount importance. Simply put, the *Encyclopedia* had to be beautiful. To his credit, Carlson could not have secured more effective and committed people. He hired the full-time services of two pivotal women: Christine A. Lunardini, office editorial director, and Mary Wyer, editor-in-chief. He retained a sixteen-member editorial staff and employed four additional persons to work on production and to do research for photographs.

Salaries, production, design, and promotional brochures made this a very costly project. A conservative estimate puts costs in the half-million-dollar range. My fund-raising efforts netted loans of $70,000. Instead of cash, each contributing author received a set of the *Encyclopedia*, more as a token of our appreciation than as any pretense of adequate compensation. To have promised contributors even modest financial remuneration simply would have been prohibitive. Additional costs accumulated in the closing months of the project. When you are counting on over four hundred people to write entries, invariably a few individuals will fail to deliver on their commitment. With backs up against the wall and some important entries long overdue, Ralph and I surveyed our options. We paid Chicago based free-lance writer Kathleen Thompson to write several important essays, including the entry on sexual harassment.

The enthusiastic media reception of and individual responses to the *Encyclopedia* have fully justified our efforts. Everyone seems to have gotten the point. While a few reviewers have questioned the amount of space accorded one black woman versus another, or mused about who was missing, they all conclude that the *Encyclopedia* is an "astounding" achievement. Columbia University law professor Patricia Williams in an insightful review in *MS* declared that the existence of the *Encyclopedia* renders all the standard references and histories of America suspect and inadequate. She and others have concluded that we are now in a position to judge and to assess earlier and future historical scholarship in quite different ways. *Black Women in America: An Historical Encyclopedia* has ushered in a new meaning system grounded in the intersectional analysis of the historical constructions of race, gender, and class. At minimum, the historical profession must now take action to end the exclusion, distortion, and marginalization of black women.

PART **3**

Speak Truth to Power

For Pleasure, Profit, and Power

The Sexual Exploitation of Black Women, or Anita Hill and Clarence Thomas in Historical Perspective

Shortly after the Anita Hill–Clarence Thomas hearings, Harvard University sociologist Orlando Patterson wrote an op-ed piece for *The New York Times* in which he argued that the future black United States Supreme Court justice was justified in denying all charges of sexual harassment made by University of Oklahoma Law School professor Anita Hill. Patterson's embrace of the politics of denial rested on his belief that even if the allegations of sexual harassment were true, the punishment, that is, the loss of the appointment, would far outweigh the severity of the transgression. He wrote:

> If my interpretation is correct Judge Thomas was justified in denying making the remarks, even if he had in fact made them, not only because the deliberate displacement of his remarks made them something else but on the utilitarian moral grounds that any admission would have immediately incurred a self-destructive and grossly unfair punishment.[1]

The fact that a "liar," not to mention a harasser of a woman, would occupy a position on the nation's highest tribunal seemed inconsequential to Professor Patterson.

Perhaps more than any of the events of that emotionally draining weekend, Patterson's espousal of moral pragmatism and rationalized deceit encapsulated vividly the centuries-long sexual harassment and exploitation experiences of black women. Since the hearings, I have given Patterson's comments considerable thought. The sexual exploitation of black women in the United States has a long and inglorious history that persists to this day. Yet the true dimension and nature of this exploitation remains shrouded in denial, metaphor, ignorance, and silence. Perhaps as much effort has been expended to deny, rationalize, and ignore the sexual exploitation of black women by some white and black men, and by white women, as went into the commission of these egregious offenses. Earlier I had advanced the idea that black women's reluctance to discuss publicly their experiences of sexual abuse and exploitation grew out of the culture of dissemblance they had developed as a resistance or survival strategy.[2] A companion to this notion, however, is the politics of denial practiced by white men, white women, and black men. Thus, dissemblance and denial combined in the larger society's mind to obscure, nullify, or render unimaginable the possibility that a black woman could be raped, sexually exploited, and harassed.

Although the vast majority of black women, for understandable reasons, remain silent, Anita Hill belongs to a rather select group who have spoken publicly about harassment and exploitation. These women, like Hill, braved a disbelieving and hostile public. Even so, during slavery a few black women told of their sexual experiences in slave narratives, novels, poems, and deeds.

The antislavery lecturer and poet Frances E. W. Harper wrote, in a poem entitled "A Double Standard" (1896), the following stanza that captures the pain and the price exacted for revealing that a black woman has been sexually active:

> Crime has no sex and yet to-day
> I wear the brand of shame;
> Whilst he amid the gay and proud
> Still bears an honored name.[3]

A quick perusal of library shelves yields other examples, for instance, Harriet Jacobs's *Incidents in the Life of a Slave Girl* (1861) and the historical account of the murder trial of *Celia, A Slave* (1991). To read both volumes is to glimpse the terror and humiliation slave women endured and the lengths to which they went to protect their sexual selves. In recent memory, there is the 1974 case of Joan Little, who killed Clarence Alligood, her jailer, as he tried to rape her. Like Celia over a hundred years earlier, Joan Little would go on trial to face murder charges and the death penalty for attempting to defend herself against a white rapist. The intersections of race, gender, and class are deeply embedded in all their stories.

Harriet Jacobs, Celia the slave, Joan Little, and Anita Hill all told stories of sexual harassment, met different fates because of their disparate responses, and encountered the politics of disbelief and denial. Few Americans wanted to hear the voices or confront the reality of the depth of violence and exploitation these shadow women endured. Few powerful white males wanted to take them or their stories seriously. Almost no scholar wanted to go to the trouble of weaving into the basic fabric of America's largely mythological view of itself as the land of democratic equalitarianism and virtue the blood-soaked threads of black women's exploitation. Why this disinclination to see or hear their stories? To do so, to take black women seriously, would necessitate reckoning with the complicity of some white men, some white women, and some black men in the enduring project to dehumanize and to degrade the most nonprivileged and vulnerable segment of the American population. Ironically, however, to take black women seriously is also to recognize their culture of resistance and survival and the strength of their will to be free and sexually autonomous. In the case of Celia and Joan Little, they were capable of killing.

Before proceeding, perhaps it would be useful to revisit briefly the experiences of these four black women: Harriet Jacobs, Celia the slave, Joan Little, and Anita Hill. Perhaps a retelling of these resistance stories, and the placing of them in a larger social-historical and theoretical context, may motivate us to help black women bring to an end this long reign of exploitation and terror. At least by engaging their stories, we empower and encourage present and future generations of black women to continue the struggle for dignity and freedom from sexual exploitation in spite of society's penchant for denial and disbelief.

Harriet Jacobs

In 1861, Harriet Jacobs, under the pseudonym Linda Brent, published *Incidents in the Life of a Slave Girl*, a narrative that even today generates controversy. One of the unique features of this narrative is Jacobs's personal testimony of the sexual harassment and exploitation she experienced as a slave. But most compelling is her description of her creative means of resistance and ultimate escape from Dr. Flint's relentless entreaties and bribes for sex. Dr. Flint even threatened her at one point, saying that it was within his rights to kill her for resisting his advances. For seven years Jacobs secluded herself in a garret, assisted only by her grandmother. Prior to the hiding, Jacobs resisted Dr. Flint by voluntarily submitting to sex with another white man. "It seems less degrading to give one's self, than to submit to compulsion," she explained. "I knew nothing would enrage Dr. Flint so much as to know that I favored another; and it was something to triumph over my tyrant even in that small way."[4] But Jacobs's entreaties for understanding resonate throughout black women's history. She confided:

> You never know what it is to be a slave; to be entirely unprotected by law or custom; to have the laws reduce you to the condition of a chattel, entirely subject to the will of another. You never exhausted your ingenuity in avoiding the snares, and eluding the power of a hated tyrant; you never shuddered at the sound of his footsteps, and trembled within hearing of his voice.[5]

Eventually Jacobs made a successful escape to freedom via the Underground Railroad.

Celia

In 1850, sixty-year-old Robert Newsom, a prosperous Callaway County, Missouri farmer, purchased fourteen-year-old Celia, and over a period of years he repeatedly raped her and forced her to bear at least one child. Historian Melton A. McLaurin succinctly described the process: "a healthy sixty years of age, Newsom needed . . . a sexual partner. Newsom seems to have deliberately chosen to purchase a young slave girl to fulfill this role, a choice made the more convenient by the ability to present the girl as a domestic servant purchased for the benefit of his daughters."[6]

On June 23, 1855, a pregnant Celia repulsed Newsom as he attempted to force her yet again to have sexual intercourse. On that night of her resistance, Celia struck him twice with a stick. She then burnt his dead body in the fireplace. Charged with first degree murder, Celia's attorney asked the critical question: Did this black slave woman have the right to defend her sexual self? Her counsel wanted specifically to receive a verdict that would establish that the masters' economic prerogatives did not include the right of sexual molestation. Implicitly he wanted an answer to the question: Was Celia a woman entitled to the right of self-defense assured all free white women under Missouri statute? He requested that the judge give the following instruction to the jury:

> If the jury believe from the evidence that Celia did kill Newsom, but that the [k]illing was necessary to protect herself against a forced sexual intercourse with her on part of said Newsom, and there was imminent danger with such forced sexual connection being accomplished by Newsom, they will not find her guilty of murder in the first degree.[7]

The judge's negative answer came with dispatch, as he rejected Celia's lawyer's request and instead offered the prosecutor's instructions to the jury:

> If Newsom was in the habit of having intercourse with the defendant who was his slave and went to her cabin on the night he was killed to have intercourse with her or for any other purpose and while he was standing in the floor talking to her she struck him with a stick which was a dangerous weapon and knocked him down, and struck him again after he fell, and killed him by either blow, it is murder in the first degree.[8]

Armed with these instructions, the jury deliberated only briefly before finding Celia guilty of murder in the first degree to be punished by death. And just as U.S. Supreme Court Justice Roger B. Taney would rule in the famous March 6, 1857, Dred Scott case that a black man had no rights a white man was bound to respect, the Missouri courts declared that in the eyes of the law, black women, in particular slave women, were not women. The court delayed execution until the birth of her child so as not to deprive the Newsom estate of the profit of Celia's rape. The baby, however, was stillborn. This case lends a special poignancy to Sojourner Truth's often repeated alleged query, "Ain't I a Woman?"

Of course Newsom's daughters refused to comment on their father's abuse of Celia or to respond in any way to her entreaties for help. Their silence was in keeping with the politics of denial. For these plantation mistresses to have aided Celia would have meant that they and other similarly situated white women had to acknowledge openly that their fathers, brothers, and husbands were rapists. Similarly, the black slave with whom Celia was involved ran away so as to avoid public collaboration of her rape and any personal implication in the killing. As Orlando Patterson might suggest, the punishment would have exceeded the friend's tangential involvement in the whole affair.

Joan Little

On August 27, 1974, the Beaufort County district attorney claimed that twenty-year-old Joan Little, incarcerated on robbery charges on August 27, 1974, lured sixty-two-year-old jailer Clarence Alligood into her cell, stabbed him to death with an ice pick, and fled. One of the white lawyers who helped to prepare the initial defense for Little saw in the case the opportunity to raise a number of legal and social issues, including "the right of a woman to defend herself against a sexual attack; prison conditions for women; the discriminatory use of the death penalty against poor people and blacks; and the right of a poor person to an adequate defense."[9] Eventually Little was freed, but not because anyone believed her version of the events. Ultimately, asserted one juror, the state failed to prove its case. Undoubtedly, had Little not attracted the assistance of the Southern Poverty Law Center and national media attention, the outcome would have been different. This acquittal, unfortunately, did not end her engagement with the criminal justice system. She was arrested in 1989 at the New Jersey entrance of the Holland Tunnel on weapons and stolen property charge.

Anita Hill

I used to wonder how American history would read if it were told from the perspective of sexually exploited black women. The Anita Hill–Clarence Thomas sexual harassment hearings and the aftermath answered my question. As Anita Hill spoke in her calm, controlled voice about the harassment and indignities she had suffered, she became a powerful metaphor for the telling of the black woman's tale in America. As the Democrats on the Senate Judiciary Committee and a startled nation sat transfixed, Republicans Orrin Hatch, Alan Simpson, and Arlen Specter let loose. The last voice that elite white male power brokers want to hear in this society is that of the black woman. Although their questions, innuendos, and demeanor sought to shatter her credibility, Anita Hill persevered. In this last decade of the twentieth century, she opened the door through which all black women must enter or forever remained closeted in silence and secrecy, in denial and disbelief.

The magnitude of her courage to tell her story is revealed most effectively when viewed against the historical reluctance of black women to draw attention to their inner lives. Because of the interplay of racial animosity, class tensions, gender role differentiation, and regional economic variations, black women as a rule developed a politics of silence and adhered to a cult of secrecy. The dynamics of dissemblance involved creating the appearance of disclosure, or openness about themselves and their feelings, while actually remaining enigmatic. Only with secrecy, thus achieving a self-imposed invisibility, could ordinary black women acquire the psychic space and gather the resources needed to hold their own in their often one-sided and mismatched struggle to resist oppression.

Pleasure, Profit, and Power

The sexual exploitation of black women occurs on many different levels, as the above examples testify. On the physical level, they can be forced to give sex—that is, raped. This appropriation of their sex for pleasure and for profit reinforces male domination.

The profit gained from the sexual exploitation of black women falls into two separate categories: economic and psychological. During slavery, some black women were sold as concubines or mistresses, and their offspring enriched the pockets of owners and lovers, for the child inherited the status of the mother. So obviously there was economic incentive to possess a black woman. But there was also the psychological or psychic profit gained from degrading and dehumanizing in one person the two characteristics most threatening to white males: blackness and femaleness. The domination of white women meant control only of a subordinate sex, just as the control of black men translated into domination only over race. With the black woman securely under control, white men imagined themselves true masters of the universe and all its inhabitants. Historian Joel Williamson offers a succinct summation: "By its very nature slavery created commanding imperious persons. Slaveholding planters saw themselves as the lords of their little earths, and of all the bodies dwelt thereon." He reminds us that "however much white society might denounce as wretches those who used their power to extract sex from their slave subjects, it positively defended their right to do so, even under circumstances that were blatantly outrageous."[10]

    The achievement of total domination and the extraction of maximum psychological profit dictated the reduction of black women into something totally undeserving of human consideration. Accordingly, as historian Winthrop Jordan illustrates, white men demonized and villainized black women's sexuality and femininity.[11] This process gave rise to an array of negative stereotypes. Historians Deborah Gray White and Patricia Morton elaborate at length on the Jezebel, Mammy, and Sapphire stereotypes and how such negative depictions of black women operate as invidious mechanisms of control.[12] The victim was transformed into culprit as the black woman became the ultimate other. One of the common themes in the idea of "otherness" is objectification. As the other becomes object, it is perceived as a thing to be managed and possessed. The object is thence seen as dangerous, wild, and threatening; but ironically it also inspires curiosity and invites inquiry, giving rise to intense desire for knowledge, possession, and domination. The corollary to the notion of woman as personification of nature is the conviction that it is man's responsibility to penetrate nature's mysteries. The black woman came to exemplify nature untamed, unknown, unmastered. That black women were dark in color lent credence to notions that they were indeed more like nature, or even more natural sites for white man's explorations and aggressions.[13]

    Profit, both psychic and economic, from the dehumanization and degradation of black women cut across gender lines. White women gained from the exploitation of black women in a culturally inscribed way. The slave and free black woman's sexuality stood in stark contrast to the "ultrafeminine" images of Southern white womanhood. It is daunting indeed to unravel the interlocking images of the slave woman and her dominating white mistresses, but we do know that white female sexual status rose in proportion to the diminution of black women. White women's virtue was protected as long as lustful passions could be released upon powerless black women. Even today, popular culture is replete with a range of dichotomized images of the good white woman and the evil black woman, the feminine white woman and the masculinized black woman, the chaste, demure, virginal white woman and the sluttish, whorish, depraved black woman, the immoral, unmarried black welfare mother and the dutiful white housewife.

Unraveling black men's relationship to the exploitation of black women is problematic. Black men won advantage because of the negative stereotyping of black women. In bell hooks's accounting of the consequence of the scapegoating of black women through matriarchal mythology, for example, white men forged psychic bonds with black men "based on mutual sexism." To be sure, matriarchal mythology often helped to deflect black men's attention away from the serious social and economic policies and employment shifts that have worsened and today seriously impair their ability to provide for themselves and their families. For a long time, charges of matriarchal domination led to the conclusion that black women were responsible for the "pathological status of black families" and the demasculinization of black men. Such accusations successfully deflected concern about growing economic and political disparities between white and black males in the society. At the very moment in time that black males bonded with each other and with white men in defense of Clarence Thomas, unemployment of blacks in general reached an all-time high. To the extent that justifiable anger over deteriorating economic, political, and social conditions is diffused into intraracial conflict and black male–black female disquiet, elite white males profit.

The Clarence Thomas–Anita Hill sexual harassment hearings hit me hard. Actually, I cannot remember when an event affected me more deeply and profoundly. Of all the things that got to me during that tense weekend in October 1991, the most disturbing was the way the Republican members of the Senate Judiciary Committee treated Hill. Perhaps too deep familiarity with the history of the sexual exploitation of black women over the past four centuries on American soil ill-prepared me for one more public assault. That they were disrespectful is putting it mildly. She came to tell her story, to share her experiences, and to shatter the silence—to use her own voice in a quest for a fair hearing. Hill was scorned, ridiculed, threatened, and denigrated. As she left the chambers, I saw through my own tears and anger the shattered remnants of another black woman's dignity. We stand on the threshold of the twenty-first century, and still black women must seek, plead, and even die for the freedom, justice, and equality of opportunity so glibly promised white males in the Constitution of the United States, black males in the Fourteenth and Fifteenth amendments and, for all intents and purposes, to white women in the Nineteenth Amendment to the Constitution. I wrestled with the same question that echoes across the decades of her unique history—what will it take for the black woman to be free and considered fully human? Black women will be free only when we are all brought to oneness as human beings, when we all love and care for each other simply because we are human beings and it is our duty and right. Yet an enlightened future is possible only if we are finally able to comprehend and to confront the damage that historic sexual exploitation has done to black girls and women. Further, we must fully understand the importance of close friendship and family ties between black women. Only within the realm of these critical relationships can they receive the psychosocial support that has helped them escape the paralysis of being the country's greatest and most total victim.

Still, it would be naive to expect that a group of women so victimized and exploited have managed to escape with their identities intact. Actually low esteem and virulent self-hatred afflict a great many black women and preclude any possibility of mutual support in countless times and places. Divisive impulses were and continue to be fanned by the existing hierarchy of status and color privilege prevalent within the black community and by the often disastrous competition for male attention. While America has a penchant for blaming the victim, the victims often blame themselves and others similarly situated. This explains in part why so many black women, if media reports are accurate, denounced Hill and supported Thomas.

Even so, the most fundamental tensions exist not between black women and black women, but between black women and the rest of society—especially white men, white women, and to a lesser extent black men. All are involved in a multifaceted struggle for control of black women's productive and reproductive capacities and sexuality. But there are additional factors that warrant consideration. Since sexual exploitation constitutes such a central force in the historical and contemporary lives of most black women, especially working-class or poor black women, they were undoubtedly astonished at what Professor Hill described as constituting her experience with sexual harassment. In other words, Thomas's allusion to "pubic hair on his coke can," for example, seemed mild in comparison to the rape, beatings, and verbal and psychological abuse that figure so prominently in poor black women's daily lives.

Given their culture and history and the success of the politics of denial, it is encouraging to note that black women are disproportionately represented among those who have filed sexual harassment suits in recent years. Sexual harassment and exploitation, whether for pleasure, profit, or power is a significant concern of all women, but for black women it is a cancer with which they have lived too long.

Booker T. Washington and Madam C. J. Walker

Madam C. J. Walker deserves a special place in the annals of black women's history. While directing the Black Women in the Middle West archive project, along with Shirley Herd, Virtea Downey, and Patrick Bidelman I traveled across Indiana and Illinois in the early 1980s searching for primary records, photographs, and other documents that would shed light on the historical contributions of black women on local, state, and regional levels. Nearly every long-term black resident in Indianapolis, Indiana, spoke of Madam C. J. Walker—and always with pride and reverence. Gradually, I learned more about this unique woman entrepreneur who so embodied the teachings of her prominent contemporary, Booker T. Washington, a man whose name literally defines the era in which they lived. Her story, like his, sounds mythical in the retelling. In the era of Booker T. Washington, or the age of Jim Crow, lived a woman who had moved from a sharecropper's cabin in Delta, Louisiana, where she had been born on December 23, 1867, to achieve the enviable feat of turning a black hair and scalp treatment formula into a million-dollar business and who moved into a thirty-four-room mansion in New York shortly before her death in 1919.

For this impoverished sharecropper's daughter of the delta, life turned out to be a grand adventure of which she was the star. One of three children born to former slaves, Sarah Breedlove was in quick succession an orphan at six, married at fourteen, mother of Lelia at seventeen, and a widow by twenty. Like so many other working-poor black women, she had to take the only job available to support herself and her young daughter; she became a washerwoman. She washed for white families in Louisiana and Mississippi, and in an effort to improve her life she migrated to St. Louis, Missouri. Again, the only work available was in domestic service. Within time the harshness of her work, combined with inadequate diet, insufficient rest, and endless stress, took its toll. Always mindful of the importance of grooming and personal appearance, she despaired over her hair falling out, especially around the temples. In her own retellings of her story, Walker claimed that she dreamed the secret formula for a hair and scalp product that miraculously restored her hair and the health of her scalp. Others have speculated that she more than likely discovered the formula for a hair and scalp treatment manufactured by Annie Malone's Poro company in St. Louis.

Migration, or mobility, is a recurring theme in her life. Usually poverty was reluctant to release its grasp. But the move to Denver proved propitious. Leaving St. Louis, Walker, with all of $1.50, arrived in to Denver to live with her widowed sister-in-law. There she produced and sold the hair growing and scalp restoring product to other black women, door to door at first. In 1906 she married newspaperman Charles J. Walker, began calling herself Madam C. J. Walker, and soon reaped the benefits of advertising her products in the black press. Convinced that greater profits awaited her in the more densely populated East, Walker moved her business to Pittsburgh, but after two years she relocated to Indianapolis. During the last decade of her life, Walker amassed a remarkable personal fortune and charted a path to personal and economic autonomy for thousands of black women on three continents. Students traveled from the Caribbean, England, and Africa to attend the Walker Colleges in Chicago, Washington, D.C., and Kansas City, Missouri.

In describing Walker's impact on black women, columnist George S. Schuyler wrote:

> What a boon it was for one of their own race to stand upon the pinnacle and exhort the womanhood of her race to come forth, lift up their heads and beautify and improve their looks. . . . The psychological effect of Madam Walker's great activity has been of great importance and can hardly be overestimated. Besides giving dignified employment to thousands of women who would otherwise have had to make their living in domestic

service, she stimulated a great deal of interest generally in the care of the hair.[1]

Paula Giddings succinctly describes the innovative and original system Walker designed to empower black women economically:

> Though she began by offering her formula door to door, Walker understood that that was not the way fortunes were made. She established a chain of beauty parlors throughout the country, the Caribbean, and South America. She had her own factories and laboratories, said to be the most advanced of their kind. Walker set up training schools in hair culture, and employed black women agents to sell the products—including hair growers, salves for psoriasis, and oils—on a commission basis.[2]

Historian Leroy Davis in an informative and insightful essay, asked was Madam C. J. Walker "A Woman of Her Time?" He posed two additional questions that still await an adequate response: "To what extent did the accomplishments of Madam Walker represent the overall aspirations of Afro-American women?" and "Was she primarily an exemplar of Booker T. Washington's philosophy of accommodation and economic self-advancement, or did she find in that philosophy a convenient vehicle for meeting the aspirations of black women?"[3]

Davis's questions inspire others. Given the magnitude of her accomplishments, why aren't the decades between 1890 and 1920 referred to as the Age of Madam C. J. Walker, or perhaps the Age of Booker T. Washington and Madam C. J. Walker? Was not her ascension equally as impressive, and even more dramatic than, as that of Washington, considering that she had to overcome combined racial and sexual discrimination? Judging that her legacy, as Washington's, continues to affect millions of African Americans in their daily lives, what did Walker do, or fail to do, to bring about her comparative historical obscurity? Regardless of the answers to these specific questions, an altered periodization of black history is necessary. Thus, the decades from 1890 to 1930 are best referred to as the First Era of Black Women. Although the important community building and women's club formation work yielded many outstanding and notable black women, none was more important or powerful than Madam C. J. Walker, who was indeed a woman of her time.

In the early 1980s I was delighted when my friend, historian Gwendolyn Keita Robinson, indicated her intent to transform her dissertation into a full-length biography of Madam C. J. Walker and the history of black beauty culture. Since then, Walker's great-granddaughter Alelia Perry Bundles has published a useful biography for young adults. Only recently, however, in 1992 to be exact, did the Indiana Historical Society open the Madam C. J. Walker Papers. I examined those papers as soon as they were available and thus began the process of satisfying a gnawing curiosity about the interior consciousness and the entrepreneurial genius of one of the most complex "race woman" in our past. The multilayered work of this significant African American who is still perhaps best known to the general public as the answer to a Trivial Pursuit–like question, "who is America's first woman self-made millionairess?" is in need of major excavation and analysis.

Madam C. J. Walker has been trapped in an intellectual void created in large part by the race relations/social problems paradigm that historians constructed during the 1960s. In the absence of a language of gender and a consciousness of the complex matrix of domination and female resistance, black women, rich and poor alike, remained invisible to most black scholars. The historian Evelyn Brooks Higginbotham has observed that the metalanguage of race silenced all other discourses. Consequently, the male-biased/race relations/social problems paradigm seemed best suited to advance interpretations of black life and leadership at the turn of the century. Black women could be comprehended and treated as historical subjects only if they were attached to a man, an institution, or an organization.

Madam C. J. Walker was representative of hundreds of female entrepreneurs who facilitated black community development and made it a part of a process of defining and expanding their role in postemancipation black culture and society. She and cosmetic and beauty culture rival Mrs. Annie M. Turnbo Malone, were among the leaders of the late nineteenth and early twentieth centuries black women's movement that demanded sexual respectability and created a new aesthetic of feminine beauty as part and parcel of their quest to give a gendered meaning to freedom. As the archetype "race woman," Walker was a major force in black charitable giving and a critical supporter of key institutions that were instrumental in the many antiracism struggles.

Madam C. J. Walker's unique discourse of resistance to both sex and race subordination that undergirded an economic empire built on new ideals of black feminine beauty and sophisticated marketing technologies proves the inadequacy of earlier paradigmatic models. A more complex analytical framework is needed in order to assess the impact of Walker on the black community and on gender relations within that community. A superficial analysis of her business products frequently invites easy ridicule and dismissal. Even some of the black leaders wondered how liberating it could be to concoct a salve to grow longer hair and nurture the scalp. Even the names of the products, such as Wonderful Hair Grower, are suspect and hardly indicative of an oppositional consciousness. Is it likely that patriarchy would find threatening her inspirational lectures given before tens of thousands of black women with titles such as "From the Kitchen to the Mansion" or "The Negro Woman and Business" when the vast majority of women entrepreneurs were seamstresses, laundresses, and hairdressers who conducted modest businesses in their own homes? Does not the very nature of her manufacturing enterprise and her spoken words and written advertisements suggest an unquestioning embrace of Western capitalist ideology and acceptance of Horatio Alger mythology?

Madam C. J. Walker could not be romanticized like a Harriet Tubman or a Sojourner Truth or an Ida Wells Barnett. Her resistance did not lead to dramatic physical encounters with white slave masters or require her to demonstrate masculinist cunning, wizardry, or heroic exploits. She was no literal Moses or general or legendary defender of black men against lynch mobs. She never asked, "Ar'n't I a woman?"

All Walker did was to create and launch the most subversive challenge to and assault against the proscriptive belief systems and negative definitions of black femininity. She implicitly, if not explicitly, declared war against white and black patriarchy and undermined the ongoing battles to control black women's sexuality and to appropriate and exploit their reproductive and productive labor by manipulation of negative stereotypes and slander. Contrary to the white myths, Walker told black women that they were beautiful. Of course she emphasized that use of her products would enhance their beauty, increase self-esteem, and raise their expectations and demands. She also demonstrated by her own example that producing and selling her products would generate higher wages and income than most African Americans dared to imagine. She urged black women to lift themselves up as a way to uplift the race, and in a 1912 speech she proclaimed, "I am a woman who came from the cotton fields of the South. I was promoted from there to the washtub. Then I was promoted to the cook kitchen, and from there I promoted myself into the business of manufacturing hair goods and preparations. I have build my own factory on my own ground."[4]

In contrast to Booker T. Washington, Walker did not advise black people, as he did in his infamous speech at the Atlanta Cotton States and International Exposition in 1895, to drop their buckets where they were and to acknowledge that the Southern white man was the black man's best friend. Never in the twenty years of her ascendancy did she have lunch at the White House or receive $600,000 from philanthropist Andrew Carnegie, or any amount from the ubiquitous Julius Rosenwald, or from John D. Rockefeller's corporate philanthropic trusts. Nor did she build a political machine to dominate black higher education and the black press.

To compare them is not to belittle or diminish Washington, but to clear the lens for a sharper view of Madam C. J. Walker and other black women activists of this "woman's era." Finally, Walker refused to have anything to do with white Americans once she got rid of her washtubs and cook's apron. Indeed, her Indianapolis factory employed only local black men and women. By 1912 Walker, newly divorced from newspaperman Charles Walker, employed 1,600 agents and was making $1,000 per week. She built a mansion in New York and moved there in 1916. Throughout the years she continued to give generously to black schools, organizations, and individuals.

To be sure, Walker's black feminist ideology or her womanist communal consciousness and carefully orchestrated philanthropy were distinguishing characteristics. Her relentless adherence to a philosophy of black self-help, mutual aid, separate institutional development, and racial solidarity gave her common ground with Washington. According to historian Nancy Cott, "Women's communal consciousness ought to be explicitly recognized for its role in women's self-assertions, even while those self-assertions are on behalf of the community that women inhabit with their men and children." For Walker and her agents, such communal consciousness was reinforced by "womanist" consciousness. The historian Elsa Barkley Brown states the point well: "many black women at various points in history had a clear understanding that race issues and women's issues were inextricably linked, that one could not separate women's struggle from race struggle." Certainly Walker was aware of this. To be a womanist was a big order, because it required holding together many constituencies and multiple purposes all at once.[5] Perhaps it is better to say that Walker possessed a communal womanist consciousness that enabled her to fight one struggle on many different fronts, using and devising strategies according to their effectiveness in a given space and time.

The National Negro Business League that Washington founded in 1900 and its annual conventions allowed few black women space in the public life of the race. While the Tuskegee Wizard supported her, Washington and Walker differed on at least two major points. She more than he believed in the efficacy of migration and urbanization, and she stressed the importance of economic autonomy for black women as women, celebrated their agency, and disdained victimhood. One of her advertisements read, "A Real Opportunity for Women who wish to Become Independent. Mme. Walker's System of Scientific Scalp Treatment and Sales of her Hair Preparations are giving support to more than 100,000 people in this Industry. Come in and learn how."[6]

To a noteworthy degree, Walker's life and work effectively captured the gender dimension obscured in or missing from Washington's prescriptions for black progress. While Washington's National Negro Business League was important to her, it bears underscoring that the national beauty shop system that Walker created provided a uniquely separate public space and nurtured, as did the club movement and as Evelyn Brooks Higginbotham's study of the Black Baptist Woman's Convention demonstrates, a distinct black women's culture.[7] Walker's beauty shop system paved the way for politicization and mobilization of black women across class and color lines. In 1916 Walker announced plans for a national club organization of her beauty agents. A letter she wrote to Freeman B. Ransom, lawyer and manager of her business since 1911, allows a close revealing of Walker's mind and method.

... I meant to organize clubs all over the country, and at some time call a meeting of all the agents and form a National which would be similar to the Women's federated clubs; only there would be no handling of moneys other than just to pay for literature and the like. Each club will handle its own money.
... I am thinking that it would be a good idea to put such women as Miss Lynch to treat, teach, and organize, deliver lectures on The Negro Woman in Business, and show ... pictures. I talked with Miss Lynch while in Salisbury, and she is very anxious to take up the work. I thought to give her $125. per month and let her pay her own expenses, and after the first year if she has sent in sufficient business to warrant it to give her an increase.
... I would like you to fix a contract which would apply to such agents as Miss Lynch and give them some dignified name other than agent and submit it to me at your earliest convenience providing you think my proposition a good one. Also would like you to form a letter to be sent to all the agents concerning my proposed organization and make a special appeal to them for one dollar each for the Memorial Fund. Address them as Dear Friend. Show them the reason why they should contribute. It will show to the world that the Walker Agents are doing something else other than making money for themselves.

The Madam Walker organization grew into a far-reaching network of clubs that resulted in increased sales of Walker products and greater prominence for and engagement of the company in the internal affairs of disparate black communities. The Madam C. J. Walker Hair Culturists Union of America assessed each member dues of twenty-five cents a month, and at their death their estates were entitled to a fifty-dollar payment. Every city that boasted at least five agents had a Walker Club and each year sent one representative to the national convention, the first of which occurred in Philadelphia in 1917.

The national conventions honored and granted cash prizes to the clubs and individuals that had the largest number of agents, the greatest sales volume, and the most outstanding record of benevolent work. The conventions cemented a sense of community, promoted professionalism, and enabled black women to engage in political discussions even though they could not yet vote. The politicization of black beauty culturists was quickly manifested. For example, following the bloody East St. Louis riot, Walker and her agents sent a telegram to President Woodrow Wilson declaring that they represented twelve million Negroes who "keenly felt the injustice done our race and country through the recent lynching at Memphis, Tenn., and horrible race riot at East St. Louis, and knowing that no people in all the world are more loyal and patriotic than the colored people of America, respectfully submit to you this our protest against the continuation of such wrongs and injustice in this land of the free and home of the brave, and we further respectfully urge that you as President of these United States use your great influence that Congress enact the necessary laws to prevent a recurrence of such disgraceful affairs."[8] President Wilson did not respond to these black women who spoke truth to power. In spite of their disfranchised status, the agents attending the 1918 convention held in Baltimore, Maryland, passed a resolution supporting the enactment of a federal antilynching bill. Harmony did not prevail in every instance, for the following convention witnessed a rift among the agents over the issue of whether the Walker products should be sold in drugstores and other retail outlets.

Walker possessed a sharp grasp of the political economy of black cosmetics. In September 1917 she spearheaded the founding of the National Negro Cosmetic Manufacturers Association and served as its first president. It was a bold, if ultimately futile, move to consolidate black dominance in the black cosmetics market. In her preliminary opening statement she explained that "inasmuch as Bankers, Wholesale and Retail Merchants found it necessary to organize for the purpose of regulating and nearly as possible making uniform their business operations and prices [I] felt it was equally necessary and urgent that the Hair Growers and Manufacturers of Hair Preparations, organize along such lines, especially in light of the fact that Manufacturers of Hair Preparations often suffer because of the activities of unscrupulous persons who placed fake preparations on the market." The charter is a cogent statement of Walker's understanding of the politics of an increasingly competitive and profitable industry. Clearly structured to preserve—indeed, to monopolize—economic gain for black businesses through cooperation, the charter reads:

> Realizing that the Manufacturers of Hair Goods, and Preparations have carved for themselves a place high in the business and commercial life of the Country, that such manufacturers owe it to themselves and their business to serve the good will and confidence of the business world: That the present good standing of such Manufacturers was attained by virtue of great sacrifice and bitter fights against fakes and impostors; that the future of such business can best be safeguarded through organized efforts; therefore in order to better protect Hair Growers and Manufacturers of Hair Goods against fraud and false representation, to properly regulate prices, to encourage business against the dishonest and illegitimate, to develop and inculcate the spirit of value for value, to protect the uninformed and unsuspecting, to promote the spirit of business reciprocity among ourselves, to encourage the development of Race enterprises and acquaint the public with the superior claims of high class goods, the product of negro business men and women, we the undersigned have associated ourselves together for the purpose of forming an organization which shall be known as THE NATIONAL NEGRO COSMETIC MANUFACTURERS ASSOCIATION.

Walker became involved with national and international issues of concern to peoples of African descent. In late 1918 and early 1919 she considered going to the Versailles Conference as an alternate delegate of the National Equal Rights League to ask for a provision concerning the rights of Americans of African descent in the treaty. She, like other members of the delegation, was unable to obtain a passport. Internationally, she was briefly involved with Adam Clayton Powell Sr. in the formation of an International League of the Darker Peoples early in 1919, a precursor to Marcus Garvey's Universal Negro Improvement Association.[9]

This essay touches the high points of Madam C. J. Walker's life and work. Clearly there is much more to learn. New scholarship on her remarkable odyssey promises to deepen our understanding of gender roles and relationships in the lives of people who lived behind the veil of Jim Crow.

Paul Robeson
Truth and Punishment

Paul Robeson added the collective experiences of black Americans in their struggles against segregation, discrimination, and disfranchisement to his own unique triumphs and tribulations to construct a lens through which he viewed and interpreted the big issues and events on the world stage. In 1950, the U.S. government placed Paul Robeson under "house arrest" with the revocation of his passport. He could no longer travel abroad to pursue his singing career. Never had a black performer of his stature and talent crashed so profoundly against the wall of white power. To be sure, by midcentury Robeson had become synonymous with protest against the continued subjugation of colonial peoples throughout the world. His outspokenness sealed his fate, and he who had entertained millions for decades was effectively silenced and ostracized. Outraged white politicians banned biographies from library shelves and withdrew recordings from record stores. Theater owners across America closed their doors as Robeson's earnings shrank from more than $100,000 a year to a little over $6,000. Paul Robeson, in short, was rendered invisible, a nonperson, and generations of young African Americans "knew his name not" and certainly would not have recognized his voice. What did this black man do or say to deserve such unmitigated silencing?

From 1950 to 1958, Paul Robeson fought against the combined might of the United States government and the business community to retrieve his passport. In so doing, he challenged the power of the State Department to make decisions as to which individuals had the right or privilege to travel abroad. While the essential constitutional issue involved focused on the right to travel, the case was complicated by Robeson's political views. His "crime" was speaking and singing for the cause of freedom—not just for black Americans, but for all oppressed peoples in Asia, Africa, and in Latin America. To understand fully Robeson's relentless determination to win back the right to travel, and his symbolic role in the liberation struggles of colonial peoples, it is necessary to review transformations of the 1940s.

The "straw" that the State Department used to justify stripping Robeson of his passport and denying his right to travel was the statement he made in 1949 in Paris at the World Peace Congress. Robeson allegedly declared that President Harry Truman's Four Point program for colonial development meant a new slavery. He argued that as demonstrated in Africa, the program amounted to an invasion by the former secretary of state, Edward Stettinius, and "his millions." Then Robeson boldly declared, "It is unthinkable that American Negroes could go to war on behalf of those who have oppressed them for generations against the Soviet Union, which in one generation has raised our people to full human dignity."[1]

Historian Lamont Yeakey analyzed both the implications of Robeson's words and activities and the response of the United States government. Yeakey asserted that "the fact that he [Robeson] made seemingly irrefutable analogy between the plight of his people here and those of the Third World abroad alarmed the government. His comparison between those who exploited and oppressed colonial peoples in the Third World and the structure of that dominance, and those who oppressed blacks in this country through institutional racism was simply too much for the white political and economic establishment to bear. Robeson made sense, not only to those government officials and opponents of democracy in America, but he made sense to the hundreds of thousands who heard him."[2] Throughout the 1940s Robeson fought the twin evils of international and domestic racism and "linked the struggle of black America with the struggles of black Africa, brown India, yellow Asia, and the blacks of Brazil and Haiti and the peons of Mexico and South America."[3]

Robeson's words may have shocked and alarmed some white Americans, but even a facile reading of black history demonstrates that these thoughts and utterances were not new. Actually, Robeson spoke out of the revolutionary black oratorical tradition shaped by such nineteenth-century leaders as David Walker, Henry Highland Garnet, and Bishop Henry McNeal Turner.

As historian Sterling Stuckey noted, David Walker as early as 1829 had said that black men could not fight in earnest for a country that did not accord them their rights. Henry Highland Garnet argued, in 1841, that if the government should attempt to arm black men in the North to send them to Kentucky to put out a slave rebellion, blacks would never go for that. In 1868, in the Georgia State Legislature, Bishop Turner proclaimed that he would not fight to protect the flag of either Georgia or America until those flags began to protect American citizens who were black.[4] Superimposed on this revolutionary tradition out of which Robeson spoke and acted were the alienation, anger, and frustration born of his concerted efforts to help America and the Allies defeat Hitler's Nazism during the Second World War. Black Americans became permanently angry while fighting a war for a democracy they did not enjoy at home.

The war years were a rude awakening for most black Americans, particularly for Paul Robeson. Concerning these years, James Baldwin wrote: "The treatment accorded the Negro during the Second World War marks . . . a turning point in the Negro's relations to America. To put it briefly, and somewhat too simply, a certain hope died, a certain respect for white America faded."[5] Robeson pondered rhetorically: "What difference is there between the Master Race idea of Hitler and the White Supremacy Creed of Eastland? Who can convince the European peoples that the burning cross of the white-robed Klan is different from the swastika of the Brownshirts?"[6]

World War II unveiled the hypocrisy and paradox of sending a segregated military to fight an enemy preaching a master race ideology while simultaneously upholding racial segregation and white supremacy at home. While the marines and air corps excluded blacks entirely, the navy allowed them to join an all-black messman's branch. Initially the military established a quota of fifty-six black nurses to work in the segregated hospitals reserved for black wounded servicemen.

The black press launched an all-out assault on government sanctioning of segregation in the armed forces. A daily barrage of articles assailed those agencies and policies that practiced discrimination in employment, housing, and social services. As the black press intensified its protests, the government retaliated.

Individuals within the federal government pressured the White House and the Justice Department to indict some black editors for sedition and interference with the war effort. Virginius Dabney, the Southern white liberal editor of the *Richmond Times Dispatch,* made one of the most widely publicized attacks on the black press. He charged that "extremist" Negro newspapers and Negro leaders were "demanding an overnight revolution in race relations," and as a consequence they were "stirring up interracial hate." Dabney concluded his indictment by warning that "it is a foregone conclusion that if an attempt is made forcibly to abolish segregation throughout the South, violence and bloodshed will result."[7]

The democratic rhetoric unleashed during the Second World War motivated black Americans to reexamine their second-class position in American society. During the postwar years, Robeson and others such as W.E.B. Du Bois raised awareness of America's counterrevolutionary posture in numerous anticolonial struggles. From 1945 to 1949 millions of people in Asia, Africa, and Latin America attempted to throw off the shackles of colonialism and achieve self-determination. Under the leadership of Mahatma Gandhi and Jawaharlal Nehru, the Indian National Movement reestablished India's political independence from Britain in 1947. In a three-year struggle, 1946 to 1949, the Indonesian people successfully ended centuries of Dutch rule. Ho Chi Minh, whom Robeson dubbed "the Toussaint L'Ouverture of Indo-China," led the Vietnamese in their fight for independence against France.[8] In 1949 the Chinese people won out over the feudal landlords and foreign rule and established the Chinese People's Republic.[9]

Paul Robeson clearly understood how and why America exacerbated the difficulties these nationalists confronted in their struggles against colonial oppressors. In an address before the National Labor Conference for Negro Rights in Chicago on June 10, 1950, Robeson proclaimed that "our nation has become the first enemy of freedom and the chief tyrant of the mid-century world." He elaborated:

> How well and how bitterly do we recall that soon after Roosevelt died, American arms were being shipped to the Dutch—not for

> the protection of the Four Freedoms, not to advance the claims of liberty—but for the suppression of the brave Indonesian patriots in their fight for Independence.
>
> That was in 1946, and today—four years later—we have the announcement of another program of arms shipments to destroy a movement for colonial independence—this time arms for the French imperialists to use against the brave Vietnamese patriots in what the French progressive masses call the "dirty war" in Indo-China.[10]

Again in 1954 Robeson spoke out on Vietnam. Had power heeded his words, perhaps America could have avoided the soul wrenching tragedy of the Vietnam War, and the millions of people who lost their lives could have been spared.

> Now, when France wants to call it quits, Eisenhower, Nixon and Dulles are insisting that Vietnam must be re-conquered and held in colonial chains. "The Vietnamese lack the ability to govern themselves," says Vice President Nixon.
>
> Vast quantities of U.S. bombers, tanks and guns have been sent against Ho Chi Minh and his freedom-fighters; and now we are told that soon it may be "advisable" to send American GI's into Indo-China in order that the tin, rubber and tungsten of Southeast Asia be kept by the "free world"—meaning white Imperialism.[11]

Paul Robeson reiterated the question he asked in 1949 as to whether black men shall fight for a country that oppressed them. "What business did a black lad from Mississippi or Georgia share-cropping farm have in Asia shooting down the yellow or brown son of an impoverished rice-farmer?"[12] No one in government answered him. Dr. Martin Luther King Jr. repeated the same question in 1967 and 1968. He, too, received no response from white governmental and military authorities. Apparently, a black man could ask no question a white man was bound to answer.

Robeson saw and experienced an America that has only recently become visible to most other citizens. Columnist Jack Anderson wrote: "The heirs of George Washington and Thomas Jefferson actively have aided and abetted the rise of military dictatorships in the Western hemisphere. In a few short years, Latin America has become largely a martial Pan Americana, with the pentagon as its Vatican." In 1963 four Latin American nations—El Salvador, Honduras, Nicaragua, and Paraguay—were ruled by military dictators. By 1973 these four had been joined by the military dictatorships of Brazil (1964), Panama (1968), Bolivia (1969), Ecuador (1972), Chile and Uruguay (1973). Over a period of thirty years the Pentagon squandered $2 billion for hardware and training on the military establishments of Latin America.[13] Murder, torture, imprisonment, and poverty were the lot of the poor masses in these countries. Robeson foresaw this tragedy of human suffering and waged a heroic, yet doomed, struggle against the tyranny.

Robeson spoke out on behalf of all colonial peoples, but those occupying a special place in his heart were the Africans. In 1941 he joined in the founding of the Council of African Affairs, which called attention to the vital economic and political role Africa would play in the postwar world. Robeson appreciated Africa's potential economic clout. He observed that four thousand tons of uranium ore were extracted yearly from the Belgian Congo (now Zaire), which was the main source of the United States supply. Africa, Robeson maintained, provided more than half the world's gold and chrome, 80 percent of its cobalt, 90 percent of its palm kernels, one-fifth of its manganese and tin, one-third of its sisal fiber, and 60 percent of its cocoa.[14]

An astute political commentator, Robeson stressed the inseparability of African liberation from imperialist overlords and the black American's resistance to American racism. Robeson wrote, "the free peoples of the free colored nations are our natural friends: their growing strength is also ours."[15] In a 1957 address before the United Nations, the minister of justice of Ghana, Ako Adjei, underscored Robeson's personal convictions:

> Ghana has a special responsibility and obligation towards all African peoples or peoples of African descent throughout the world who are struggling to free themselves from foreign rule, or even who, by the mere reason of their color, are denied the enjoyment of very elementary civil and political rights which the Constitutions of their own states guarantee to all citizens. I should like to request all Members of the United Nations to take note that the new State of Ghana is concerned with the freedom of all African peoples and also with the treatment that

is meted out to all peoples of African descent, wherever they may be in any part of the world. . . .[16]

There is a direct correlation between Robeson's passport revocation and his involvement in liberation struggles and his leadership in the Council of African Affairs. When Secretary of State Dean Acheson revoked Robeson's passport in 1950, he explained that Robeson's travel abroad "would be contrary to the best interests of the United States."[17] Robeson sought redress through the courts, and in February 1952 the Court of Appeals upheld the denial of his passport. The State Department's brief is quite revealing:

> . . . Furthermore, even if the complaint had alleged, which it does not, that the passport was canceled solely because of the applicant's recognized status as spokesman for large sections of Negro Americans, we submit that this would not amount to an abuse of discretion in view of appellant's frank admission that he has been for years extremely active politically in behalf of independence of the colonial people of Africa.[18]

Robeson reapplied for a passport in 1953, 1954, 1955, and 1956. To reclaim his passport "became the central factor in his life"; for as he wrote, "From the days of chattel slavery until today, the concept of travel has been inseparably linked in the minds of our people with the concept of *Freedom*." Drawing on the nineteenth-century black struggle for freedom and that of his own father who escaped from slavery via the Underground Railroad, Robeson persevered. In his autobiography he declared:

> From the very beginning of Negro history in our land, Negroes have asserted their right to freedom of movement. Some of the runaway slaves went to foreign countries not to secure their own freedom but to gain liberation for their kinsmen in chains. The good work they did abroad lives on in our own time, for that pressure which comes today from Europe in our behalf is in part a precious heritage from those early Negro sojourners for freedom who crossed the sea to champion the rights of black men in America.[19]

During the seven years of litigation, the State Department's and the court's rationales for denying travel privileges to Robeson went from the sublime to the ridiculous. Initially the court held that the American citizen does not have a right to travel abroad; travel is a privilege granted at the convenience of the government. Later the court ruled that the State Department had the right to restrict the travel of any American citizen in the national interest. And finally it held that Robeson had failed to exhaust administrative remedies open to him. He had, for example, declined to execute an affidavit concerning past or present membership in the Communist party.[20]

By 1958 enormous international pressures on the American government to release Paul Robeson produced results. Everyday peoples, leaders and statesmen in India, China, the Soviet Union, and in African countries, agitated for Robeson's freedom. As one biographer succinctly put it: "The detention of Paul Robeson within the national limits of the United States during these years was the single most costly act America might have taken in terms of propaganda to the colored peoples of the world."[21]

Because of this international pressure, the Supreme Court of the United States in 1958 ruled on two cases that contested the secretary of state's arbitrary authority to revoke passports. The decision in those cases had a direct bearing on Robeson's petitions, which were again locked into the legal machinery. In the five-to-four decision in *Rockwell Kent v. John Foster Dulles*, Justice Douglas ruled that the secretary of state did not have the authority to withhold a passport because of an individual's political views. To make the issuance of a passport contingent upon the filing of an affidavit as to his membership in the Communist party was to deny a constitutional right (not privilege) without the due process of law of the Fifth Amendment.[22] Paul Robeson received his passport in June 1958, and in July 1958 he went to Europe.[23]

The striking and invaluable legacy Robeson left to black and white America—and thus his impact on history—is a dual one. One side of the legacy was the lesson derived from his individual struggle for freedom, which was embodied in his pursuit of the passport and the right to travel. This one aspect of his life clearly reveals the extent to which white government officials were willing to go in order to nullify the Constitution and suspend the rights of American citizens who objected to the exploitation of the masses for the private gain of a few. Robeson's activities and statements in behalf of liberation for all oppressed peoples and his analysis of the role the American government played in the perpetration of national and international oppression of colored people throughout the world comprise the other side of his legacy. From him we can learn, develop, and sharpen our own commitment and resolve to participate in and support the collective international struggle for peace and freedom. Robeson's life inspires us to stand firm and to speak truth to power.

Divine Obsessions
History and Culture of Miles Davis

One music critic has written that he found *Miles: The Autobiography* a "disturbed and disturbing" book, "harrowing" to read. It is an assessment with which I concur. Yet, for all that jazz trumpeter Miles Davis reveals of himself in this problematic, often shocking, autobiography, I am more intrigued by the silences that punctuate his tale. Ironically, it is well to remember that in spite of the tell-all flavor of his autobiography, Miles considered himself to be a master of silences in his music. Indeed, one of the features that helped to make "cool jazz" of the 1950s so distinct was its orchestration, its unison work in the middle registers, and its artful and evocative use of limited solo space and silences. Inasmuch as I consider myself to be a historian of "the silent and silences," who argues a "dissemblance as resistance" motif, the controversial and mercurial Miles Davis, an accomplished architect of jazz innovation, is much too important an icon of twentieth-century black culture to be permitted the last word on himself.

To be sure, there will be many words uttered and written about Miles in the decades to come. This brief essay focuses attention on Miles Davis's multiple obsessions, divine and diabolical, and explores how his class status, race, and gender shaped and propelled his efforts to define himself as a music professional intent on transforming jazz. I use class both to denote socioeconomic status and relation to means of production. I am mindful of the contemporary sociological and philosophical use of class, and culture, as markers or signifiers for race.

* * *

Miles Davis was born at Alton, Illinois, on May 25, 1926, the son of a prosperous middle-class dentist and oral surgeon, Miles Dewey Davis II, and his wife Cleota. The year following his birth the family, including an older sister, moved to East St. Louis, where his brother was born. Miles studied trumpet with Elwood Buchanan. While in high school and shortly after graduation, Miles worked with local and visiting musicians who played the so-called chitlin' circuit. Most notably, he accompanied the band of Billy Eckstine who, along with two sidemen, Charlie "Yard Bird" Parker and Dizzy Gillespie, played an engagement at the Club Plantation in St. Louis in July 1944. The exposure to these musicians influenced Miles to eschew attending a black elite institution, Fisk University in Nashville, Tennessee. Instead, Miles traveled to New York, where with essential financial and moral support from his father, he enrolled in Juilliard, one of the most prestigious schools of classical music in the country.

In New York, Miles attended classes during the day, but at night he pursued his education in jazz from the master musicians of the era. He absorbed all that he could from Bird, a process made easier because they roomed together for a brief period. Other teachers included Dizzy, and pianist Thelonius Monk. Throughout the 1940s and 1950s Davis became saturated into jazz culture. This bifurcation of daytime formal study and nighttime informal study lasted only until, as Miles alleges, what he was learning in the company of the musical greats would help him to develop his own unique style and sound, to find his own voice far better than the classical influences of Juilliard. His rapid progress at discovering his musical self led him to form combos while still a relatively young man. By 1949 Miles had become, as Nat Hentoff put it, "the leader of, and the catalyst for, an historic group of recordings that later became known, in album form, as the *Birth of the Cool*."[1]

In the ensuing decades Davis would continue to make waves in jazz, plunging fearlessly into uncharted waters, swimming against the tide, diving deep and surfacing at once transformed and transforming. Occasionally, he became mired in the murky depths of the underworld, as was the case when he became a heroin addict in the early fifties, cured himself of the affliction, only to sink into self-imposed exile and an orgy of oblivion in the late 1970s. But, phoenix-like, he rose again and again, giving rise to fresh musical innovations, fusing rock and jazz, incorporating electric instruments, hiring European musicians, and expanding the audience for this uniquely American music, all the while feeding the myth and legend of Miles Davis, "the baddest man on the planet." He died in 1991.

Key questions impede facile understanding of Miles the man. Why is the autobiography of this self-described wife beater, drug addict, and pimp so profoundly compelling and simultaneously repulsive? How can we—indeed, should we attempt—to separate the man from his music? What do his life and work reveal about the nature of American culture and society in the twentieth century? What propelled Miles on his odyssey? What was the point of his quest? What are his contributions to jazz?

To begin to answer at least the first three of these questions necessitate a closer look at the way black American culture creates its own black male icons on the one hand, and an examination of Miles's deliberate determination to expand and transform jazz from the world of small clubs to the concert halls on the other. Complicating the transformation and expansionism was the absence of black people in control of the traditional institutional structures requisite to attracting and holding young black and white audiences. During the early years Miles played jazz in small intimate clubs that dotted Fifty-second Street in New York. These clubs gradually disappeared after the war as rising black militancy and racial consciousness and the massive infusion of drugs made whites feel unwelcome and unsafe. The venue for jazz changed.

Many, including Davis, lamented that jazz wore the legacy of its lower-class, or folk, origins. With notable exceptions, most of the musicians could not read music, although Davis may have exaggerated the extent of this ignorance. The larger American society remained grudgingly ambivalent, enjoying listening or dancing to the swing and be-bop, but rejecting and disclaiming all but the most entertaining and appealing musicians. Certainly, given the inherently racist nature of the society, it did not help matters that the majority of great jazz musicians were black men and the owners of the record companies were all white. It was onto this scene with horn in hand that the Middlewestern, middle-class Miles Davis ventured.

In the late 1940s and 1950s, there existed no formal or "legitimate" structures that conferred on able jazz musicians acceptance, recognition, status, and other socially sanctioned rewards. Although *Down Beat* and *Metronome* existed, there were no scholarly journals or academic music associations holding annual conferences of jazz students and practitioners. To gain center stage in the jazz world, Davis had to blaze his own trail. Remaining at the center of the proscenium became the guiding obsession of his life.

Before turning the spotlight on Miles Davis the man, it is important to place him in an appropriate historical context with specific attention to what was happening to people of his race and gender, that is, African-American men, in the 1940s, 1950s, and 1960s. This requires the construction of altered periodization of black history, one that takes equally into consideration the experiences and agency of both black men and women and the oppressions they endured. I divide a gendered and racialized black history into four major eras.

The onset of the Civil War signaled the First Era of the Black Man. It extends from 1860 through the collapse of Reconstruction and the return of white Southerners to power. During this tumultuous time, so eloquently described by W.E.B. Du Bois, black men acquired legislated freedom, citizenship, and the right to vote with the adoption of the Thirteenth (1865), Fourteenth (1868), and Fifteenth (1870) amendments to the United States Constitution. Black men participated in the political process, holding various elected and appointed offices including several seats in the U.S. House of Representatives and two in the U.S. Senate. They helped to enact a number of laws in Southern states that universalized education and granted more rights to women. Further, black men purchased property, founded towns, established schools and religious institutions, and inaugurated the sharecropping system. When white Southerners, with white Northern acquiescence, returned to power they launched a program of terrorism and violence, engaged in legislative subterfuges to nullify the amendments, and used the politics of assassination and lynching to silence forever those black male leaders who overtly resisted the new order.

The second period began in the 1890s and ended around 1930 and is best referred to as the First Era of the Black Woman.

Although most scholars of black history have variously labeled this period the Age of Booker T. Washington, the Age of Accommodation, the Era of Jim Crow, or as historian Rayford Logan dubbed it, the Nadir, black women were among the most active and determined agents for community building and race survival. Their style was concentrated on internal developments within the black community and is reflected in the massive mobilization that led to the formation of the National Association of Colored Women's Clubs that boasted a membership of over 50,000 by 1914. The work of antilynching crusader Ida B. Wells Barnett and the economic empire building of Madam C. J. Walker also mark this era. Black women perfected a "politics of respectability," a "culture of dissemblance," and a cult of secrecy and silence. The objective was to keep the interior life of themselves and of their communities free from the hostile scrutiny of white Americans. Black women focused on issues of interiority, and when they could not stem the tide of violence, rape, lynching, and disfranchisement they urged migration out of canaan to Northern "promised lands." The era ended with the onslaught of the Great Depression, punctuated by the deaths of Ida B. Wells Barnett and A'lelia Walker, daughter of Madam C. J. Walker.

World War II ushered in the Second Era of the Black Man, and this is the period in which Miles Davis grew into manhood and created his musical legacy. The broader historical context of this era immediately calls to mind the Scottsboro Boys rape cases, the Tuskegee syphilis experiment, the segregation of black men in the armed forces, the experiences of Jackie Robinson of the Brooklyn Dodgers, the house arrest and erasure of Paul Robeson, the humiliation of W.E.B. Du Bois before the House Un-American Activities Committee, and the lynching of Emmett Till, followed by the 1960s assassinations of Medgar Evers, Malcolm X, and Martin Luther King Jr. and the FBI persecutions of the Black Panthers and the Black Power nationalists.

Concomitantly, this historical context includes consideration of the agency and genius of black men. The agency of ordinary black men is most graphically revealed in their struggles within the U.S. military and in postwar migrations to Northern urban areas. In 1941, A. Philip Randolph of the Brotherhood of Sleeping Car Porters called for the March on Washington Movement that resulted in President Franklin Delano Roosevelt's issuance of Executive Order 8802 establishing a committee to oversee the employment of black citizens in the defense industries with government contacts. Constitutional lawyers Charles Hamilton Houston, William Henry Hastie, and Thurgood Marshall were winning major desegregation victories in the courts and tearing down the edifice and myth of white supremacy. They destroyed the Democratic white primary in *Smith v. Allwright* (1944), and ten years later overturned the "separate but equal" doctrine in *Brown v. Board of Education* (1954).

Great writers including Richard Wright, Ralph Ellison, Chester Himes, James Baldwin, and John A. Williams were publishing their classic works. Similarly, Muhammad Ali boldly proclaimed and effectively demonstrated his domination of the world of professional boxing. Black male civil rights leaders of CORE, NAACP, SCLC, SNCC, and the National Urban League joined forces to March on Washington in 1963 and effected the passage of the 1964 Civil Rights Act and the Voting Rights Act of 1965. The passage of such legislation paved the way for the rise of black elected officials, of which Richard Hatcher, Carl Stokes, and Kenneth Gibson became the most famous beneficiaries.

Clearly, Davis was not unaffected by these diverse occurrences and myriad challenges that transformed America. Further, this recitation is not to say that black women were uninvolved in, or unaffected by, the turbulent events of this Second Era of the Black Man. After all, these men were their husbands and lovers, sons and brothers, fathers and uncles, nephews and friends who added continuity and coherence to their lives as they reciprocated. Indeed, by now it is possible and necessary to emphasize the parallel and intertwined history of black women's own sexual exploitation and racial oppression, as well as their work in social transformation, community building, and oppositional consciousness. I underscore, however, that in American patriarchal culture, black men were the most visible agents of social change and the most likely targets of overt white repression and resentment.

Not surprisingly, this era witnessed a rigidification of gender roles and conventions within the black community. The ideal black middle-class arrangement was the two-parent household with the woman occupying a subordinate position. Black manhood was defined by the material resources amassed and by the extent to which he dominated and controlled (or appeared to) his woman. These conventions became deeply entrenched in the years following World War II and mirrored to a disconcerting degree what was transpiring in the overall society. A not unrelated propensity in the black community was the internal process of individualization—the celebration of the achieving black man in all arenas of public and cultural life. Given the collective resistance of the civil rights movement, for example, Martin Luther King Jr. would emerge the hero. Miles Davis mastered the art and process of individualization in his music and lifestyle, as graphically reflected in the costumes he wore, the flashy cars he drove, and the women he possessed.

Now, to return to the "baddest man on the planet." Someone had to move jazz from the clubs on Fifty-second Street to, say, the Rutgers University Institute for Jazz Studies. Miles Davis was one of the many someones who did just that. By the sheer force of his personality, the magnitude of his obsessions, Davis bridged the transformation or transition from jazz as dance music and entertainment to jazz as concert and even art music. But as is the case with most progressions, evolution does not occur in a strictly linear fashion—that is, after all, the great liberal myth. On the contrary, as he elliptically demonstrates in his autobiography, many times he had to pause, drop out, regroup, and change directions in order to move where he knew not. Such was the tortured course of his odyssey that Miles, possibly inadvertently, obscured and, some might add, undermined, with the publication of his "disturbed autobiography" the importance of his own, inarguably substantial contributions to the music he loved with such consuming passion.

Anyone who deals with Miles the man, however, must come to grips with his autobiography and the ramifications of an all-too-revealed life. His book is disturbing to some because it holds up the mirror to the contradictions and stagnation of middle-class existence in America. Miles was foremost an artist, and like Gauguin, Picasso, and Henry Ossawa Tanner, he felt compelled to reinvent himself and to forever seek new spaces for his creativity. With his constant changing, was he disingenuous? Did he work so hard at being different because he knew that musically he was an heir to, but not the equal of, Louis Armstrong or Duke Ellington? Or was it that, like Charlie "Bird" Parker, John Coltrane, W.E.B. Du Bois, and Paul Robeson,

Miles was a black man in a society that imposed its own special kind of marginality on people of his race and gender? Finally, did his alternate embrace and ultimate rejection of prescribed codes of middle-class virtue and morality as reflected in his aggressive sexuality, drug abuse, and familial irresponsibility reflect an inability, or a refusal, to learn how to live within the mainstream and yet maintain a creative edge?

Without apparent hesitation, apology, or remorse, Miles chronicles his abuse of wives and women friends, including the beautiful and vivacious dancer Francis Davis, and the enormously talented and popular actress Cicely Tyson. He admits he was often neglectful, if not unloving, of his four children and of their mothers whom he did not marry. To be sure, he treated the people who loved him no worse than he treated himself. Still, this does not absolve him or excuse his misogynistic behavior. That he was a disturbed and tortured man, husband, father, and lover he makes clear. His badness speaks for itself without extenuation. Why he reveals so much of the negative aspects of his private life and personality is where the silence resides.

What is most intriguing about Miles Davis is the great pains and labor he expended trying to construct a definition of himself as the ultimate in hip, bad black man. In a series of oral interviews with ordinary "moral-hearted" (a phrase I borrow from Earnestine Jenkins) or good black men ranging in age from middle twenties to late seventies, I discovered a reserved reverence for Miles Davis. Aware of his dark side, these men eschewed making excuses for Miles by elaborating on his musically or socially redeeming qualities. Still, Miles spoke to ordinary "moral-hearted" black men in a way that was unique. He spoke to them not only through his music but also through the clothes he wore, the confrontations with white police authority, the way he distanced himself from audiences, the angry unsmiling countenance, and the outspoken critique of music corporations and white industry moguls. He spoke to them eloquently through the conspicuous material possessions, the red and canary yellow Ferraris and Lamborghinis, and the beautiful women at his side.

While Martin Luther King Jr. was marching, Thurgood Marshall was defending, Malcolm X was exhorting, and Murry DePillars was painting, to ordinary "moral-hearted" black men Miles, though rich and acclaimed by the white society that he often mocked and disdained, was the modern bad black man. Flawed to be sure, he was the icon of cool. The work of historians Lawrence Levine and Robin D. G. Kelley provide some insights into black folk culture and consciousness that may unwrap the Miles Davis mystique and the enduring significance of a pantheon of secular hero figures. As Levine observes, the traditional secular hero figures "symbolized the strength, dignity, and courage many Negroes were able to manifest in spite of their confined situation."[2]

It was the growth of the individualist ethos among Second Era Black Men that prepared the "moral-hearted" ones to embrace those bad black men who "operated by eroding and nullifying the powers of the strong; by reducing the powerful to their level." Bad black men like Miles, Adam Clayton Powell Jr., Mike Tyson, or Marion Barry often paid a price for their badness. Yet they provided a measure, or taste, of sweet vengeance vicariously enjoyed by ordinary "moral-hearted" black men too "circumscribed by the limits of reality." Near the end of his autobiography Miles declared, "Black people are acting out roles every day in this country just to keep on getting by. If white people really knew what was on most black people's minds it would scare them to death. Blacks don't have the power to say these things, so they put on masks and do great acting jobs to get through the fucking day."[3] I submit that Miles Davis, too, put on a good acting job. His autobiography, however, was not his greatest performance. *Sketches in Spain*, *Kind of Blue*, and *Bitches Brew* are far more eloquent and enduring testimony to his genius.

A Statement

In his autobiography Miles Davis rejects the politics of respectability. He paints a picture of himself as being raw and real. He took all the things denied black men of his era, including white women, money, and control over the music he played and created. He refused to engage in self-sacrifice or delayed gratification. Some critics may have objected to his later body adornment, platform shoes, psychedelic costumes, and jheri curled and weaved hair. He commodified himself and his music as he saw fit. It was the aura of freedom, of a black man unchained, that captured the imagination of ordinary "moral-hearted" black men who pressed their lips and went silently to work at the steel mills and post offices and who returned home to crowded flats and overburdened women after, perhaps, a stop at the local tavern or a visit with their own women on the side.

Vicariously through Miles ordinary black men glimpsed the possibility of another life with tongues unbitten and bank accounts not overdrawn. If as Ossie Davis has said, Malcolm X was our bright and shining revolutionary prince, and Sam Cooke was the shining black revolutionary prince of sweet soul music, then Miles Davis the prince of darkness was surely one of the baddest of bad black men. Miles Davis culture style was not without consequence. Those who embraced his culture too uncritically paid hell. By 1968 the forces of white repression took deadly aim. The FBI pursued the destruction of perceived bad black men such as the Black Panthers with a single-minded determination. Fred Hampton and Mark Clark were assassinated by Chicago police. In 1985 Davis released a prophetic album entitled *You're Under Arrest*. A few years later Rodney King would barely escape with his life and become yet another symbol of violent white police power.

While Davis's culture may have spoken to ordinary black men, it carried intensely threatening, and alternately alluring, messages to average white American men. Miles was not unmindful of this, as his descriptions and analyses of his own confrontations with white police authority attest. In October 1969 he called the police after a shooting incident in Brooklyn. The police arrived, searched him, and took him to the station. Davis insists, "They just didn't like it that a black guy was in this expensive foreign car with a real beautiful woman. They didn't know what to make of that. When they looked up my record I guess they found out that I was a musician and had trouble in the past with drugs, so they were going to try and pin some shit on me just for the hell of it. Maybe they would get a promotion for busting a famous nigger."[4]

The weapons of the oppressor are many and ever-changing. By the middle of the 1970s, coinciding roughly with Miles's resignation, or self-exile, the Second Era of the Black Man crashed as unemployment rose, new drugs flooded the black community, black-on-black homicide rates exploded, and AIDS sunk deadly root. While a few blacks prospered—especially those in higher education and in upper echelons of government work—a great number were caught in a downward spiral. Welfare rates skyrocketed, and the black man, became, according to some, "obsolete and endangered."

The upswing of the women's liberation movement coincided with the decline of the Second Era of the Black Man. Like the rhythmic cycles of nature, black women found their own voice and articulated a new consciousness as they again assumed center stage with a renaissance of powerful writings that unveiled the rampant sexism within the black community. As Pearl Cleage metaphorically put it, black women were mad at Miles and told the world of their displeasure.

While attention shifted to black women, some black men felt displaced and betrayed. They fought back on several levels, as some negative rap lyrics on MTV videos attest. And as their anger and frustration grew, many everyday black men stopped coming home. I think it is time for black men to leave the Miles Davis culture and come back home. Bring your divine black selves and unique geniuses on home. As Roberta Flack sang in the 1970s, "Black people we've been down too long." It is time to let Pharaoh go.

PART 4

Race, Gender, and Change

An Angle of Vision
Black Women and the Constitution, 1787–1987

Introduction

American history is a rich tapestry of interwoven threads. Each thread represents the experiences of men and women of diverse ethnic and racial groups who have collectively shaped the patterns and contours of this increasingly pluralistic society. Fully to understand and appreciate past and present America requires an examination of the total fabric and all of its components. To ignore, to ridicule, to distort any portion is to diminish the significance of the whole and to render a flawed version of the American polity. No nation can remain strong and viable with an image of its past based upon half-truths, self-serving myths, and blurred visions. The task of the historian is to probe the evidence, to examine critically those values, traditions, and beliefs held most dear in order to understand that delicate balance between the ideal and the reality.

The challenge to the historian is a daunting one, made manageable only with the aid of an array of analytical concepts. To comprehend American society in all of its complexity, the historian must dissect the interconnections among race and ethnicity, gender, socioeconomic and political status, region, and the self-determination strategies of both the privileged and the underprivileged.

This essay on black women and the United States Constitution represents an attempt to answer two questions. How can we use the angle of vision of black women to arrive at a deeper understanding, a more accurate portrayal, of the successes and failures of the men who met in Philadelphia two hundred years ago to create a more perfect union? Related to this question is the corollary. By what strategies have black women attempted to make the Constitution's promises to establish justice, ensure domestic tranquility, and secure the blessings of liberty applicable to themselves?

I feel compelled to declare at the outset that this focus on black women is not intended to diminish the struggles of black men, white women, poor white men, Naive Americans, or any of the other groups ignored and omitted from consideration by the authors of the Declaration of Independence and the framers of the Constitution. Nor is this an intellectual exercise to determine who among them was most oppressed. Suffice it to say that even a little oppression is too much for any people to bear. Why then do I single out black women? Given the nature and extent of black women's oppression in American society under slavery and in freedom, it is revealing indeed to analyze the ways they fought for and won basic rights and thus helped to transform the Constitution, bringing it into closer harmony with the ideals of the Declaration.[1]

Black women viewed the Constitution in dynamic terms. Through almost total reliance on the judiciary, especially after the passage of the Fourteenth Amendment, politically powerless and invisible black women struggled to effect social change. It is their determined faith in struggle and belief in judicial remedies to Constitutional inequality that provide a window onto the larger unceasing political and legal freedom quests of America's dispossessed. Black women, along with members of minority rights organizations, have cared about the nation's injustices to help make the Constitution the framework for "a more perfect union."

The first part of this essay will be necessarily brief. Prior to 1865 there existed no special relationship between black women and the Constitution. In short, their original legal position was "extra-constitutional." This is not to suggest, however, that the Constitution was irrelevant to antebellum black women. Although the Constitution neither mentioned slavery by name nor addressed the fact that one-fifth of the population were slaves, several clauses and sections did cover slavery, by providing for the continued importation of slaves until 1808, by requiring interstate cooperation in return of fugitive slaves, and by counting slaves as three-fifths of white persons in determining direct taxation and representation.[2]

Article 1, Section 2

"Representatives and direct taxes shall be apportioned among the several States . . . according to their respective numbers, which shall be determined by adding to the whole number of free persons . . . three-fifths of all other persons."

Article 1, Section 9

"The migration or importation of such persons as any of the States now existing shall think proper to admit shall not be prohibited by the Congress prior to the year 1808."

Article 4, Section 2

"No person held to service or labor in one State, under the laws thereof, escaping into another, shall in consequence of any law or regulation therein, be discharged from such service or labor, but shall be delivered up on claim of the party to whom such service or labor may be due."

The Constitution was clearly infected by the evils of slavery; in no way can it be construed an antislavery document. But it is, perhaps, an overstatement to assert that it legitimized or fastened slavery and the ideology of black inferiority on the states. Rather, the Constitution reflected the compromises made by framers more intent on having it accepted by the entire country, including South Carolina and Georgia, than creating a true democracy. The Constitution, therefore, mirrored customs and practices as they were. Yet, as Jefferson feared, slavery was the firebell in the night. In taking the long view, it is safe to argue that given the inevitable conflict between states' rights and federal power, the framework of the national government created by the Constitution made emancipation possible if not inevitable. By extension, while the original Constitution failed expressly to address the rights of blacks, women, and other dispossessed groups, as shown below, it was capable of amendment, and in the hands of a fair-minded federal judiciary it certainly proved to be advantageous to late nineteenth- and twentieth-century challengers to legalized inequality.

I

Black women never enjoyed the luxury of self-delusion concerning their legal or social status in American society. They occupied neither gilded cages nor lofty pedestals. One black woman political activist bitterly declared that at the birth of the new nation the woman of African descent "was the most pathetic figure on the American continent. She was not a person, in the opinion of many; but a thing—a thing whose personality had no claim to the respect of mankind. She was a house-hold drudge, a means of getting distasteful work done; she was an animated agricultural implement to augment the services of mules and plows in cultivating and harvesting the cotton crop. Then she was an automatic incubator, a producer of human livestock, beneath whose heart and lungs more potential laborers could be bred and nurtured and brought to the light of toilsome day."[3]

If this sober assessment suggests anything it is that black women did not rely on statutes, judicial opinions, the Declaration of Independence, or the United States Constitution to define the parameters of their existence. These daughters of Africa questioned not the importance of the Declaration of Independence or the Constitution in laying the political and legal foundation for an ostensibly democratic America.

Indeed, the moral forces unleashed by the War for American Independence and the rhetoric of equality, democracy, freedom, and inalienable rights fanned within black women and men a grim determination to loosen and obliterate first the shackles of involuntary servitude, then grueling poverty and debilitating ignorance, and finally political powerlessness.[4]

Doubly proscribed, as slaves and as females, black women were considered little more than mindless brutes, and as women, even when free, they were discouraged from openly addressing political issues. A few black women of the revolutionary generation did break the imposed silence and defy restrictive gender and racial conventions to plead, cajole, petition, and sue for manumission. As early as 1781 a slave woman, Elizabeth Freeman, sued for her freedom, which she won when a Massachusetts court ruled that the state's Constitution of 1780 had indeed abolished slavery.[5] The *Freeman* case possesses a dual significance: It reflected the rising antislavery sentiment among certain Northern white communities, which would in the following decades lead to a gradual legislative and judicial destruction of slavery in that region. Antislavery momentum peaked in some circles with the passage of the Northwest Ordinance of 1787. Article Six of the Ordinance declared, "There shall be neither slavery nor involuntary servitude in said territory, otherwise than in punishment of crimes whereof the party shall have been duly convicted. . . ." This is not to suggest that slavery never existed in Illinois, Indiana, Ohio, Michigan, or Wisconsin, but it was much attenuated and prevailed largely under the guise of long-term apprenticeships. As slavery loosened in the Northeast and lost ground in the Middle West, it became even more deeply entrenched in and peculiar to the South. This would have dire consequences a half century later. The *Freeman* case is also important as an illustration of the way black women immediately embraced the privileged white man's claims to freedom and equality. With alacrity and skill, antebellum black women, like white women and black men, appropriated revolutionary concepts as ideological bases for their freedom quests through the courts.

Thus, for the first generation of Revolutionary War black women, the equation was a relatively simple one. When black women would be free, all of American society would be redeemed. True freedom, however, does not come by merely wishing or even suing for it. Again the experiences and beliefs of the Founding Fathers taught black women a cardinal lesson. Those who would be free must fight for it—and die if necessary. Actually, it is essential to point out that black women meant several things when they wrote and talked about freedom. Just as there was for them no one kind of oppression, there was no one kind of freedom. Black women desired three inseparable kinds of freedom: control over their bodies or personal freedom; political and legal freedom; and freedom from racial discrimination.

The first African-American woman to speak before a mixed audience in public was Maria Stewart (1803–1879). In 1832 she began her brief tenure as a public lecturer by addressing the recently formed Afric-America Female Intelligence Society in Boston. Stewart's speeches and early writings were preserved in the pages of the abolitionist newspaper *The Liberator*. Stewart took pains in her initial speeches and writings to rationalize breaking the taboo of female silence. In her mind the call to speak in public came from the very highest authority. She declared: "Me thinks I heard a spiritual interrogation—'Who shall go forward, and take off the reproach that is cast upon the people of color? Shall it be a woman?' And my heart made this reply—'If it is thy will, be it even so, Lord Jesus!'" And with this Stewart called for all black women to "awake, arise: no longer sleep nor slumber, but distinguish yourselves."[6]

Undoubtedly imbued with the fervor of the Revolutionary era, Stewart nevertheless refrained from calling upon her fellow victims of tyranny to liberate themselves by force. Instead she, like so many black leaders to follow, appealed to the moral consciousness of white countrymen to accord her race the same rights to freedom from slavery they possessed:

> Did every gentleman in America realize, as one that they had got to become bondmen, and their wives, their sons, and their daughters, servants forever, to Great Britain, their very joints would become loosened, and tremblingly would smite one against another; their countenance would be filled with horror, every nerve and muscle would be forced into action, their souls would recoil at the very thought, their hearts would die within them, and death would be more preferable. Then why have not Afric's sons a right to feel the same? Are not their wives, their sons, and their daughters, as dear to them as those of the white man's?[7]

She knew well the futility of attempting to secure black liberation through rebellion. Unlike Nat Turner, Denmark Vesey, or Gabriel Prosser, Stewart conceded:

> We will not come out against you with swords and staves, as against a thief; but we will tell you that our souls are fired with the same love of liberty and independence with which your souls are fired. . . . We will tell you, that it is our gold that clothes you in fine linen and purple, and causes you to fare sumptuously every day; and it is the blood of our fathers and tears of our brethren that have enriched your soils.[8]

With that she concluded, "WE CLAIM OUR RIGHTS." And for Stewart the central right was freedom from slavery.

If Stewart was America's first black woman political writer, Sarah Parker Remond (1824–1894) of Salem, Massachusetts, was one of the foremost participants in the antislavery movement, whose speeches fired international audiences. The daughter of a Revolutionary War veteran, Remond was denied a passport following the infamous 1857 Dred Scott decision in which the United States Supreme Court had ruled that blacks had no rights inasmuch as they were not citizens of the United States.[9] Undaunted, Remond, without a passport, toured England, Scotland, and Ireland under the sponsorship of the Ladies and Young Men's Anti-Slavery societies, lecturing to as many as two thousand people at a time. Remond, according to a family friend, "was dedicated from birth to the cause of freedom. The parents and other women of the family looked after her training, supplying all her personal needs, only requiring of her that when ready [she was] to war against the traffic in human flesh."[10]

In March 1859, Remond spoke at a meeting of the Dublin Ladies' Anti-Slavery Society. She focused on the sexual exploitation of black women under slavery. According to one account of the lecture, Remond declared that the female slave was "the most deplorably and helplessly wretched of human suffers. . . . For the male slave, however brutally treated, there was some resource; but for the woman slave there was neither protection nor pity. If the veriest scoundrel, the meanest coward, the most loathsome ruffian, covets the person or plots the ruin of a defenseless female, provided she be known to be, ever so remotely, of African descent, she is in his power."[11] In a similar speech before a London audience, Remond again spoke of the sexual exploitation of the female slave. Obviously appealing to a sorority of consciousness, she remarked that, "If English women and English wives knew the unspeakable horror to which their sex were exposed on southern plantations, they would freight every westward gale with the voices of moral indignation and demand for the black woman the protection and rights enjoyed by the white."[12]

Thus far I have presented samplings of the oratorical and literary expressions of free black women political figures who, perhaps mistakenly, believed that appeals to Christian love and moral suasion would bring down the house of slavery. But politics, when considered from the black woman's angle, is more than written and spoken words. Slave women, illiterate and uneducated, downtrodden and exploited as they unquestionably were, we now know still behaved in ways that reflected resistance to their status as chattel property.[13] The fact that they survived, bore and nurtured children, and attempted to preserve family, culture, and self-respect throughout the slave experience is in itself a political statement.

To be sure, slave women rarely assumed leadership roles in the scores of organized revolts and conspiracies of the colonial and antebellum periods, the best known of which were the Stono Rebellion in South Carolina in 1739, Gabriel Prosser's revolt in Virginia in 1800, Denmark Vesey's conspiracy in South Carolina in 1822, and the Nat Turner insurrection in Virginia in 1831. These men anticipated what perhaps few whites appreciated, that the end of slavery would cost 500,000 white and black lives. Concern for their children and a desire to preserve the family at all costs, however, prevented large numbers of slave women from violent expressions of disdain for slavery.

Nevertheless, slave mothers deserve at least passing reference in any discussion of female resistance. Although they may have eschewed running away, truancy, or armed rebellion as standard forms of resistance, these captive women did play a major role in instilling the fighting spirit into their children, especially their daughters. One slave recalled, "The one doctrine of my mother's teaching which was branded upon my senses was that I should never let anyone abuse me. 'I'll kill you gal, if you don't stand up for yourself,' she would say. 'Fight, and if you can't fight, kick; if you can't kick, then bite.' "[14]

Historian Deborah Gray White in speaking of female slave resistance maintained that for the most part their "resistance in the United States was seldom politically oriented, consciously collective, or violently revolutionary. It was generally individualistic and aimed at maintaining what the slaves, masters and overseers had, in the course of their relationship, perceived as an acceptable level of work, shelter, food, punishment, and free time."[15] Actually White's observations are equally appropriate to black male slave resistance. The point that needs emphasis and clarification, however, is that the black female slave experience was marked by sexual exploitation. However similar or identical their slavery experience may have been, the essential distinction between black men and women even after slavery was that black women were powerless to protect their sexual selves.

II

A systematic study of the role of black women in hastening the defeat of the South and the concomitant destruction of slavery during the Civil War remains to be written. That the freedwomen were very much concerned with gaining citizenship and voting rights in the Reconstruction period is well documented. Sojourner Truth (1797–1883), the legendary veteran of the antislavery crusade, continued to travel and lecture on behalf of the rights of women after the demise of the peculiar institution. At one postslavery meeting, Truth, undaunted by the occasional hostility of various audiences, declared, "I know that it feels a kind o'hissin and ticklin' like to see a colored woman get up and tell you about things, and Woman's Rights. We have been down so low that nobody thought we'd ever get up again; but we have been long enough trodden now; we will come up again, and now I am here."[16] Truth had more to say than to announce that black women, as Stewart had cajoled a half century earlier, would rise again. She doggedly asserted, "But we'll have our rights; see if we don't; and you can't stop us from them; see if you can. You may hiss as much as you like, but it is comin'. Women don't get half as much rights as they ought to; we want more, and we will have it." In her own inimitable fashion she continued, "I have lived on through all that has taken place these forty years in the anti-slavery cause, and I have plead with all the force I had that the day might come that the colored people might own their soul and body. . . . We are now trying for liberty that requires no blood—that women shall have their rights—not rights from you. Give them what belongs to them."[17]

In Sojourner Truth's mind, as long as the country denied women full citizenship and human rights, then slavery was only partially destroyed. She declared, "I come from another field—the country of the slave. They have got their liberty—so much good luck to have slavery partly destroyed; not entirely. I want it root and branch destroyed. Then we will all be free indeed. I feel that if I have to answer for the deeds done in my body just as much as a man, I have a right to have just as much as a man."[18] Reflecting a keen understanding of the dangers of patriarchal politics, Truth exclaimed, "There is a great stir about colored men getting their rights, but not a word about the colored women, and if colored men get their rights, and not colored women theirs, you see the colored men will be masters over the women, and it will be just as bad as it was before."[19] In spite of her speeches and appeals, the nation's politicians, preoccupied with issues of reunification, economic development, and westward expansion, turned deaf ears to her, to her voice, and to white women's entreaties for the vote.

To be sure, nothing would ever again be as bad as it was prior to the December 18, 1865, ratification of the Thirteenth Amendment abolishing slavery. The adoption of the Fourteenth Amendment three years later, defining and conferring national and state citizenship on the four million Afro-Americans, and the ratification of the Fifteenth Amendment in 1870 represented near fulfillment of those promises embodied in the Declaration of Independence and in the United States Constitution. Clearly the Civil War was not launched to destroy slavery. President Lincoln and other Republican leaders made it known that the objective of the war was to preserve the Union, to establish the primacy of federal authority over state laws. Only with the negation of states' rights could the federal government strike at slavery and obliterate, if it so desired, all related forms of racial oppression.

From the perspective of black women, however, the Civil War was the true American Revolution, and the Fourteenth Amendment the most potent weapon they would possess throughout subsequent decades of struggle for personal, legal, political, and civil freedom.

The first section of the Fourteenth Amendment provided that "No State shall make or enforce any law which shall abridge the privileges or immunities of citizens of the United States; nor shall any State deprive any person of life, liberty or property, without due process of law; nor deny to any person within its jurisdiction the equal protection of the laws." In an oblique attempt to coerce states toward enfranchisement of black state citizens, Section 2 prescribed penalties for states interfering with or denying voting right to state citizens, including blacks. On March 30, 1870, the Fifteenth Amendment was added to the Constitution. It had as its primary objective the enfranchisement of black males. This last of the Reconstruction amendments prohibited all state racial restrictions on voting: "The right of citizens . . . to vote shall not be denied or abridged by the United States or by any State on account of race, color, or previous condition of servitude." Each of the three amendments ended on virtually the same note: "The Congress shall have the power to enforce this article by appropriate legislation."[20]

In an attempt to provide the appropriate legislation to protect blacks' rights as guaranteed by the Fourteenth Amendment, Congress in 1875 enacted the first Civil Rights Act. The Supreme Court of the United States, however, was of a different mind. In a series of decisions in 1883, the top tribunal ruled the public accommodations provisions of the act unconstitutional, leaving to local option the definition of black rights. Black men and women were outraged at this major assault on and restrictive interpretation of the Fourteenth Amendment. This decision, in Frederick Douglass's view, not only sealed the casket on the Reconstruction experiment but also contained the makings of a "black Ireland in America."[21]

It was at this juncture that the albeit small numbers of educated professional black women moved the battlefield for rights and the equal protection of those rights into the courts. For the next one hundred years black women, often acting independently, sued repeatedly those parties thwarting their enjoyment of citizenship rights. The courts became their ongoing constitutional convention. It was not enough to have the black freedom amendments on the books. The courts had to be persuaded to interpret broadly the meanings of those laws.

Immediately after the Supreme Court delivered its devastating decision in 1883, teacher, newspaperwoman, and soon to be internationally known antilynching crusader Ida B. Wells (1862–1931) purchased a railroad ticket in Memphis, Tennessee, and took a seat in the section now by state policy legally and constitutionally reserved for whites. When she refused to move, she was bodily thrown off the train, whereupon she hired a lawyer and sued the Chesapeake and Ohio Railroad for damages. The *Memphis Daily Appeal* headlined the federal circuit court's verdict: "Darky Damsel Obtains a Verdict for Damages Against the Chesapeake and Ohio Railroad—What it Cost to Put a Colored School Teacher in a Smoking Car—Verdict for $500." Upon appeal, the Supreme Court of Tennessee reversed the lower court's ruling, concluding: "We think it is evident that the purpose of the defendant in error was to harass with a view to this suit, and that her persistence was not in good faith to obtain a comfortable seat for the short ride."[22]

Although they more often than not lost their legal suits, black women persisted in their uphill struggle for unfettered access to places of public accommodation. For educator Charlotte Hawkins Brown of North Carolina it became a matter of principle to bring suit whenever she was insulted on a train or forced to leave a pullman coach and enter the Jim Crow smoking car. In an October 19, 1921, letter to her attorney she explained why she behaved and believed as she did: "I feel that the time has come when absolute justice for Negroes who are not seeking social equality ought to at least be tested in the Courts." She continued,

> As for me, a Negro woman, I feel so intently the insults that are heaped upon me by the Railroad Company that I am willing to become a martyr for Negro womanhood in this instance and give up my chance of holding, as friends, people who would withdraw because of my attitude. . . . A few of us must be sacrificed perhaps in order to get a step further.[23]

As Hawkins continued her solitary assault against Jim Crow, other middle-class black women educators carried forward the tradition of demanding from the courts protection of basic civil rights. In 1895, Mary Church Terrell (1863–1954) became the first black woman to serve on the Board of Education in Washington, D.C. Terrell, like Ida B. Wells and Charlotte Hawkins Brown, led a multiyear campaign and initiated numerous legal challenges to end discrimination in eating places in the nation's capital. In an article entitled "What it means to be colored in the capital of the United States," Terrell charged:

> Surely nowhere in the world do oppression and persecution based solely on the color of the skin appear more hateful and hideous than in the capital of the United States, because the chasm between the principles upon which this Government was founded, in which it still professes to believe, and those which are daily practiced under the protection of the flag, yawn so wide and deep.[24]

In 1949, her persistence bore fruit when the courts outlawed discriminatory practices in Washington, D.C., restaurants.

Bringing suit in the local, state, and federal courts constituted but one aspect of the contours and substance of professional black women's activism and political ideology. Their concentration on legal action and dependence on judicial institutions to guarantee and protect rights was born of limited opportunity to influence the elective branches of government. As long as the ballot remained beyond reach, black women had few avenues to impress their political wills on legislation or to make their voices heard with effect. Within the confines of the domestic sphere, black women could and did put pressure on their enfranchised men. In the late nineteenth century, ex-slave women urged and cajoled their husbands, sons, and fathers to vote whenever they could. In the 1893 poem entitled "Deliverance," Frances Ellen Watkins Harper captured well the covert influence black women exerted on the political activities of black men:

> And if any man should ask me
> If I would sell my vote,
> I'd tell him I was not the one
> To change and turn my coat....
> But when John Thomas Reder brought
> His wife some flour and meat,
> And told her he had sold his vote,
> For something good to eat,
> You ought to see Aunty Kitty raise,
> And heard her blaze away;
> She gave the meat and flour a toss,
> And said they should not stay....
> You'd laughed to seen Lucinda Grange
> Upon her husband's track
> When he sold his vote for rations
> She made him take 'em back.
> Day after day did Milly Green
> Just follow after Joe,
> And told him if he voted wrong
> To take his rags and go.
> I think that Curnel Johnson said
> His side had won the day,
> Had not wee women radicals
> Just got right in the way....[25]

The history of the woman suffrage movement in the aftermath of the Civil War was marred by white suffragists' willingness, for the sake of political expediency, to sever all ties with black women and even to advocate their continued disfranchisement in Southern states in exchange for white male support of the Nineteenth Amendment in that region. As one recent student of the suffrage movement put it, "Suffragists not only compromised with racism and ethnic prejudices in organizing on behalf of the vote; they also turned such prejudices into a tool with which to earn the franchise. They argued explicitly that woman suffrage would benefit society since it would ensure Anglo-Saxon dominance at the polls."[26] Unwelcomed and abandoned by their white sisters, black women continued to fight for and support passage of the Nineteenth Amendment.

Self-interest was but one of may compelling reasons black women fought for the ballot. Some argued that black mothers and teachers needed the ballot in order to better protect the interests of their children. Carrie W. Clifford proclaimed that the ballot was a useful tool for black women, for "it is the ballot that opens the schoolhouse and closes the saloon."[27] Black women believed that a democratic society depended on an educated citizenry and that the black struggle for rights and against segregation and discrimination was inextricably tied to the proper education of the future generations of black children.

Religious leader and famed educator Nannie H. Burroughs, widely known for her candor and combative spirit, asserted that with the ballot black women could ensure the passage of legislation to win social protection against rapists. Calling the ballot a "weapon of moral defense" she exploded, "When she [a black woman] appears in court in defense of her virtue, she is looked upon with amused contempt. She needs the ballot to reckon with men who place no value upon her virtue."[28]

While the ballot was important, acquiring it did not bring about all of the social and civil reforms women envisioned. To their dismay, black women learned very quickly the distinction between possessing the right to vote on the one hand and having the freedom to exercise the hard-won franchise on the other. The quasi-legal subterfuges invented by white Southerners to disfranchise black men after the passage of the Fourteenth and Fifteenth amendments, including the white primary, complex registration laws, literacy tests, and the poll tax, worked similarly to nullify black female voting. The poll tax not only limited black voting but also effectively restricted the political participation of poor white Southerners. The National Association for the Advancement of Colored People had, since its inception in 1909 and throughout the Great Depression and World War II, spearheaded numerous legal cases designed to persuade the United States Supreme Court to declare unconstitutional these disfranchisement measures. It would take, however, the Twenty-fourth Amendment (1964) to the Constitution to overturn the payment of poll tax as a prerequisite for voting in *national* elections,[29] and the Voting Rights Act of 1965 to protect black voters against discriminatory literacy tests and ended poll taxes in *state* elections.

By the 1930s, leading black political women had arrived at the conclusion that they needed to create one massive political organization through which they could make their voices heard. This movement toward collective political action represented a real departure from the past pattern of individual assaults by black women against Jim Crow social and civil customs and adverse public policies. In 1935 Bethune and Terrell founded the National Council of Negro Women (NCNW) dedicated to the development of "competent and courageous leadership among Negro women and [to] affect their integration and that of all Negro people into the political, economic, education, cultural, and social life of their communities and the nation."[30] When contemplating the creation of the NCNW, Bethune confided to Terrell, "The result of such an organization will, I believe, make for unity of opinion among Negro women who must do some thinking on public questions; it will insure greater cooperation among women in varied lines of endeavor; and it will lift the ideals of not only of the individual organizations, but of the organizations as a group." By the mid-1940s the NCNW had become the largest black women's organization in America, numbering 800,000 members. In addition to fighting for a constitutional amendment to outlaw the poll tax, the NCNW was committed to securing the passage of an antilynching law and to the establishment of a Fair Employment Practices Commission.[31]

The post–World War II years witnessed a significant shift in the location of black political activity. Increasingly black politics focused on local issues, and black women seemingly were more concerned with removing local, political, civil, and legal barriers to their citizenship. Recent scholarship has just begun to note the key roles black women such as Rosa Parks, Ella Baker, and Fannie Lou Hamer played in the modern civil rights movement. The autobiographies of Jo Ann Robinson, Daisy Bates, and Ann Moody shed much-needed light on this too-long-obscured dimension of the grass-roots black struggle for justice and freedom and an end to constitutional inequality. Historian Sara Evans presents countless recollections of black women's centrality to the civil rights movement: "In addition to their warmth and courage in taking in civil rights workers, these black women also furnished the backbone of leadership in local movements. Volunteers wrote home of 'Mama' doggedly attempting to register again and again or of a rural woman attending a precinct meeting. [And when] . . . no one showed up . . . with a neighbor as a witness, she called the meeting to order, elected herself delegate and wrote up the minutes."[32]

As a result of Fannie Lou Hamer's (1917–1977) relentless determination to vote and the equally intractable determination of white Mississippi Democrats to keep her and other blacks from full political participation, a group of the state's black citizens founded the Mississippi Freedom Democratic Party. Hamer became vice chair. Later in the summer of 1964 Hamer led a delegation of Mississippi citizens to the Democratic National Convention in Atlantic City. There the MFDP challenged the seats of the regular Mississippi delegation. The result of the challenge was an unprecedented pledge from the national Democratic Party not to seat delegations that excluded Negroes at the 1968 national convention.[33]

I have painted with broad strokes this canvas of black women's political history. Time and space preclude a detailed analysis of the triumphs and failures of the most recent generation of black women political writers, thinkers, and activists. It would take another paper of longer length to detail the variety and scope of the impact of these women on the political process and the ongoing struggle to make the Constitution a truly egalitarian document.

Such an examination would reflect on the 1952 Progressive Party's vice presidential candidacy of Charlotta A. Bass of California, the 1968 presidential campaign of Shirley Chisholm of New York, the exemplary legislative career of Barbara Jordan of Texas who in 1972 became the first Afro-American from the South to be elected to the United States House of Representatives since Reconstruction. It would entail discussion of Septima Poinsette Clark who in 1965 led a Southern Christian Leadership group that registered approximately 7,000 black voters in Alabama. Attention would have to be devoted to Constance Baker Motley of New York who in 1966 was appointed the first black female federal judge.

The relationship between black women and the Constitution is a direct one. They never viewed the Constitution as a fixed body of legal principles. Had they done so they would have passively accepted exclusion and denigration. Rather, black women embraced the Constitution and the ideals it represented and used it to acquire the rights, privileges and immunities, and protection needed to effect a transformation of American society. Constitutional litigation, especially after the adoption of the Fourteenth Amendment, was the single most important instrument for challenging minority exclusion from the political process. In tracing the unique struggle of this one group of America's dispossessed we are able to understand exactly how and by what process the United States Constitution became the people's political law. America may not yet be truly the land of freedom with all of the multifaceted meanings of that term. If black women have anything to say about it—and they do—all the people in this nation conceived in liberty and dedicated to the proposition of universal equality may one day soon claim their birthright.

Black Lawyers and the Twentieth-Century Struggle for Constitutional Change

The fact that the Constitution of the United States is not only alive after two hundred years but is still evolving as the fundamental law of the land has been attributed to the wisdom and genius of its framers, the majority of whom were lawyers. Most especially, credit is accorded to James Madison, principal architect of the system of checks and balances. Madison ensured, or so he must have imagined, political stability by providing for a bicameral legislature, an executive, and a judiciary. The framers of the Constitution nevertheless left unresolved two discordant issues. At birth, therefore, the new republic was marked by an ambiguous line separating and defining state and national power. In the years to come, this ambiguity would severely test the resiliency of the new government.

Even more problematic than the controversy over state versus federal rights was the struggle to resolve the contradiction inherent in the coexistence of democracy and constitutionally sanctioned slavery, and later, racial inequality. Actually, the two issues became so closely intertwined that it would require two reconstructions—one in the aftermath of the Civil War and another several generations later—to restore the primacy of federal authority over state power and equality of rights over racial subordination. It is the second reconstruction that commands attention because of its important accomplishments. As political scientist Charles V. Hamilton has pointed out: "Blatant, overt laws requiring segregation of the races were declared unconstitutional, and laws denying and impeding the rights of black Americans to vote were ended. In this sense, the civil rights movement that most people joined (or opposed) was won."[1]

Many individuals, groups, and organizations contributed to the victories of the modern civil rights movement. A wealth of scholarly literature details the changing fortunes of the U.S. Supreme Court and the ideologies of the justices comprising the high tribunal since the 1930s. Scores of autobiographies and biographies examine the lives and contributions of national and of local community black protest leaders in the movement. For the most part, however, historians have neglected to analyze the roles played by the individual local black attorneys who labored behind the scenes, in the shadows of the larger-than-life black protest figures, but without whose labor and expert legal guidance there would have been no second reconstruction or civil rights revolution.[2]

The business of this essay is not to diminish the brilliance of James Madison's achievement. Rather, I propose that we share the spotlight for the efficacy, longevity, and vitality of the U.S. Constitution with a very special cadre of American citizens, the members of the twentieth-century black bar. It is a daunting task to unravel the tangled tapestry of factors that explain how such a small group of African-American lawyers, never at any point exceeding 2 percent of the legal profession, wrought a second emancipation. Between 1910 and 1920 the number of black lawyers increased from about 800 to 950. By 1940 there were 1,350 black lawyers serving a population of thirteen million African Americans. In 1950 the black lawyer population stood at approximately 1,450, and in 1960 it jumped to more than two thousand. The number of black physicians throughout this period was well over four thousand.[3] Unfortunately, little has yet been written about the educational and professional handicaps black lawyers endured and their responses to them.

In their relentless pursuit of equality and freedom for black Americans, black legal soldiers revolutionized constitutional jurisprudence, derailed the strange career of Jim Crow, and made civil rights, as opposed to state rights, the moral imperative of the twentieth century. In other words, black lawyers, working with a number of organizations over long periods of time, transformed constitutional jurisprudence to embrace the primacy of civil rights over state rights, and replaced the doctrine of "separate but equal" with one of equality.

This "equalitarian revolution" was the hidden revolution within the modern black rights movement.[4]

This chapter examines the role of the black bar and the institutional infrastructure that sustained it throughout the critical years of 1945 to 1965. During this period black lawyers were involved in more than a dozen favorable cases in the U.S. Supreme Court. Because it is first necessary to identify the black bar, its national leaders, chief strategists, and community-based lawyers, this discussion devotes considerable attention to the development of key black-led legal institutions: the National Bar Association (NBA), Howard University, and the National Legal and Educational Defense Fund, Inc., of the National Association for the Advancement of Colored People (NAACP). These institutions, along with the pivotal civil rights organizations, the Southern Christian Leadership Conference (SCLC) and the Student Nonviolent Coordinating Committee (SNCC), generated the court cases that enabled lawyers to win the substantive judicial decisions. To be sure, the relationship between the black bar and the civil rights protestors was a symbiotic one. The street protests and demonstrations provoked oppressive responses from white police and municipal governmental authorities based on, as the lawyers put it, a "misapplication of preexisting constitutional laws."[5] This is not an attempt to overemphasize the work of the lawyers and to subordinate the contributions of the leaders of these protest organizations and the demonstrators who bore the brunt of imprisonment and white brutality.

The second part of the discussion highlights a few of the precedent-setting U.S. Supreme Court decisions won by the black bar during the second reconstruction. A series of brilliantly orchestrated cases secured decisions that desegregated transportation and public schools, reapportioned districts, extended and protected black voting rights, and finally ended restrictive housing covenants. Yet it is well to recognize that although judicial decisions expanded on the meaning of the Constitution of the United States, they alone would not have effected a revolution in American race relations. Judicial decisions in and of themselves did not contain political or moral authority to force compliance. Judge J. Skelly Wright correctly reminds us that "a compelling moral principle, banned from the political system, was taken up by the Supreme Court and given formal legitimacy, then, when the political system refused the legal principle, as it had the moral one, the idea traveled back into the private sector, back to the people, and created a whole new politics."[6] And much of this new politics was played out in the streets—in demonstrations, marches, sit-ins, and freedom rides.

Still, throughout the period of the modern civil rights movement, the black lawyer was an essential force. As one student maintained, "Black lawyers have been fulcrums on which the see-saw of the civil rights movement was balanced." During this turbulent period, the black lawyer was adviser, mediator, educator, and defendant, depending on the needs of the hour. Black lawyers worked with the civil rights organizations, dealt with opposition attorneys, negotiated with members of white city board and county officials, joined interracial commissions, posted bonds to liberate thousands from Southern jails, and not infrequently suffered physical attack and had their homes bombed.[7] Burke Marshall has pointed out that "the protestors, demonstrators, and so forth acted at all times with careful legal advice, under a claim of right under the federal constitution to do what they did. . . . To put it another way, the action taken by the members of the protest movement merely asserted legal rights guaranteed by the federal constitution, but denied to them by unconstitutional, and therefore unlawful, local police action."[8] In an exuberant tribute to the black bar, former Atlanta mayor Maynard H. Jackson exclaimed, "When considered in light of the impediments and shackles born of a system of racism and systematic exclusion, the gains of the black lawyer are nothing short of phenomenal."[9] No less effusive, Robert L. Carter declared that the black lawyers "succeeded in transforming the Fourteenth Amendment, and to a lesser extent the Fifteenth Amendment, into a Negro Magna Carta."[10]

Most discussions of the role black lawyers played in the transformation of constitutional jurisprudence, that is, in the elimination of constitutional support for racial segregation and discrimination, begin with Charles H. Houston. The reverence accorded this man and his deeds is not without merit. Houston, born on September 3, 1895, in Washington, D.C., was a graduate of Amherst College. He earned his first law degree in 1922 from Harvard Law School and his doctorate in juridical science the following year. He continued his studies at the University of Madrid, where he studied civil law. From 1924 to 1929, in the firm of Houston and Houston, Charles Houston practiced law with his father in Washington, D.C. Although his legal work was demanding, Houston managed to find time to take an active interest in the fortunes of the Howard Law School and to research the general status of the black lawyer. In 1929 Houston's life changed irrevocably when he accepted the post of vice-dean of the Howard University School of Law, where he served as a full-time administrator until 1935.

No less talented and essential to the black rights struggle than Houston was William Henry Hastie. In 1930 Hastie, a recent graduate of Harvard Law School, joined Houston as a faculty member at the Howard Law School. Hastie was born on November 17, 1904, in Knoxville, Tennessee. He completed his undergraduate study at Amherst College. While engaged in work for the S.J.D. at Harvard, and on leave from the Howard Law School, Hastie participated in his first major black rights case. He assisted (on behalf of the NAACP) Conrad Pearson and Cecil McCoy in defending the right of Thomas R. Hocutt to enter the School of Pharmacy at the University of North Carolina.[11] After Houston resigned from Howard in the mid-1930s, Hastie stepped in to continue the revitalization process.

The Howard Law School had opened on January 6, 1869, with an integrated faculty and student body. Until 1898, students pursued a two-year course of study for the LL.D. degree. In 1898 the course for the LL.D. degree was extended to three years. Before 1904 no tuition fees were charged, only a matriculation fee of $10. Up to 1924, the only entrance requirement was a high school education or its equivalent. The administration raised the admission standards in 1924 to two years of standard college work. Clearly, as conditions were in the mid-1920s, Howard Law School was far from becoming what attorney Robert L. Carter later described as "the center of intellectual ferment in black legal circles."[12] Nevertheless, Howard Law School was still deemed to be of higher quality than the only two institutions in the entire South that offered legal training to black students, Simmons University in Louisville, Kentucky, and Virginia Union University in Richmond, Virginia. Most white law schools, which with a few exceptions were located in the Northeast, excluded blacks.[13]

As early as 1926, Houston had become involved in the affairs of the Howard Law School. Three years before assuming the deanship he had undertaken the challenge of spearheading a special faculty campaign committee charged to raise money to improve the school's law library. Houston believed that the inadequacies of the law library accounted for the refusal of the Association of American Law Schools to recognize the institution. In a widely circulated fund-raising letter, he offered potential contributors a candid assessment of existing conditions: "It has no endowment. It has no student loan funds or scholarships. Most of the professors are employed only on part-time; and even in the case of full-time professors their salaries fall below those of the academic professors by hundreds of dollars. The Law Library is not up-to-date."[14] Warming to the task of persuading others to give, Houston provided even more specific details of the law library's needs: "The Howard University Law Library now consists of some 5482 volumes, of which more than 1000 are duplicates and an additional 500 antiquated and out-of-date, leaving a working library of less than 4000 volumes." According to the December 1925 report of the Association of American Law Schools, a recognized law school was expected to own a library of not fewer than 7,500 volumes.[15]

Thus when Houston accepted the vice-dean's position at Howard Law School, he did so fully cognizant of the needs and challenges. As with so many things in his life, in this he proved successful. With singleminded purpose and unremitting drive, Houston transformed the unarguably marginal enterprise into a school fully accredited and highly respected. Propitiously, Houston's work between 1929 and 1935 at the law school enabled him to train a cadre of young black lawyers imbued with a desire to go south and do legal battle with Jim Crow. At the outset of his tenure as vice-dean, Houston carefully unveiled his vision of what the school would accomplish: "The aims . . . should be to equip its students with the direct professional skills most useful to them, and to give them as deep and as broad a societal background as possible." But Houston articulated an even higher purpose when he declared, "From the standpoint of public function, the Negro lawyer ought to be trained as a social engineer and group interpreter. . . . To qualify such group leaders, the law school must give its students a thorough understanding of the administration of Law with its inherent limitations superimposed with a brief societal background."[16]

Under Houston's leadership, the Howard Law School faculty produced a generation of black lawyers very different from the ones he had criticized in a 1928 report on the status of the black bar financed by the Laura Spelman Rockefeller Memorial Fund but sponsored by the Howard Law School. Researching the project had been an illuminating and frustrating experience. Perhaps the most significant benefit Houston derived from making the survey and preparing the report was the unique opportunity to travel across the country and to meet and talk to virtually all of the major practicing black lawyers and a few he needed not to have met. While the lack of social conscience of many black lawyers disappointed him, he did manage to identify a handful of key Southern black lawyers who exemplified an admirable spirit of public service. He singled out for special praise N. P. Frederick of Columbia, South Carolina; S. D. Redmond of Jackson, Mississippi; S. D. McGill of Jacksonville, Florida; Scipio A. Jones of Little Rock, Arkansas; and A. T. Walden of Atlanta, Georgia. He acknowledged that "there are some men in the South who are doing real pioneer work for the Negro lawyer . . . trying cases in many instances at the risk of their personal safety."[17] Along more critical lines, Houston railed against the appalling incompetence and absence of social reform work among many black lawyers. He charged, "I think it may be said without much fear of contradiction that the lawyer exerts less influence on the community than any other class of professional man." He elaborated:

> Along strictly professional lines the Negro lawyers have come to the front when racial controversies have cropped out in the courts. Scipio A. Jones saved the lives of the Elaine rioters by his disinterested work; N. P. Frederick paved the way for the ultimate acquittal of the Lowmans altho the mob subsequently lynched them. The Chicago lawyers and the Washington lawyers came to the defense of the Negroes arrested during the race riots of 1919 and 1920. W. Ashbie Hawkins is the grand old man who has fought every form of discrimination in Baltimore during the last forty years. But these instances are sporadic. There is no court committee in any town to fight oppression of

undefended Negroes; no legal relief organization, and no enthusiasm [a]bout starting one.[18]

The contacts Houston made while working at Howard proved invaluable when in 1935 he left the law school to serve as the first full-time salaried attorney and special counsel for the NAACP. A close colleague and admirer described Houston's work with the NAACP in reverential terms: "He was the architect and dominant force of the legal program of that organization. He guided us through the legal wilderness of second-class citizenship. He was truly the Moses of that journey."[19] Shortly before he relinquished the reins on this position in 1939, the NAACP separated the litigative functions of the organization in order to receive tax-exempt status and created the NAACP Legal and Educational Defense Fund.

Between 1929 and his death in 1950, Houston devoted his entire professional life and all of his considerable legal talents to laying the groundwork, as historian and biographer Genna Rae McNeil puts it, for the judicial battles that all but dominated the Supreme Court's docket from 1939 through 1965. His colleague, William H. Hastie, in a moving testament to Houston's significance declared, "He lived to see us close to the promised land of full equality under the law, closer than even he dared hope when he set out on the journey and so much closer than would have been possible without his genius and his leadership."[20] Houston possessed many characteristics that won converts to his cause. As described by Dean Erwin N. Griswold of the Harvard Law School, "He was handsome, in a dignified yet forceful way. He was a man who created respect."[21] Griswold announced what the black bar already knew, "It is doubtful that there has been a single important case involving civil rights during the past fifteen years in which Charles Houston has not either participated directly or by consultation and advice. He was a tower of strength in the legal field."[22]

Shortly after Houston assumed the reins of the NAACP's legal work, he drafted what he called the "Tentative Statement Concerning Policy of NAACP in Its Program of Attack on Educational Discrimination." In it, Houston delineated the three "glaring and typical discriminations" destined to be the targets of concentrated legal action: differentials in teachers' salaries along color lines, inequalities in transportation facilities (which he deemed the basic barrier to the consolidation of rural schools), and inequalities in graduate and professional education offered to whites in universities supported by state funds but denied to black students. Houston was especially concerned with the denial of professional and graduate study to blacks. He believed that the denial of advanced educational opportunity to black students was a white ploy "to perpetuate the inferior status of Negroes" and to prevent the race from developing a viable pool of leaders.[23]

In the 1930s and 1940s, in tandem with his work at the Howard Law School and the NAACP legal program, Houston oversaw the emergence and maturation of the black bar. Through the force of his personality, the clarity of his vision, and the sheer determination of his will, Houston sparked a new social consciousness among black lawyers. He persuaded them to join him in the battle for black rights before the courts. Thus, by the eve of World War II, Houston had forged critical working relations with dozens of local black lawyers across the country. These linkages became a tightly woven network of the best black legal minds available. On one occasion Houston encouraged a young man contemplating law as a career, "There is an unlimited field in the law for young Negroes who are willing to make the fight." He predicted that "the lawyer is going to be the leader of the next step in racial advancement." If the lawyer was destined to be, as Houston phrased it in 1935, "the trouble shooter," then the site of all the action would, in the coming decades, occur in the South. He declared, "It is obvious that our greatest problems are in the South, where the masses of Negroes suffer the greatest handicaps and discriminations. The Negro lawyer in the South in the next twenty-five years has a chance to reconstruct the entire southern picture."[24]

An abiding conviction that Southern black lawyers would play pivotal roles in the reconstruction of race relations fed Houston's desire to forge close associations between the NAACP Legal Committee and the black bar. He was keenly aware that revolutions of any stripe depended for success on the depth of the infantry. These local lawyers, or the lieutenants and foot soldiers, often initiated, massaged, and argued in the lower courts the precedent-setting cases. Their involvement in and subsequent cooperation with the NAACP led to the U.S. Supreme Court victories in *Smith v. Allwright* in 1944 (ending the white primary), *Shelley v. Kraemer* in 1948 (nullifying restrictive housing covenants), and *Brown v. Board of Education* in 1954 (desegregating public schools in the South). Then in the years after *Brown*, the local lawyers became the advisers to the leaders of the civil rights movement, playing instrumental roles in linking the courtroom struggles with those battles raging in the streets of Birmingham, Montgomery, Albany, Greensboro, and Selma.

The problems and obstacles impeding the professional development of black attorneys cannot be exaggerated. Some scholars have suggested that in the 1930s the black bar existed in a state of segregated disarray. The problems black attorneys encountered entering the profession and their difficulties in earning a living by practicing law during the 1930s and 1940s have been discussed elsewhere in great detail and need only brief mention here. For the most part, black lawyers possessed inadequate education, substandard training, limited opportunities for professional development and growth, and low professional esteem. Even when highly competent, the American Bar Association refused them membership on the basis of race; potential clients, even black ones, regarded black lawyers as inferior; white judges in the South sometimes barred black lawyers from courtrooms; and few law libraries were open to them. The vast majority of the 1,200 black lawyers were relegated to the least desirable and least remunerative areas of practice—criminal offenses, domestic relations, personal injury, and small claims.[25]

Houston's supervision of one of the key agencies for social and legal reform, the NAACP Legal Committee, and his involvement with significant members of the National Bar Association, during the 1930s provided the essential institutional base from which he orchestrated the multifaceted attack on Jim Crow and black second-class citizenship. Contemporaries graciously and generously accord Houston a place of honor and readily acknowledge the debt owed his leadership. Houston, however, would have been the first to admit that the major legal victories of the 1930s and 1940s were accomplished precisely because of the collaboration of an array of talented barristers, including Raymond Pace Alexander, William H. Hastie, Thurgood Marshall, Leon A. Ransom, and James M. Nabrit. These men, virtually all having received their legal training at Howard or Harvard law schools, constituted an elite stratum of the black bar.

Shortly after Houston settled into his new position with the NAACP, he moved to balance the racial composition of the NAACP National Legal Committee, which for most of its existence had been composed of prominent white attorneys. There were exceptions. Black attorneys William Andrews and James Cobb had worked with the legal committee during the 1920s. Among the new black attorneys whom Houston nominated for membership on the committee was Z. Alexander Looby of Nashville, "the best trained and most outstanding lawyer in Tennessee," Houston wrote. He described Alexander P. Tureau of New Orleans as "a leader of the fight against disfranchisement in Louisiana." Earl Dickerson of Chicago, an assistant attorney general of Illinois, was noted as being "one of the best lawyers in the Middle West." A former president of the National Bar Association, Raymond Pace Alexander of Philadelphia was dubbed "an outstanding trial lawyer of the East." Houston offered special praise for one attorney, Leon A. Ransom of Washington, D.C., describing him as one "of the best legal minds in the Negro race," who had done "more than anyone else upon the Howard University faculty to inspire young law students with social purpose."[26] Scholars August Meier and Elliott Rudwick contend that "with the association of Houston to the post of special counsel, the transition from white preeminence to black control of the NAACP's legal work was essentially complete."[27]

The black lawyers whom Houston added to the NAACP Legal Committee belonged to a closely knit professional and personal brotherhood. They shared similar educational backgrounds; most of the older ones were trained at Harvard, Yale, and other elite Eastern law schools. The majority of the younger men were products of Howard University Law School, where they received instruction from Houston, Hastie, and James Nabrit. These black lawyers maintained a great degree of contact through fraternal, social, business, and professional organizations, especially the National Bar Association.

Houston, ever on the search for outstanding black legal talent, continuously enlarged the fold. Roy Wilkins, former executive secretary of the NAACP, lauded Houston's special talent for persuading black lawyers to become involved in the civil rights struggle. Wilkins recalled that Houston "was able to get black lawyers interested in civil rights cases because he talked it wherever he went." Similarly, James Nabrit reminisced that "when Houston selected a person to work with him, it was as if the mantle of the Lord had dropped on them, and they would do anything for him."[28]

In September 1936, while in Reno, Nevada, Houston, wrote a revealing memorandum to four black lawyers: Leon Ransom, Z. Alexander Looby, Carl Cowan, and Thurgood Marshall. The memorandum was loaded with praise and instructions concerning the University of Tennessee desegregation case then being sponsored by the NAACP. Ever the cheerleader, Houston first exclaimed, "Congratulations Andy, Looby and Carl. Splendid work; the case seems to be in good shape." What Houston found especially gratifying about the case against the University of Tennessee's School of Pharmacy denial of admission to William B. Redmond II on account of race was the potential it held for mobilizing the black community. He maintained, "That hunch about inspecting the minutes of the board of trustees of the University of Tennessee was one of the best inspirations we have had. When the story is told to Negroes, I think it will furnish one of the most inspiring episodes in the educational campaign. It shows Negroes that the minutes of so-called white universities are public records, open to inspection of Negroes the same as any other citizen, and that Negroes in proper cases will insist on their rights."[29]

In the case against the University of Tennessee, the university's attorney argued that a Tennessee act of 1901 made it a criminal offense to teach white and Negro students in the same class, school, or college building. Accordingly, the law prohibited the enrollment of any Negro students in the university. The plaintiff, William Redmond, contended that this act of 1901 applied to the physical separation of the races and was entirely consistent with the provisions of the act of 1869, which provided for the admission of Negroes to the University of Tennessee but required that they be instructed in separate classes. The black lawyers argued that William Redmond was not seeking to enter the same classes with the white students in the School of Pharmacy, but rather that he was entitled to admission to the school and that it was incumbent on the trustees of the university to provide him separate instruction in accordance with the acts of 1869 and 1901. The black lawyers further insisted that the University of Tennessee's denial of admission to him on account of color violated the Fourteenth Amendment to the Constitution. The Chancery Court of Shelby County, Tennessee, in Memphis, dismissed the petition for mandamus, holding that "there was no pharmaceutical school in Tennessee in which a Negro student was eligible to enroll but ruled that the State of Tennessee did not violate the Fourteenth Amendment by limiting the School of Pharmacy of the University of Tennessee to white students only."[30]

During the local court arguments, Ransom and Houston introduced two strategies that would become standard features of desegregation litigation over the next twenty years. Ransom identified and called for testimony from black professionals, in this instance two practicing pharmacists. He used their testimony to establish "conclusively that there is a real need for Negro pharmacists in the State of Tennessee as well as the entire South, and that Negroes are not confined, in this profession, to practice solely within their own race." The second point hammered home by Houston focused on the state's failure to provide adequate pharmaceutical training for blacks and that this created a "great menace to the health of the good white people of the South." Eventually, after a couple of adverse decisions, the NAACP abandoned the case. Its significance lies in being the mirror reflecting Houston's leadership style and thoughts on the roles of the black lawyer.[31]

The memorandum, however, goes far beyond commenting on the specifics of the Tennessee desegregation case. In it Houston explained why he removed himself from direct formal involvement in the case and elaborated on the philosophical rationale for including as many top-notch, well-trained, carefully selected local black attorneys as possible in the civil rights cases. Further, he discussed relations between the antisegregation court cases of the black bar and the activism of community leaders.

After the first round of arguments in *Redmond v. University of Tennessee School of Pharmacy*, Houston withdrew, declaring, "This is no star performance." Houston believed that no one person or lawyer should ever be indispensable to a given case. He insisted, "My ideal of administration is to make the movement self-perpetuating so that the loss of the head or any set of members will not hamper progress." The achievement of a "self-executing" administration, Houston asserted, is possible only "where all subordinates have been so well trained and posted about the program that any one of them is able to step into the chief's shoes any minute and carry on with no loss of stride." He concluded with characteristic modesty, "My greatest satisfaction in these cases is to find I can let go and the colleagues carry on as well, if not better than I can."[32]

In positing this philosophy of "self-executing" leadership, Houston was in no way attempting to drop out of the legal battle against segregated education. Rather, it was critical to his overall program to take a backseat in the early years of this desegregation of education campaign. Houston's decision was based on a desire for self-protection and the protection of other black lawyers, and on a realization of the importance of maintaining local black confidence and support: "There is safety in sudden switching and changing, and rotation of counsel. If the opposition gets the belief that I am the only person to worry about and that if I am removed all trouble will be over, it will concentrate on removing me by disbarment proceedings, public embarrassment, criminal charges, or otherwise." Houston desired to spare local black lawyers the threat of white reprisals and retaliations. He reasoned that if the white opposition understood that "it will not accomplish anything by my removal or by removal of any set of lawyers, it will not waste time on personal reprisals but will accept the fact that it has to fight a movement and concentrate on technical defenses and defenses to the merits."[33]

Wisely, Houston urged his colleagues to continue to emphasize, when speaking to the press or local audiences, that "these cases are not my cases, but the manifestation of a spontaneous local demand on the part of the citizens, and that for every one of us who for any reason drops out, there remains a dozen to take his place." Houston resolved that white opposition and harassment of the black attorney along with the "cry of outside interference and agitation" would be muted if "we can show a bushel of lawyers than if we have to have one or two men running all over the country on emergency calls just like a fire engine or wrecking crew."[34]

Houston's decision to move into the background in order to maneuver behind the scenes did not reflect either a diminution of personal interest or decreased professional involvement in the local school desegregation cases. To his "boys," as he referred to them, Houston demanded, "just keep me fully advised of everything." He warned them, "and for God's sake don't let them catch us asleep on technicalities and don't let anything go by default." Houston remained ever mindful of the powerful white personal and institutional resistance they confronted. At one juncture, he lamented that "against us we have all the forces of state governments." He knew that any losses or mistakes would be blamed on him, "as the responsible authority." After all, he recalled having once advised "Andy and the boys the line between a bitch and a son-of-a-bitch was mighty fine." More seriously, he reiterated, "The only thing I can do is pick our associates with all possible care and insist on being kept advised of all developments so as to be able to counsel with the fellows if I think things are not developing as they should." He added, in wry humor, "If success comes the boys can have it, and I won't have such a long distance to fall when the reaction comes and the second-guessers get busy."[35]

The caring and cooperative working pattern Houston evidenced with the trio of black attorneys handling *Redmond v. University of Tennessee* became his trademark. He offered advice, encouragement, and attention to detail. To Sidney Redmond, black attorney in St. Louis, Missouri, whom Houston retained to handle the local legal work in the more successful *Missouri ex rel. Gaines v. Canada*, he cautioned, "Remember that it is not your job to find a client. I don't want you to be put in the position of fomenting litigation. I want the newspapers or interested laymen to find you your client. All I want you to do is make the investigation and disclose the rotten conditions."[36]

When Redmond expressed anxiety about not moving quickly enough, Houston cautioned him, "I am not anxious for you to rush the case simply to get action. . . . The issues involved are so big that we cannot afford to omit any detail of preparation in a hasty attempt at grandstand play. So as long as you are working, be assured that I will not become impatient because suit is not filed within the next few days."[37] Moreover, when the beleaguered Redmond encountered difficulties working with the local leaders of fraternity and sorority groups, Houston wrote with empathy, "I appreciate the difficulty you face in working with your group. The same thing has happened in every state we have entered. Frankly, the university program has slowed down to a walk for lack of suitable candidates both in the front line and in reserve." He emphasized that the work with the fraternities and sororities, albeit often frustrating, was necessary in order "to undergird the educational program with more popular support." He reminded his colleague, "What we must realize is that we are marking out new ground and that very few persons have the pioneer spirit. Consequently, do not be dismayed by the timidity and general unreliability of many of those with whom you come in contact."[38]

The same determination, patience, guidance, and commitment Houston demonstrated while working with the local black lawyers in the aborted *Tennessee* case can be seen in his interactions with the members and leaders of the National Bar Association. As mentioned earlier, many have stated that the black bar was in a state of segregated disarray during the 1930s (some would add the 1940s). Certainly the legal profession was segregated, but the notion that the black bar was in disarray depends on the perspective of the observer. Actually, the allegation of disarray is more a testament to the vast differences in status and resources between the black and white bars than a comment on individual black lawyers. Fully a generation before the black lawyers organized the National Bar Association, white lawyers of the American Bar Association (ABA) had already engaged in and completed the whole process of professionalization. Of course, the issue of admitting blacks to membership was not resolved until much later.

That blacks found it virtually impossible to win admission into the majority of law schools in the country is well documented. It is also important to recognize the treatment meted out by the American Bar Association. In 1912 the ABA expelled black member William H. Lewis, a graduate of Amherst College and Harvard Law School, who in 1910 had been an assistant attorney general for the United States. Apparently he had gained membership in the ABA before his racial identity was known. The leaders defended their purge by arguing that the ABA was intended to be a social organization. It was only the concern and adamant protests of former ABA president and NAACP official Moorfield Story that persuaded the organization to ameliorate the racial policy.

In response to Story's objection, the ABA amended a resolution so as to permit all existing black members to remain, but it barred all future African Americans. Refusing to give in, Story argued, "in my judgment the American Bar Association is not a social organization. It claims to represent the whole American Bar, and its recommendations are made on that basis. I think, therefore, it cannot exclude from membership persons who are in other respects entirely fit, merely because their complexion is dark, or their race different from that of other members."[39] Although the ABA convention in 1914 lifted the color bar, a new resolution was adopted calling for full disclosure of race on all applications. Needless to say, this tactic allowed local and state bar associations to weed out all black applicants and thus effectively preserved the ABA's racial purity. Not until 1943 would black lawyers shatter the color bar of the ABA.

By any measure, the difficult terrain separating the black and white legal professionals posed major challenges to the few black lawyers practicing in the 1920s. None of these men and women possessed the resources, time, and institutional support necessary to surmount the obstacles in the path of their professional development. By the end of World War I, all of the dozen or so black law schools lacked endowments, adequate operating expenses, libraries, enough full-time teachers, or scholarships for their impoverished students. The majority of the black lawyers engaged in the least remunerative practices. To add to these difficulties, there was a deeply entrenched public stereotype of the black lawyer as an incompetent, shady character whose race prevented him from winning respect from either judges or juries. According to one student of the profession, "the legal insecurity of the Negro is such that the Negro lawyer has but little chance before a Southern court. Protection by a 'respectable' white person usually counts more in the South for a Negro client than would even the best representation on the part of a Negro lawyer."[40]

As the experiences of early black attorneys in Tennessee illustrate, white colleagues and white citizens proved intractable in their resolve to drive black lawyers out of the profession. Historian Lester Lamon observed, "Black lawyers who fought legal discrimination too vigorously often found themselves in professional or physical danger from irate white citizens." In 1920 the Tennessee Bar Association barred the combative Robert L. Mayfield, a graduate of Howard Law School, who had fought for eight years to keep his license. When Chattanooga attorneys Noah W. Parden and Styles L. Hustchins saved

Ed Johnson, convicted of rape, by appealing to the U.S. Supreme Court in 1906, they suddenly found it safer to move to Oklahoma. After Justice John Marshall Harlan granted Johnson a stay of execution, the white citizens took him from the Hamilton County jail and lynched him.[41]

What is remarkable about the black bar during the 1930s is not its disarray but the professionalization of the approximately 1,300 black lawyers then practicing in the country. The 1930s saw the rise of a more militant definition of the proper role the black lawyer should play in black and American society. This coming together of the black bar occurred during the first phase of the modern civil rights movement.

In the first decade of its existence, the National Bar Association accomplished more in the realm of elevating the black lawyer's self-esteem than in contributing to the science of law, or removing the shackles of legal oppression from the black community. But self-esteem, pride, and respect were urgently needed if black lawyers were to assault Jim Crow and repair the derogatory stereotypes of their profession prevalent across the country.

Charles Houston was preeminent among the small cadre of well-trained, visible, and respected black lawyers who shaped the militant, activist twentieth-century role of the black lawyer. Houston preached the gospel, holding that the Constitution was the chief weapon to demolish the edifice of legal inequality. Going one step further, Houston asserted that the judges serving on the U.S. Supreme Court more often than not decided cases on the basis of previous principles established in earlier cases. He continued that these judges showed a marked reluctance to decide cases on constitutional grounds. The strategy was clear. In order to effect fundamental constitutional change and to remove the legal barriers thwarting black advance, black lawyers had to take up to the Supreme Court a series of cases that would establish important precedents. All engaged in the struggle knew that this course would take decades to execute fully.[42]

Jesse Heslip of Toledo, Ohio, a graduate of Harvard Law School and student of Felix Frankfurter, counseled his colleagues in his 1932 NBA presidential address, "We must become thoroughly grounded in constitutional law; we must be ready to face the nation's highest tribunal in search of justice for ourselves."[43] Houston similarly declared that blacks needed their "own constitutional lawyers" because, as he contended, "no one can prepare or present Negroes' cases as well as a trained Negro."[44]

Each president of the NBA echoed identical sentiments emphasizing the black lawyer's obligation to honor the social contract that had gradually emerged with the black community. No one questioned the necessity of the black lawyer to recognize that his fate and that of the black community were inextricably interwoven. Indeed, succeeding NBA presidents consistently preached the centrality of court litigation in the whole quest for black rights. Eugene Washington Rhodes, president in 1933, declared, "The cause of the race will be advanced in exact proportion to the strength and militancy of the bar. . . . The sole bulwark of protection for Negroes are courts of the law. There is no other way out."[45]

Throughout the 1930s and early 1940s, leading black barristers accepted and exhorted that the Constitution of the United States was not only an important expression of values and principles but also the source of authority for legal and political rules and the institutions that could affect the course of social change. Houston and his colleagues advocated that blacks and other minorities, since they were unable to influence significantly the executive and legislative branches of the government by means of the ballot, should try to achieve their social, educational, and political rights through the courts. For the dispossessed, disfranchised, and disinherited, the law was, in Houston's opinion, the most accessible instrument with which to win civil rights.[46]

Houston's definition of the black lawyer's role grew out of his belief that the lawyer, while at heart a troubleshooter, was also a social critic and activist. Houston, in short, believed that the lawyer should devote his skills and talents to winning black rights through litigation. Yet, while this litigation was under way, the lawyer should also be engaged in activities to mobilize black community residents to protest and agitate for their rights in other arenas.[47] Houston himself attempted to stir up the black communities. In numerous articles published in the NAACP's *Crisis*, he provided instruction on "How to Fight for Better Schools," how to find suitable plaintiffs, raise funds, and organize suits, and the importance of educating white Americans to the true nature and extent of black oppression.[48]

Actually, Houston's views were entirely consistent with those of the early leaders of the National Bar Association, which was founded in 1925. The moving force behind the formation of the NBA was George H. Woodson of Des Moines, Iowa. Woodson was born in Wytheville, Virginia, in 1865 and graduated from Howard Law School in 1895. He practiced law in Iowa until his death in 1933.[49] The men and women who planned and organized the black bar agreed that its objectives would be

> the advancement of the science of jurisprudence, and in addition to form a nationwide organization of practicing attorneys of the Negro race in an endeavor to strengthen and elevate the Negro lawyer in his profession and in his relationship to his people; to improve his standing at the bar of the country, and to stress those values that would serve to enhance the ethics of his practice and conduct, to condemn actions that have a tendency to lessen respect for the lawyer and to create a bond of true fellowship among the colored members of the Bar of America for their general uplift and advancement and for the encouragement of the Negro youth of America who will follow their choice of this profession.[50]

Indeed, little philosophical difference distinguished Houston from NBA stalwart Raymond Pace Alexander. A native of Philadelphia, Alexander was educated at the University of Pennsylvania, Columbia University, and Harvard Law School, from which he was graduated in 1923. He then returned to Philadelphia to practice law. At the first NBA convention, Alexander declared, "We owe the law more than merely using it as a means of making a livelihood.... We owe to our people, who, more than any other people are in need of our services, a duty to see that there shall be a quick end to the discrimination and segregation they suffer in their everyday activity."[51] Subsequent NBA presidents adhered to the social contract of race service. For years, Leon Ransom served without pay as the chief counsel of the *University of Tennessee* cases.[52] In exchange for the support, respect, and loyalty of the masses of blacks, the race lawyers prepared the legal cases designed to overthrow the constitutional foundation for white supremacy and to remove the shackles of black subordination.

Writing in the first issue of the NBA's *National Bar Journal* in 1941, Raymond Pace Alexander asserted, "The National Bar Association is really the development of the American Negro's belief in himself." He concluded, "As the American Negro lawyer began through this Association to develop a belief in himself, his efforts in crusading for equal justice for the Negro citizens in their fight to improve their civic status took on a new and vastly important aspect." To substantiate his conclusions, Alexander enumerated the twenty cases heard by the U.S. Supreme Court between 1923 and 1940 that dealt with black rights. Each case had a black lawyer on the defense team, and every black lawyer so involved, according to Alexander, was a member of the National Bar Association.[53]

It was during the 1940s that the NBA came of age. The annual conventions were well attended, membership soared, and black lawyers launched their own official organ, the *National Bar Journal*. The topic of most of the articles published in the journal concerned the various civil rights activities of the members. Charles Houston, William Hastie, Thurgood Marshall, and other members of the NAACP Legal Defense Fund delivered papers and reported on the various litigations sponsored throughout the country. Virtually all of the key NBA performers had some connection with the Defense Fund. Indeed, so much cross-fertilization of ideas and strategies occurred that it is difficult to determine where the NBA ended and the Legal Defense Fund began.

It is significant that between 1938 and 1954 the NAACP and NAACP Legal Defense and Educational Fund, under the leadership of Houston and his successor, Thurgood Marshall, argued six antisegregation education cases before the U.S. Supreme Court.[54] These cases fell into three broad categories: "suits seeking to equalize the desegregation of public graduate and professional schools, suits seeking to equalize the salaries of black and white teachers, and suits occasioned by the equalities in the physical facilities at black and white elementary and secondary schools."[55]

Inexorably, black lawyers—beginning with Houston, Hastie, and Marshall, aided by Ransom, Nabrit, Lovett, and scores of unheralded local attorneys—persuaded the U.S. Supreme Court in litigation from *Gaines* to *Brown* to reject the doctrine of "separate but equal." Through their compelling arguments they persuaded the Court to reinterpret constitutional equal protection of the law and establish a new standard of equality. In so doing they revolutionized constitutional jurisprudence and made civil rights, as opposed to states' rights, the moral imperative of the twentieth century. Black lawyers have made a most significant contribution to the evolution of a living Constitution. Their efforts have benefited all Americans. Thus no celebration of the U.S. Constitution can justifiably ignore the feats of Charles Houston and the black bar.

The Intersection of Race, Class, and Gender in the Nursing Profession

Nurses are among the most critical components of the entire health care delivery team. Physicians, hospital administrators, social workers, and community leaders are quick to attest to the significance of the nurse as a key professional involved most directly in hospital patient care and in health care delivery in general. In spite of the strategic importance of nurses' special skills, there continues to exist a chronic shortage of nurses. No racial-ethnic community or geographic region has escaped the many adverse consequences of an inadequate pool of trained nurses. Moreover, since the 1960s an ever-expanding number of communities have wrestled with severe problems of dilapidated hospital facilities that have forced many closings across the country. In addition, the alarmingly short supply of physicians has especially exacerbated health care delivery problems in poorer rural and urban inner-city areas.

Contemporary economic exigencies, gender stratification, and a history of racial exclusion interacted in ways that shape and sustain the current nursing and medical personnel crisis. In recent years increased media attention has heightened our sensitivity to the external, or societal, and internal, or professional, forces that result in high incidence of "nurse burnout." Articles, reports, and surveys have delineated all the variables contributing to burnout, including low pay, long and irregular hours, and the demeaning, subservient roles nurses are expected to play in the medical and hospital hierarchies. Further, as nurses seek advanced educational credentials, the profession itself has been forced to confront a deepening stratification along racial and ethnic lines.

Racial-ethnic and working-class white women occupy the lowest rung in the professional nursing hierarchy. Supervisory positions in hospitals, private agencies, and the nursing professorate remain, with few exceptions, the exclusive preserve of middle-class white women. The nursing profession is a potent laboratory for the study of the convergence of factors and forces that helped to create the structural underrepresentation or exclusion of women and men of color from virtually all of the controlling institutions and learned professions in this country. More specifically, against the backdrop of nursing, it is possible to examine the historical difficulties that black Americans have encountered in their struggle for greater access to the medical and legal professions throughout the first half of the twentieth century.

In *Black Women in White: Racial Conflict and Cooperation in the Nursing Profession, 1890–1950* I examine the struggle of black nurses to win integration and acceptance into the mainstream of American nursing. Fully one half of the book, however, traces the establishment and evolution of the institutional infrastructure of black health care, that is, hospitals, nursing training schools, and collegiate programs in nursing. In two works in progress, one a history of black physicians, and the other a history of black lawyers in the twentieth century, I continue this line of investigation, but with a slightly different shading. I move from a horizontal to a vertical level of analysis as I probe the ways the black struggle for professional integration helped to lay the basis for the emergence of the modern civil rights movement during the 1950s and 1960s.

Infusing all of my work on the history of blacks in the professions is the desire to demonstrate how essential it is for scholars of women's history to incorporate race as a category of analysis, and for black studies scholars likewise to pay greater attention to the construction of gender roles within the black communities that they investigate. And, of course, both black and women's history scholars should be ever mindful of class, or where people in any given group stand in relation to the means of production, and differences growing out of regional location. Finally, when examining those groups considered or relegated to marginal status by the larger society, it is critically important to use agency as an analytical category. Agency can be defined as a consciousness of resistance or as a process whereby subordinate groups acquire the skills needed to effect social change, modification, or reform.

In sum, I am urging my colleagues in both areas, and reinforcing those who already do, to employ more sophisticated multidimensional conceptual categories in their analyses of black and women's subjects. The categories or concepts that work for me are race, gender, class, regionalism, and agency. Only by employing them and probing their intersection was I able to approach a more comprehensive understanding of the conflict and cooperation that permeate the nursing profession and that punctuate the past and present of black women.

The contours of black nurses' struggle for acceptance and recognition, like those of the black doctors and lawyers, were shaped by factors as diverse as regional location, economic depression, and the catastrophe of war. The decades between the world wars witnessed first a hardening and eventually a softening of racial animosities between black and white nurses. Racism was a pervasive ideology during the period from the 1890s through the 1950s. This ideology of black inferiority and white supremacy dictated the subordination of blacks in every key area of American society.

Although slave women had for generations provided nursing care for both blacks and whites, when the first nursing schools opened their doors in 1873 few administrators expressed interest in training black women. The New England Hospital for Women and Children in Boston was an exception. In 1879 the school graduated the first black professional nurse in the United States, Mary Eliza Mahoney (1845–1926). But even here, the reception of black women was restricted. The charter of this pioneering nursing school stipulated that only one Negro and one Jewish student be accepted each year. No school in the South admitted black women.

The conflict and tension, as reflected in the attempts of white nurses to bar black women from entry into the profession, to deny them appointments to supervisory positions, to exclude them from membership in professional organizations, to restrict their access to training schools and postgraduate education, and to ensure that they received less pay for the same work, go beyond racist ideology. White nurses feared economic competition with black nurses who, for understandable reasons, would sometimes work for less money and perform household tasks shunned by their white counterparts. Further, black women's long association with domestic service provoked status anxiety among those white nurses who labored to distance the profession from any taint of servitude.

While investigating the history black women in the nursing profession, my attention soon focused on the larger political arena in which they worked. In order to effect social change and to improve their status in the nursing profession, black nurse leaders had to cultivate the necessary organizational skills and had clearly to articulate an integrationist political agenda. Simultaneously, they had to create a consciousness of resistance to demeaning stereotypes of themselves as women and as nursing professionals.

The leadership of black nurse Elizabeth Carnegie captures well this consciousness of resistance so essential to survival and self-esteem. In keeping with long-established patterns of racial etiquette, all the white administrators, physicians, and nurses at St. Philip Hospital in Richmond, Virginia, addressed white nurses as "Miss" and black nurses as "Nurse." In the 1930s this practice was, as Carnegie notes, "a step up from being addressed by first names." As if to compound black subordination within the hospital hierarchy, Carnegie recalls, "Not only were Negro nurses addressed this way by the white nurses and doctors, they were instructed to address each other and refer to themselves in this manner." Refusing to acquiesce to this social affront and professional slight, Carnegie, then a new clinical instructor, exhorted her black coworkers, "You can't control what someone else does, but you can control what you do." She admonished the black student nurses to "address themselves and each other as 'Miss.'" She insisted that the black students extend this courtesy and show respect by addressing all their black patients as "Miss, Mrs., or Mr.," in spite of the fact that white nurses and doctors also addressed the Negro patients by their first names.[1]

Nursing, a predominantly female profession, existed in the shadow of the male-dominated medical establishment. Early dreams of an autonomous profession of women health care providers had quickly faded into a subordinate reality. Within ten years of the founding of the first nursing schools, hospital administrators dominated virtually every aspect of nursing training. Insufficient capital and endowment and the demand for more scientific-based instruction enabled hospital administrators quickly to gain hegemony in nursing education.

Through the opening decades of the twentieth century, white nursing leaders had no alternative but to leap into the political fray. They struggled to gain control over admission standards, curriculum, work practices within the hospitals, and nursing licensing and registration. When male hospital administrators, motivated chiefly by a desire to secure an obedient, subservient, cheap labor force to clean the hospitals and care for the patients, accepted impoverished, poorly educated, unrefined women into their diploma programs, nursing leaders objected. As long as the young women lured into nursing came from impoverished backgrounds, hospital administrators enjoyed absolute control over their dominions. Nurse leaders rightly reasoned that the convergence of traditional female subservience and class disparity between student and administrator, nurse and physician, actually strengthened and secured male authority over the nursing profession.

As early white nursing leaders devised strategies to raise the status of nursing, they ignored the adverse consequences that their actions and policies had on the career aspirations of black women. Thus, white leaders emphasized the need to attract the "superior type" of woman into the training schools. Obviously this "superior type" mirrored the Victorian ideal of true womanhood: middle class, native-born, white, unmarried, and Protestant. The vision of the ideal nurse excluded black women, who not only suffered the legacy of slavery but were, as a rule, members of the class of working poor.

The efforts of nurse leaders to recruit "superior types" converged with the modernization of American hospitals. By the turn of the century, administrators recognized the need for a more reputable and efficient supply of cheap labor to maintain the hospital and to attend to the demands of a growing middle-class patient clientele. Not surprisingly, the class lines initially drawn in the late nineteenth century hardened considerably during the early decades of the twentieth century.

As a second strategy to raise the status of the nursing profession, white nurse leaders organized professional associations. In 1894, spurred by the call of Isabel Hampton, superintendent of the Johns Hopkins School of Nursing, nurse leaders formed a body that subsequently became the National League of Nursing Education (NLNE). Soon thereafter, American and Canadian graduate nurses organized what would be renamed in 1911 the American Nurses' Association (ANA). The leaders of the NLNE, ANA, and the many other emergent national societies fought to upgrade the status of nursing and to transform a "calling" into a profession. Again, black women, in the absence of specific provisions that would have overcome the racial exclusion practiced by Southern state organizations, were, with few exceptions, denied membership in these national associations and thus rendered professional outcasts.

In this respect the experiences of black women in nursing parallel those of blacks in both medicine and law. Two medical schools, Howard Medical School in Washington, D.C., founded in 1868 with support from the federal government, and Meharry Medical School in Nashville, Tennessee, bore the responsibility of training over 80 percent of all black doctors in the country prior to the modern civil rights movement. While Howard and Meharry effectively preserved the presence of black men in medicine, so effective were the exclusionary practices and sexually discriminating policies of the vast majority of medical schools that women, especially black women physicians, all but disappeared by the start of the Great Depression.

In 1890 there were 909 black physicians, approximately 90 of whom were black women. By 1920 the figure had jumped to a total of 3,885, but the number of black women doctors declined to only about 65 by 1925. A similar reduction is also true for white women. It is reasonable to suggest that black women desiring health care careers turned in larger numbers to nursing.

That black women did secure a place, albeit a negligible one, in the early nursing profession reflects the self-determination, sacrifice, and self-denial of hundreds of black community residents and the leaders who founded the hospitals and nursing training schools. Beginning with Chicago's famed black physician, Daniel Hale Williams, who in 1891 founded Provident Hospital, scores of black professionals and educators, along with black women's clubs, launched a veritable "black hospital and nursing training school" crusade. Under the leadership of Booker T. Washington, the Tuskegee Institute School of Nurse Training in Tuskegee, Alabama, opened in 1892. In the same year the Hampton Nurse Training School and Dixie Hospital in Hampton, Virginia, accepted its first class. In 1894, Williams was instrumental in creating another black nursing school, the Freedmen's Hospital and Nurse Training School in Washington, D.C. Two years later, in October 1896, black women of the Phillis Wheatley Club founded the only black hospital and nursing training school in New Orleans, which eventually became the Flint Goodridge Hospital and School of Nursing.

By 1920 there existed 36 separate black nursing training schools. Of course, in 1926 there were 2,150 predominantly or exclusively white institutions. It is difficult to exaggerate the extent to which black communities, with their meager resources and handmade supplies, sustained these fledgling and perpetually struggling institutions. Many of the hospitals and nursing schools courted financial disaster and seemingly always existed on the brink of collapse. The community contributions to their survival ranged from cash donations to that of an elderly black woman who in 1905 donated to Douglass Hospital in Philadelphia, "a mince pie, 1 leg of lamb, 3 cakes of hard soap, and 4 pounds of grits."[2] Organized groups of black clubwomen raised funds to purchase linen, food, and equipment and to repair physical plants.

Any discussion of black women in the nursing profession necessarily involves an examination of the institutions that trained, and to a limited extent employed, them. These early black nursing schools were, for the most part, as deficient in quality and standards as were many of their white counterparts. In keeping with prevailing practices, the students nurses were exploited as an unpaid labor force. In every institution they performed all the domestic and maintenance drudgery, attended the patients, and dispensed medicine. The trials and tribulations endured were such that many student nurses at Tuskegee Institute required extended leaves of absence to recover from damage done to their health while working in the hospital. It was not inconsequential, therefore, that one of the early Tuskegee catalogs noted that the major admission requirement into the nursing program was a strong physique and stamina to endure hardship.

Clearly the most oppressive aspect of black nursing training at some of these early schools involved the hiring out of student nurses to supplement the hospital's income. At the Charleston, South Carolina Hospital and Nursing Training School, the student nurses were required to turn over to the hospital the dollar a day they earned on private cases. These students also managed the hospital's poultry operation, tended the vegetable gardens, and organized public fund-raising activities. At Tuskegee the extensive hiring-out practices and unrelieved toil in an unhealthful environment provoked a student nurse revolt and a threatened mass walkout. The embattled hospital administrator, physician John A. Kenney, eventually persuaded Booker T. Washington to accede to some of the students' demands. Kenney later blamed this unique demonstration of belligerence on women who were, as he maintained, "not prepared for the serious study of nurses."[3]

The meagerness of primary sources prevents a detailed analysis of the Tuskegee Training School's culture that made such an organized expression of discontent possible. The letter quoted earlier (p. 60) from Bessie Hawse, a 1918 graduate of Tuskegee Institute, does, however, shed some light on the kinds of services the student nurses were expected and able to provide upon completion of the training program.

In spite of the attendant hardships and the mediocre instruction, hundreds of black women like Hawse were graduated from these segregated hospital nursing programs and proceeded to render lifesaving service to the black sick. It is little wonder that given the service they provided, and the fact that they were often the only available health care professionals, black nurses enjoyed a high level of respect and esteem within the black communities. Indeed, many black hospital administrators and physicians agreed that the black nurse had helped rural blacks to overcome their abhorrence, often justified, of hospitals. Physician J. Edward Perry founded the small proprietary Wheatley Provident Hospital and Nurse Training School in Kansas City, Missouri. In a particularly candid appraisal of the nurse, Perry declared: "The nurse is a co-partner of the doctor. Without her, in many instances, his efforts in the battle of disease would be futile." Perry admitted that "since the inception of the work of Wheatley Provident Hospital the nurses have played a conspicuous part." He confided,

"But for their loyalty and devotion, the institution would early have been grounded upon a sandbar of disaster and chaos."[4]

One caveat is in order at this juncture. Few of these black institutions would have been able to survive without the substantial financial contributions of white philanthropists. Throughout the first half of the twentieth century, white philanthropic foundations, most notably the Chicago-based Julius Rosenwald Fund, the Rockefeller trusts, and the General Education Board, provided sums for building construction and renovation. Foundations established graduate and postgraduate fellowships for nurses and physicians, granted salary supplements for special personnel, and offered operating expenses for clinics and training programs.

The role of the philanthropic foundations in the overall struggle to provide adequate health care for black Americans is a complex one. On the one hand, philanthropic donors could not escape the charge that their contributions to black hospitals and nursing training schools actually strengthened racial discrimination and preserved segregation. To the extent that blacks maintained and operated parallel institutions, their demands for admission into white or public institutions fell upon unsympathetic ears. While it is tempting to interpret philanthropic largesse in simple altruistic terms, here again the underlying motivations are more complex.

Between 1929 and 1942 the Julius Rosenwald Fund distributed over a million and a half dollars to black health care enterprises. Rosenwald explained that improving black health was the only way to protect and preserve the health of the white population. He advised all to heed that "It is well to remember that germs recognize no color lines and the disease in one group threatens the health of all."[5] Certainly mindful of his admonition, the General Education Board (GEB) launched an ultimately doomed million-dollar experiment. The GEB attempted to entice the University of Chicago to cooperate with Provident Hospital to provide clinical experiences for the university's black medical students who were not allowed to work in the institution's own hospital. A 1922 interoffice memo gives additional insight into beliefs and assumptions underlying philanthropic benevolence:

> The GEB's interest is neither sentimental nor merely humanitarian, it is practical. The Negro race is numerous and widely

scattered; it is with us to stay. Aside from any concern which on humanitarian grounds might be felt for the Negro for his sake, it is clear that the welfare of the South, not to say the whole country—its prosperity, its sanitation, and its morale—is affected by the condition of the Negro race.[6]

Here it is important to underscore that racism within the health care professions not only restricted the numbers of black men and women who became physicians and nurses but also endangered the health of African Americans in general. The most tragic example of the disregard for black health and life was reflected in the infamous Tuskegee syphilis study conducted at Tuskegee, Alabama, under the aegis of the United States Public Health Service. The experiment, begun in 1932, doomed approximately four hundred black sharecroppers who were deliberately denied treatment for their syphilitic infections in order that researchers could study the course of the disease.

Historian Allan M. Brandt pointed out the two essentially racist percepts undergirding the experiment: "First, the doctors who designed the study believed that virtually all southern blacks were infected. Second, they contended that the men involved would never be treated anyway." During the forty-year duration of the study, Brandt notes that the Public Health Service "actively sought to prevent the men from receiving therapy, all the while telling the subjects that they were being treated by government doctors. Many of the men—perhaps more than 100—died as a result of tertiary syphilis."[7]

As indicated, black leaders and communities with white philanthropic allies created institutions that provided black men and women the opportunity to become physicians, nurses, and even lawyers. But earning the nursing diploma or the medical or legal degree did not signal acceptance into the professions. Most professional associations, including the American Medical Association, the American Nurses' Association, and the American Bar Association, denied membership to blacks. In order to belong to these hierarchically structured groups, nurses, physicians, and lawyers had first to win membership in local affiliates. Of course, all Southern-based affiliates prohibited blacks from becoming members.

Left with little alternative, black professionals embraced the ideology of self-determination and commenced in the late 1890s the arduous task of creating a separate network of professional associations. Black physicians meeting in Atlanta, Georgia, in 1895 founded the National Medical Association. In August 1908, fifty-two black nurses met at St. Mark's Episcopal Church in New York City to found the National Association of Colored Graduate Nurses (NACGN). And finally, in 1925 black lawyers established the National Bar Association at a meeting in Des Moines, Iowa. To be sure, the separate associations played a significant role in the ongoing struggle against racial exclusion and segregation. One of the most important contributions these associations made was the promotion of positive self-esteem among the black professionals. Their annual conventions and deliberations enabled black professionals to build networks, make business contacts, share information, and sharpen leadership skills. Still, not all black professionals approved of the separate black organizations and institutions. Some Northern black professionals, especially those who had been trained at elite white institutions, argued that the existence of separate black units took the pressure off whites to integrate. Black nurses rarely seemed to participate in this debate.

In 1912 the NACGN had 125 members and by 1920 it boasted a membership of 500. Beginning in 1934, at the height of the Great Depression, under the leadership of NACGN president Estelle Massey Riddle and executive director Mabel K. Staupers, with funds provided by white philanthropic foundations, especially the Julius Rosenwald Fund, the organization launched a sustained attack against discrimination and segregation in the nursing profession. At this juncture, white nurse leaders, perhaps alarmed by the possibility that black nurses would accept the invitation of black physicians to become an auxiliary of the National Medical Association, for the first time seriously entertained dropping exclusionary barriers to membership in the American Nurses' Association. Under no circumstances, they reasoned, should any group of nurses affiliate with the male-dominated medical profession. Such action would set a precedent injurious to the autonomy of the nursing profession.

It was this decades-long and often frustrating quest for integration that distinguished the black nurses' engagement in the process of professionalization from that of their white counterparts. Riddle's and Stauper's relentless struggle against the discriminatory quotas imposed by the military establishment during World War II eventually won for black women full integration into the mainstream of American nursing.

The struggle for acceptance and recognition impelled black nurses to develop a finely tuned political consciousness and to devise innovative battle plans. They had to nurture relations with an array of public agencies, civil rights organizations, media representatives, and prominent individuals outside the boundaries of the profession itself. The inescapable realty of entrenched racism within and without nursing, therefore, necessitated and reinforced in them a dual consciousness. At a fundamental level their professional struggle simply mirrored the larger war for first-class citizenship waged by black people across the centuries.

In 1951, their integration goal achieved, black nurse leaders took an unprecedented step. They dissolved the NACGN. Never before had any male- or female-dominated black professional or civil rights protest organization deliberately folded. Ironically, in 1971, a new generation of black nurses, dissatisfied with the limitations of the integration meted to them, created the National Black Nurses Association, suggesting that the earlier dissolution had been premature. Nevertheless, the existence of the National Black Nurses Association bears witness to the resilience and intransigence of racism that infect not only American nursing but the entire society. In sum, the trials and tribulations of blacks in the learned professions mirror the larger war for a truly diverse and pluralistic society where the content of one's character is the only viable measure of worth.

To Heal the Race

African-American Health Care Professionals in Historical Perspective

Only within the past few decades have historians and other scholars launched investigations into the evolution of African-American health care institutions or focused attention on the roles that African-American health care professionals have played in the survival struggles of African Americans and their communities. Of all the African-American institutions created in the years following the end of slavery—the church, schools and universities, insurance companies, funeral homes, barber and beauty shops—the African-American medical institutions have received the least scholarly notice. Long-standing scholarly neglect has impeded our understanding of the complex relations among African Americans, health care professions, and the attendant institutions created to serve them.

It is important to examine the history of African-American health in slavery and in freedom and to discuss the emergence of African-American health care professionals. And no discussion of the health of African Americans in the modern era is complete without a historical analysis of the health care delivery system. A historical perspective lays a foundation for understanding the strategies devised to address the problem of high African-American mortality and morbidity during the past century. Undiagnosed and untreated disease continues to ravage the African-American community. The high incidence of AIDS, heart disease, and hypertension, to name only three life-threatening diseases, and the fact that African Americans die from chronic diseases at an alarming rate, are directly related to poverty, lack of insurance, inaccessible hospitals and clinics, and declining numbers of health care personnel serving impoverished communities. In this essay, I concentrate on the initiatives African Americans launched in order to improve their health and to create opportunities for those desiring to become nurses and physicians.

It is frustrating to contemplate how little progress has been made in the long struggle to provide adequate access to health care for African Americans. During slavery, a fatalistic attitude existed among most African Americans toward illness. They often chose to rely on their own remedies or on the talents of slave nurses and doctors to bring them through. Planters were often perplexed by slave behavior. As one Mississippi planter lamented, "the Negroes unfortunately for Themselves and Equally so for us had no confidence in our treatment—they Said it was certain death to take our medicine and we were compelled to stand by and See them die."[1]

African-American antipathy toward hospitalization continued well into the twentieth century. Prior to World War II, virtually every white-owned and -managed hospital in the country either denied admission or placed African-American patients in segregated basements, rooms, wards, or halls. Rigid adherence to Jim Crow policies not only discouraged African-American patients from seeking hospital care but also severely restricted the professional development of African-American physicians and nurses. Hospitals that routinely denied African-American physicians attending privileges in effect denied the African-American patient treatment by his or her own African-American doctor.[2]

Conditions within white-administered hospitals that were specifically restricted to a African-American clientele left much room for improvement. In the 1930s, Walter White, the executive secretary of the National Association for the Advancement of Colored People visited the ward reserved for African Americans at Grady Hospital in Atlanta, Georgia. According to White, "Overworked Negro nurses and orderlies scrubbed and swept incessantly, but with dismal failure, to keep the closely packed wards reasonably clean. The obsolescent building and facilities had too great a head start. . . . Dinginess, misery, and poverty pressed so hard on one from every side that even a well person could not avoid feeling a little sick in the surroundings."[3] Much later, Whitney Young, former leader of the National Urban

League, described the segregated African-American hospitals as: "generally unattractive if not repellent, and the ailing Negro avoids them if he is able. Usually he has no choice. Anxiety-ridden as to his chance of finding decent hospital facilities and apprehensive of the quality of care he will receive if and when admitted, is it any wonder that the Negro in ill health holds out against hospitalization until the last possible moment?"[4]

Prompted in large part by inadequate access to health care, African-American leaders and their communities in the last quarter of the nineteenth century addressed the problem by founding a separate, parallel network of medical and nursing schools, hospitals, and clinics. This period witnessed a growing adherence to and articulation of the ideology of self-determination and self-help and revealed a marked willingness on the part of African Americans to sacrifice for the sake of long-term improvement in the lives of their people. While African Americans, especially those who would remain in the South, launched their own institutional health care infrastructure, white policies and practices of racial segregation became institutionalized.[5]

Beginning in the 1890s, different social and educational backgrounds and regional location notwithstanding, African Americans, perhaps heeding the metaphorical advice of Booker T. Washington to drop their buckets where they were, launched and sustained a nationwide African-American health crusade. Some African-American leaders founded medical schools, others established hospitals and nursing schools, still others launched national health educational campaigns, and a few even opened community clinics. For example, in Indianapolis an African-American women's club, distressed over the high rates of tuberculosis among African Americans in the city and the reluctance of the state to provide sanatariums for them, took matters into their own hands. In 1905, the women founded an open-air clinic for African-American tuberculosis sufferers.[6] Indeed, examples abound of African-American initiative and innovation in meeting the challenge of providing treatment and care for the sick. An African-American physician, William Beck of Nashville, Tennessee, became a nationally renowned specialist who lectured throughout the South under the sponsorship of the National Anti-Tuberculosis Association. He pioneered in the use of ambulatory pneumothorax, a procedure for tuberculosis victims that was made available to those unable to gain admission to white hospitals.[7]

A final illustration of the range of African-American self-determination in the health care arena was the National Negro Health Week movement. From 1915 through 1925, for one week each winter, the executive committee of the National Negro Business League, an organization founded by Booker T. Washington, focused national attention on African-American health problems. Again, African-American clubwomen proved critical to the success of the Health Week observances. They orchestrated series of lectures, arranged for physicians and nurses to visit schools, and oversaw neighborhood clean-up campaigns. In urban Northern areas and throughout the South, African Americans pressed for the employment of African-American nurses at pubic health departments and in visiting nurses associations.[8]

As important as the indigenous efforts were, so too were the contributions of white philanthropists to the success of African-American health improvement campaigns. The financial contributions of the Julius Rosenwald Fund proved especially vital in persuading departments of health in Southern states to hire African-American public health nurses. Indeed, in 1942, the Rosenwald Fund closed a fifteen-year program designed to improve African-American health and to train health care workers. The fund distributed a total of $1,613,000 to approximately sixteen hospitals and clinics, with the largest amounts going to Provident Hospital in Chicago, Flint-Goodridge Hospital in New Orleans, and the John A. Andrew Hospital at Tuskegee Institute in Alabama. The General Education Board (GEB) of the Rockefeller Foundation likewise played a significant role in financing the creation of hospitals and clinics and in strengthening the two African-American medical schools—Meharry and Howard.[9]

The significant financial contributions of the white philanthropists complement the myriad activities of African Americans themselves in developing the African-American health care institutional infrastructure. Of course, a balanced representation of this process must consider the strong objections of those who were no less committed to improving African-American health but who saw in the creation of separate institutions a tacit acceptance of, or an accommodation to, segregation and second-class citizenship. African-American physician W. Montague Cobb characterized the creation of the network of African-American hospitals, clinics, and medical and nursing schools that flourished during the 1920s as "the Negro medical ghetto." He declared, "During the period of the building of the medical ghetto system, few voices in the power structure were raised against it. The segregated framework was like a bed of Procrustes into which every attempt at improvement had to be fitted." He lamented that, "None pointed out its injustice or inadequacy."[10]

Actually, the migration of hundreds of thousands of Southern African Americans to Northern urban communities helped to justify the medical ghetto while, at the same time, it sowed the seeds for the ghetto's destruction. Swelling African-American communities severely strained the segregation policies of large Northern municipal hospitals. Often, as neighborhoods changed from white to African American, the hospitals that had been built to serve white patients, white physicians, and a white community faced one of three choices. They could either shut down, serve the new African-American clientele, or relocate to an all-white area. In most cities throughout the country, African Americans inherited, as Montague Cobb put it, many of the secondhand hospitals.[11]

Despite the criticism of leading African-American physicians who feared accommodation to segregation, other African Americans struggled to build a system of health care institutions within the segregated parameters of American society. Yet even the separate schools they created proved susceptible to forces operating in the larger society. At one time, approximately one dozen African-American medical institutions existed. White medical reformers, however, considered only four of the schools adequate. According to M. Vandehurst Lynk, a contemporary African-American physician, the big four—Howard University School of Medicine in Washington, D.C.; Meharry Medical School in Nashville, Tennessee; Leonard Medical School of Shaw University in Raleigh, North Carolina; and the Flint Medical College (originally known as the Medical Department of New Orleans University)—labored to keep up with quickly evolving medical standards.

Although the American medical profession had been in the throes of reform since the 1890s, it was the publication of Abraham Flexner's *Report* in 1910 of medical education in America and Canada that sounded the death knell for the majority of the African-American medical schools, as well as a large number of white schools. His critical evaluation of both African-American and non-African-American schools sent shock waves throughout the entire medical profession and spurred the elimination and consolidation impulse already under way. Flexner's denouncement of the African-American schools, however, carried greater proportional consequence. By 1914, only two African-American medical schools, Howard and Meharry, survived. In addition to his stinging critique of the African-American medical schools, Flexner prescribed the role and duties of the African-American physician. Moreover, he pointedly advised that, in the interest of self-protection, whites should become concerned about African-American health:

> The practice of the negro doctor will be limited to his own race, which in its turn will be cared for better by good negro physicians than by poor white ones. But the physical well-being of the negro is not only of a moment to the negro himself. Ten million of them live in close contact with sixty million whites. Not only does the negro himself suffer from hookworm and tuberculosis; he communicates them to his white neighbors, precisely as the ignorant and unfortunate white contaminates him. Self-protection not less than humanity offers weighty counsel in this matter; self-interest seconds philanthropy. The negro must be educated not only for his sake, but for ours. He is, as far as human eye can see, a permanent factor in the nation. He has his rights and due and value as an individual; but he has besides, the tremendous importance that belongs to a potential source of infection and contagion.[12]

For nearly a century, the combination of the medical reform impulse and the work of leading philanthropists ensured that there would be at least two institutions available to train African-American physicians. The African-American population, meanwhile, exceeded ten million. Flexner's views comported well with the general societal racism, and his recommendations to philanthropists that they should support Howard and Meharry medical schools to the exclusion of others meant that the total number of African-American physicians would remain comparatively small. In sum, the reduction of the numbers and types of medical schools, the adoption of higher admission standards, the growing emphasis on professionalization, the scientific transformation of medical education and practice, and the introduction of mandatory requirements of hospital internships and residencies in an era when few hospitals offered such appointments to African Americans severely limited the number of African-American male doctors and virtually eliminated African-American women from the profession.

Begun in 1876 as the medical department of Central Tennessee College, Meharry was the first medical school in the South to provide for the education of African-American physicians. Meharry also, it should be noted, graduated the largest number of African-American women physicians (39 by 1920). Meharry and Howard, therefore, bore the responsibility for training over 80 percent of all African-American physicians in the country prior to the modern civil rights movement.

In 1890, there were 909 African-American physicians; by 1920 the number had jumped to 3,885, of which fewer than 70 were women.[13] The increase had been almost entirely due to the existence of the several African-American medical schools. There exists insufficient evidence to draw firm conclusions about the extent of the ameliorative role of African-American physicians in the delivery of suitable health care to African-American people. Nevertheless, prior to the 1960s, no Southern medical school and only a limited number of Northern ones admitted African-American students. Thus, African-American patients had insufficient access to health care providers of their own race.

In addition to the barriers that effectively limited the numbers of African-American health care professionals available to African-American communities, a tragic consequence of the "medical ghetto" and segregation was a widespread disregard for African-American life, even at the highest levels of state and federal government. While the federal government, specifically the Public Health Service, initiated and supported health programs beneficial to African Americans, it also sponsored in 1932 the infamous Tuskegee syphilis study in Alabama. The experiment made certain that approximately four hundred African-American sharecroppers would never receive treatment for their syphilitic infections so researchers could study the course of the disease when left untreated. During a forty-year period, the Public Health Service, as historian Allan Brandt points out, "actively sought to prevent the men from receiving therapy, all the while telling the subjects that they were being treated by the government doctors."[14]

The exclusion, discrimination, and restricted opportunities that run through the history of African-American medicine are also characteristics of African-American nursing. As nursing acquired the trappings of a profession, the impediments placed in the paths of African-American women mushroomed. White nursing schools denied them admission into training programs, and professional nursing associations barred them from membership and refused to list them in employment registries. White nurses viewed African-American women as a permanently alien and inferior group that could not be assimilated into the profession. Of course, part of the hostility grew out of a desire to avoid competition with African-American nurses for work.

Again, in order that African-American women should have access to professional nursing training, African-American leaders, in the name of racial self-determination and solidarity, established the appropriate institutions. Beginning in the early 1890s, African-American physician Daniel Hale Williams of Chicago and educator Booker T. Washington, founder of Tuskegee Institute in Alabama, spearheaded a movement to found hospital nursing schools for African-American women. They raised operating funds for these new institutions from the Chicago and Tuskegee African-American communities and from private philanthropies. Williams founded two African-American nursing schools. When he launched Provident Hospital and Training School in Chicago in 1891, it was the first African-American-controlled hospital in the United States. In 1894, Williams established the Freedmen's Hospital nursing school in Washington, D.C., which eventually became an arm of Howard University. In 1892, Booker T. Washington launched the nursing program at Tuskegee Institute.[15]

In addition to Provident and Tuskegee, nursing programs sprung up at Provident Hospital in Baltimore in 1894 and at Frederick Douglass Memorial Hospital and Training School in Philadelphia in 1895. In a 1900 address before the Phillis Wheatley Club of Nashville, Tennessee, Williams exhorted African-American communities to establish more hospitals and nurse training schools in the South.

He declared: "In view of this cruel ostracism, affecting so vitally the race, our duty seems plain. Institute Hospitals and Training Schools. Let us no longer sit idly and inanely deploring existing conditions. Let us not waste time trying to effect changes or modifications in the institutions unfriendly to us, but rather let us seek to promote the doctrine of helping and stimulating our race."[16]

For a constellation of reasons, the African-American nurse became one of the most highly respected and visible members of the health care team, especially in rural areas in the South, where she was often the only health professional in residence. Her role was also critical to the delivery of adequate health care to impoverished African-American urban communities, and the history of African-American nursing is inextricably tied to the creation and development of African-American hospitals. By the 1920s, the separate African-American training schools had produced approximately 3,000 nurses. By the early 1940s, 110 African-American-owned and -operated hospitals, primarily in urban areas, had been established to meet African-American needs. Many of these hospitals had fewer than 100 beds, and together they provided fewer than 10,000 beds. Of these hospitals, 70 percent were privately owned and only 22 of the 110 were fully approved hospitals (five were provisionally approved).

Because the African-American communities had contributed so much to the start-up funds that created and sustained the hospitals that operated the African-American nursing schools, the early generations of graduates were expected to repay the communities' investment. That African-American nurses amply fulfilled their part of this implicit social contract is reflected in the esteem in which they were held in the African-American community. In 1898 in Charleston, South Carolina, African-American hospital founder Dr. Alonzo C. McClennan wrote in the monthly publication *Hospital Herald*, "Physicians get better results from the treatment of the sick in the hospitals or in private practice when they have to aid them, competent nurses who are able to carry out intelligently whatever directions may be given them, and who can detect the changes in the progress of disease under treatment."[17]

The generous community support does not, however, erase the fact that African-American women constituted an exploitable, cheap labor force for these hospitals. They were required to maintain the entire hospital apparatus in addition to caring for the patients. The presence and work of these nursing students provided the added benefit of helping to attract African-American patients who would have avoided these institutions given the deeply ingrained suspicion and hostility.

African-American nurses also had to improvise strategies for professional development. As African-American physicians had done in 1895 with the creation of the National Medical Association, African-American nurses met in 1908 to found the National Association of Colored Graduate Nurses. These organizations became the chief agencies through which African-American health care professionals struggled to advance and win acceptance in the larger professional societies. For most of the twentieth century, both the American Medical Association and the American Nurses' Association denied membership privileges to African Americans. Through their own organizations, African-American physicians and nurses were able to develop a collective consciousness of resistance against forced segregation and discrimination as practiced by the larger medical establishment.

The growing professionalism of African Americans, however, never completely eradicated African-American people's ingrained antipathy nor did it radically improved their limited access to hospitals. The hospital, as Charles E. Rosenberg argues, is a major institution in American culture.[18] In the late nineteenth century, the hospital was an institution of charity that served the medical needs of the urban poor. Middle-class Americans preferred to remain in the home when ill. In the closing decades of the nineteenth century and the opening decades of the twentieth, however, medical discoveries, including the germ theory of disease and the growth of laboratory science, along with urbanization and industrialization combined to reshape the mission and significance of the hospital in American society. As the hospital became the cornerstone of modern medical education, and the medical and nursing professions became "hospitalized," so too did the white middle class. The suspicion and limited access that poor African Americans had to the hospitals, however, persisted, with African-American "hospitalization" lagging far behind that of whites.

Chicago provided an illuminating case study of the limited choices and inadequate patterns of African-American hospitalization. According to one study:

In the fifties, while black Chicagoans were increasing substantially as a proportion of the city's population, Chicago Memorial Hospital, Mercy Hospital, and St. Luke's all left Chicago's black South Side for whiter, more suburban locations. That left over 1,000 fewer hospital beds to serve an area where an estimated half-million southern blacks had settled since World War II. By the late nineteen sixties, only 13 physicians remained to serve the 63,000 black residents of the East Garfield Park area of Chicago. Nearby, in the Kenwood-Oaklawn area, 45,500 black people had only 5 physicians to meet their needs by 1968. According to one estimate, there were more physicians in one suburban medical building than in the whole westside ghetto, which housed 300,000 blacks.[19]

On the threshold of the twenty-first century, African America is witnessing an alarming shortage of health care professionals. Many of the neighborhood hospitals and community clinics established at the dawn of the century are now mere relics of a forgotten past. In one sense, the problems of inadequate access to health care facilities and the shortage of health care personnel are quite similar to conditions prevalent one hundred years ago.[20]

This brief historical overview of the obstacles that impeded African-American advance into the medical and nursing professions suggests several directions for future action. Clearly, there exists an urgent need for more African-American physicians and nurses. More competitive scholarships and other incentives must be provided to encourage young African Americans to enter the health care professions. The work to be done to improve the health of African Americans demands the full attention and cooperation of government and health care associations and institutions. African-American health professionals alone cannot provide the massive care needed to bring racial parity. Continued discrimination in all walks of life is reprehensible, but to paraphrase an observation made by Dr. Martin Luther King Jr., injustice and inequality in health and medical care are inhumane.[21]

Notes

Preface

1 This essay is based mainly on references in Joe W. Trotter, "African Americans in the City: The Industrial Era, 1900–1950" and Kenneth L. Kusmer, "African Americans in the City since World War II: From the Industrial to the Post-Industrial Era," both in *Journal of Urban History*, Vol. 21, no. 4 (May 1995): 438–457 and 458–504; J. W. Trotter, "African American Workers: New Directions in U.S. Labor Historiography," *Labor History*, Vol. 35, no. 4 (fall 1994): 495–523.

2 Taken together, useful descriptions of the black professional class over time include Carter G. Woodson, *The Black Professional Man and the Community* (New York: Johnson Reprint Corporation, 1970 [1934]); E. Franklin Frazier, *Black Bourgeoisie: The Rise of a New Middle Class in the United States* (New York: Macmillan, 1975 [1957]); Willard B. Gatewood, *Aristocrats of Color: The Black Elite, 1880–1920* (Bloomington: Indiana University Press, 1990); and Bart Landry, *The New Black Middle Class* (Berkeley: University of California Press, 1987).

3 Trotter, "African American Workers."

4 See Kusmer, "African Americans in the City since World War II," and Trotter, "African Americans in the City."

5 James Grossman, *Land of Hope: Chicago, Black Southerners, and the Great Migration* (Chicago: University of Chicago Press, 1989), 153.

6 Trotter, *Black Milwaukee*, 57–58.

7 Earl Lewis, *In Their Own Interests: Race, Class, and Power in Twentieth-Century Norfolk, Virginia* (Berkeley: University of California Press, 1991), 80–81.

8 Trotter, "African American Workers."

9 Ibid.

10 Kusmer, "African Americans in the City since World War II"; Michael B. Katz, *The "Underclass" Debate: Views from History* (Princeton: Princeton University Press, 1993), especially the essays by Thomas Sugrue and Robin Kelley.

11 Trotter, "African Americans in the City."

12 In her study of black professional women, Stephanie Shaw coins the term "socially responsible individualism" and reinforces Professor Hine's argument about the service ethic. *"What a Woman Ought to Be and to Do": Black Professional Women during the Jim Crow Era* (Chicago: University of Chicago Press, forthcoming).

13 Earl Lewis suggests that these propositions need refinement. See his "Invoking Concepts, Problematizing Identities: The Life of Charles N. Hunter and the Implications for the Study of Gender and Labor," *Labor History*, Vol. 34, nos. 2–3 (spring-summer 1993): 292–308.

14 Studies by Robin D. G. Kelley and Tera Hunter are particularly significant in helping us to begin addressing these very complex issues. See, respectively, *Race Rebels: Culture, Politics, and the Black Working Class* (New York: Free Press, 1994) and *Household Workers in the Making: Afro-American Women in Atlanta and the New South, 1861–1920* (forthcoming).

15 See discussion and quote in Trotter, *Black Milwaukee*, 101.

Introduction

1 Carl N. Degler, "An Historian Looks at *The Bell Curve*," *Contention*, Vol. 4, no. 3 (spring 1995): 3–17. Degler observes, "class is the dirty secret of white America, while race is an ancient and present tragedy" (17).

2 See Joe William Trotter Jr., *Coal, Class, and Color: Blacks in Southern West Virginia, 1915–32* (Urbana: University of Illinois Press, 1990); William Julius Wilson, *The Truly Disadvantaged: The Inner City, the Underclass, and Public Policy* (Chicago: University of Chicago Press, 1987); Earl Lewis, *In Their Own Interests: Race, Class, and Power in Twentieth-Century Norfolk, Virginia* (Berkeley: University of California Press, 1991); Robin D. G. Kelley, *Race Rebels: Culture, Politics, and the Black Working Class* (New York: The Free Press, 1994).

3 Benjamin E. Mays, *Born to Rebel: An Autobiography* (New York: Charles Scribner's Sons, 1991). Mays confided, "I have never believed that a white doctor who segregates his Negro patients and thus demonstrates that he considers them inferior could give me the same professional care as his white patients" (87).

4 Fred D. Gray, *Bus Ride to Justice* (Montgomery, Alabama: The Black Belt Press, 1995).

5 Jo Ann Gibson Robinson, *The Montgomery Bus Boycott and the Women Who Started It* (Knoxville: University of Tennessee Press, 1987).

6 The work in progress on Nurse Rivers by historian Susan Reverby of Wellesley College promises new insight into her behavior.

7 For a different response to the hearings, see Orlando Patterson, "Backlash," *Transitions Issue 62* (1993): 4–26; and "The Crisis of African American Gender Relations," *Transition Issue 66* (summer 1995).

8 Michael Schwartz, President Emeritus, to Darlene Clark Hine, February 2, 1995. Schwartz offered the following instructions: "Insofar as it is acceptable to you, I thought that you might wish to address issues of race and gender in the curriculum (and elsewhere in higher education) since May of 1970 using the student protest movement of the 1960's and early '70's as a beginning and anchoring point."

The Greater Kent State Era, 1968–1970: Personal Transformations and Legacies of Student Rebellions and State Repression

1 Jack Bass and Jack Nelson, *The Orangeburg Massacre* (Atlanta: Mercer University Press, 1984), 235.

2 I. F. Stone, *The Killings at Kent State: How Murder Went Unpunished* (New York: A New York Review Book, 1970). Also see Carol Squiers, "On Kent and Jackson State," *Artform* (summer 1991): 14–16.

3 For a very different take on this event, see Dwight D. Murphey, "Kent State: Revisited," *The Journal of Social, Political and Economic Studies*, Vol. 18, no. 2 (summer 1993): 235–255.

4 Terry H. Anderson, *The Movement and the Sixties: Protest in America from Greensboro to Wounded Knee* (New York: Oxford University Press, 1995), 183–238.

5 John Logue, "Official Violence: An American Tradition," in *Kent State/May 4: Echoes Through A Decade*, edited by Scott L. Bills (Kent, Ohio: Kent State University Press, 1982), 143–149.

6 *Newsweek*, May 7, 1990.

7 Kay Boyle, in *The Long Walk at San Francisco State and Other Essays* (New York: Grove Press, 1967), reproduces the list of fifteen strike demands made by the Black Student Union and the Third World Liberation Front. One of the demands stipulated that "fifty faculty positions be appropriated to the School of Ethnic Studies, 20 of which would be for Black Studies Program." Also see William H. Exum, *Paradoxes of Protest: Black Student Activism in a White University* (Philadelphia: Temple University Press, 1985); Dikran Karagueuzian, *Blow it up! The Black Student Revolt at San Francisco State College and the Emergence of Dr. Hayakawa* (Boston: Gambit, 1971); DeVere Pentony, Robert Smith, and Richard Axen, *Unfinished Rebellions* (San Francisco: Jossey-Bass, 1971).

8 Beverly T. Watkins, "Rutgers Weighs Moves to Meet Blacks' Demands," *The Chronicle of Higher Education* (hereafter listed as *Chronicle*), December 24, 1973. The percentage of 18- to 24-year-old black students increased from 15 percent in 1970 to 18 percent in 1974 (*Chronicle*, September 15, 1975). As the number grew, so did their alienation, estrangement, and rejection of lily-white courses in which black people made an occasional appearance as slave or exotic subaltern. Further, in an unusual move, students argued for greater involvement in community work, offering tutorial assistance to secondary school students, sponsoring cultural affairs, etc., as part of the black studies mission.

9 Cheryl M. Fields, "Women's Studies Gain: 2,000 Courses Offered this Year," *Chronicle*, December 17, 1973; Also see Catharine R. Stimpson with Nina Kressner Cobb, *Women's Studies in the United States: A Report to the Ford Foundation* (New York: Ford Foundation, 1986). Their struggles against racism continue. "Blacks Protest Campus Racism," *Newsweek*, April 6, 1987; Elizabeth Greene, "Racial Incidents at 4 Universities Spark Protests," *Chronicle*, April 20, 1988. (The four universities were Berkeley, Pennsylvania State, University of Kentucky, and Denison University.) "Students on the four campuses all charged that their administrations were too complacent about race relations and should take a more active role in improving people's understanding and appreciation of different cultures. The protesters' demands, which vary from campus to campus, include the creation of black studies requirements for all undergraduates; black, or minority cultural centers; and more black faculty members. At Pennsylvania State, students are asking for a vice-president for minority affairs."

10 Quotes in Karen J. Winkler, "The State of Black Studies," *Chronicle*, December 8, 1975; "Afro-American Studies in the Twenty-First Century: Featuring the Wisconsin Conference on Afro-American Studies, April 18–21, 1991," *The Black Scholar*, Vol. 22, no. 3 (summer 1992).

11 Jerome H. Schiele, "Afrocentricity: Implications for Higher Education," *Journal of Black Studies*, Vol. 25, no. 2 (December 1994): 150–169; Darlene Clark Hine, "The Black Studies Movement: Afrocentric-Traditionist-Feminist Paradigms for the Next Stage," *The Black Scholar*, Vol. 22, no. 3 (summer 1992): 15.

12 See Darlene Clark Hine, *Hine Sight: Black Women and the Re-Construction of American History* (New York: Carlson Publishing, 1994), Introduction.

13 Hine, *Black Women in White: Racial Conflict and Cooperation in the Nursing Profession, 1890–1950* (Bloomington: Indiana University Press, 1989).

14 Margaret L. Andersen, "Changing the Curriculum in Higher Education," *Signs: Journal of Women in Culture and Society*, Vol. 12, no. 2 (1987): 222–255. Also see Marilyn Schuster and Susan Van Dyne, eds., *Women's Place in the Academy: Transforming the Liberal Arts Curriculum* (Totowa: N.J.: Rowan and Allanheld, 1985).

15 My own work included *Black Women in America: An Historical Encyclopedia* (Brooklyn: Carlson Publishing, 1993), which I coedited with Elsa Barkley Brown and Rosalyn Terborg-Penn, and a collection of essays published under the title, *Hine Sight* (Brooklyn: Carlson Publishing, 1994). For Huggins's remark, see Nathan Irvin Huggins *Black Odyssey: The African-American Ordeal in Slavery* (New York: Vintage Books, 1990).

16 Susan Hardy Aiken, Karen Anderson, Myra Dinnerstein, Judy Lensink, and Patricia Maccorgquodale, "Trying Transformations: Curriculum Integration and the Problem of Resistance," *Signs: Journal of Women in Culture and Society*, Vol. 12, no. 2 (1987): 255–275; Kersti Yllo, "Revisions: How the New Scholarship on Women and Gender Transform the College Curriculum," *American Behavioral Scientist*, Vol. 32, no. 6 (July/August 1989): 658–667; Christie Farham, ed., *The Impact of Feminist Research in the Academy*

(Bloomington: Indiana University Press, 1987).
17 Aiken et al., "Trying Transformations," 262.
18 Gary B. Nash, "The History Children Should Study," *Chronicle*, April 21, 1995.
19 Carole Merritt, "The Power of History: Interpreting Black Material Culture," in Darlene Clark Hine, ed., *The State of Afro-American History, Past, Present and Future* (Baton Rouge: Louisiana State University Press, 1986), 213–219. Also see Karen J. Winkler, "Scholars Say Issues of Diversity Have 'Revolutionized' Field of Chicano Studies," *Chronicle*, September 26, 1990.

Ivory-Tower Reflections: A Black Woman in the Academy

1 John A. Hannah, *A Memoir* (East Lansing: Michigan State University Press, 1980), 77. I was impressed by John Hannah's philosophy and worldview because they resonated with my own. He wrote, "It seemed to me that when a person gets old and looks back over his life, what is important in it is not prestige or the amount of money in the bank, but rather whether or not he feels that this life has been useful. If he has been able to contribute, even in some small way, to making possible for people to live lives that are more satisfying to them than they might otherwise have been, that, it seems to me is probably the most meaningful of all life's satisfactions" (21).
2 Barry Gaspar, John McCluskey, and I also edit the Blacks in the Diaspora Series for Indiana University Press. Most recently Barry and I coedited a book of original essays, *More than Chattel: Black Women in Slavery in the Americas*, for the series.
3 Evelyn Brooks Higginbotham, "African American Women's History and the Metalanguage of Race," *Signs*, Vol. 17, no. 2 (spring 1992): 251-274.
4 Even though the project ended in 1983, both institutions have continued to develop their black manuscript collections. The Indiana Historical Bureau published the *Comprehensive Black Women in the Middle West Project Resource Guide: Indiana and Illinois* (1983) that describes the project and the 300 collections amassed, and contains biographical profiles of hundreds of volunteers who made it a success.
5 Much of the following information is taken from *Black Women in White* and from *Black Women in America: An Historical Encyclopedia* (Brooklyn, N.Y.: Carlson Publishing, 1993).
6 I am grateful for the comments, suggestions and good conversation of the following MSU graduate students in the History Department: LaTrese Adkins, Earnestine Jenkins, Hilary Jones, Heran Sereke-Brahan, Eleanor Shelton, Pamela Smoot, Carmen Harris, and Jacqueline McLeod. They make the journey an adventure.

Quilts and African-American Women's Cultural History

1 Quoted in Gladys-Marie Fry, *Stitched from the Soul: Slave Quilts from the Ante-Bellum South* (New York: Dutton, 1990), 1; also see Cuesta Benberry, *Always There: The African-American Presence in American Quilts* (Louisville: The Kentucky Quilt Project, 1992).
2 Gerda Lerner, ed., *Black Women in White America: A Documentary History* (Indianapolis: Bobbs-Merrill, 1972); Rosalyn Terborg-Penn and Sharon Harley, eds., *The Afro-American Woman: Struggles and Images* (New York: Kennikat Press, 1978).
3 Hine, *Hine Sight*, xxii.
4 Lawrence Levine, *Black Culture and Black Consciousness: Afro-American Folk Thought from Slavery to Freedom* (New York: Oxford University Press, 1977); also see William Ferris, ed., *Afro-American Folk Art and Craft* (Jackson: University Press of Mississippi, 1983), 67–78; Eli Leon, *Who'd A Thought: Improvisation in African-American Quiltmaking* (San Francisco: Craft and Folk Art Museum, 1987).

5 John Michael Vlach, *The Afro-American Tradition in Decorative Arts* (Cleveland, Ohio: Cleveland Museum of Art, 1978), 44.
6 Ibid., 67.
7 Ibid., 44–75; Robert Farris Thompson, "African Influences on the Art of the United States," *Journal of African Civilizations* 3 (November 1978): 44; Gladys-Marie Fry, "Harriet Powers: Portrait of a Black Quilter," in *Missing Pieces: Georgia Folk Art, 1770–1976* (Atlanta: Georgia Council for the Arts and Humanities, 1976), 16–23; Maude Southwell Wahlman, *Signs and Symbols: African Images in African-American Quilts* (New York: Viking, 1993), 64.
8 Quoted in Irene V. Jackson, "Black Women and Music: From Africa to the New World," in Filomina Chioma Steady, ed., *Black Woman Cross-Culturally* (Rochester, Vermont: Schenkman Books, 1981), 393; also see Wahlman, *Signs and Symbols*, 64.
9 Samella S. Lewis and Ruth G. Waddy, *Black Artists on Art* (Los Angeles: Contemporary Crafts Publishers, 1971), 2:ix.
10 Arna Alexander Bontemps, ed., *Forever Free: Art by African American Women, 1862–1980* (Alexandria, Va.: Stephenson, Inc., 1980), 9.

Culture, Consciousness, and Community: The Making of an African American Women's History

1 Quoted in Linda Perkins, "Education," in Brown, Hine, and Terborg-Penn, *Black Women in America*, 386.
2 John Hope Franklin, "On the Evolution of Scholarship in Afro-American History," in Hine *The State of Afro-American History*, 13.
3 Linda Gordon "Black and White Visions of Welfare: Women's Welfare Activism, 1890–1945," *Journal of American History*, Vol. 78, no. 2 (September 1991): 559.
4 For a longer discussion of the work of black women, see Jacqueline Anne Rouse *Lugenia Burns Hope: Black Southern Reformer* (Athens: University of Georgia Press, 1989).
5 Perkins, "Education," 384–385.
6 Hine, *Black Women in White*, 8.
7 Ibid., 58.
8 Ibid., 60.
9 Ibid., 24.

The Making of *Black Women in America: An Historical Encyclopedia*

1 Elsa Barkley Brown, "Womanist Consciousness: Maggie Lena Walker and the Independent Order of St. Luke," *Signs* 14 (spring 1989): 631.

For Pleasure, Profit, and Power: The Sexual Exploitation of Black Women, or Anita Hill and Clarence Thomas in Historical Perspective

1 Orlando Patterson, "Race Gender and Liberal Fallacies," *The New York Times*, October 20, 1991.
2 Darlene Clark Hine, "Rape and the Inner Lives of Black Women in the Middle West: Preliminary Thoughts on the Culture of Dissemblance," *Signs* 14 (summer 1989): 912–920.
3 Frances E. W. Harper, "A Double Standard," in *Complete Poems of Frances E. W. Harper*, edited by Maryemma Graham (New York: Oxford University Press, 1988), 176–178.
4 Harriet Jacobs, *Incidents in the Life of a Slave Girl* (New York: Oxford University Press, 1988), 85.
5 Ibid., 86.
6 Melton A. McLaurin, *Celia, A Slave* (Athens: University of Georgia Press, 1991), 81.
7 A. Leon Higginbotham, "Race, Sex, Education and Missouri Jurisprudence: *Shelley v. Kraemer* in a Historical Perspective," *Washington University Law Quarterly* 67 (1989): 673–708.
8 Ibid., 682.
9 Morris Dees with Steve Fiffer, *A Season for Justice: The Life and Times of Civil Rights Lawyer Morris Dees* (New York: Scribners, 1991), 164.

10 Joel Williamson, *New People: Miscegenation and Mulattoes in the United States* (New York: The Free Press, 1980), 54.
11 Winthrop D. Jordan, *White Over Black: American Attitudes Towards the Negro, 1550–1812* (Chapel Hill: University of North Carolina Press, 1968).
12 Deborah Gray White, *Ar'n't I a Woman? Female Slaves in the Plantation South* (New York: W.W. Norton, 1985); Patricia Morton, *Disfigured Images: The Historical Assault on Afro-American Women* (New York: Praeger, 1991).
13 Ludmilla Jordanova, *Sexual Visions: Images of Gender in Science and Medicine between the Eighteenth and Twentieth Centuries* (Madison: University of Wisconsin Press, 1989), 109–110.

Booker T. Washington and Madam C. J. Walker

1 George S. Schuyler, "Madam C. J. Walker" *The Messenger*, July 1924, 256.
2 Paula Giddings, *When and Where I Enter: The Impact of Black Women on Race and Sex in America* (New York: Morrow, 1984), 187–188. Also see Jill Nelson, "The Fortune that Madam Built," *Essence*, June 1983, 85–86.
3 Leroy Davis, "Madam C. J. Walker: A Woman of Her Time?," in *The African Experience in Community Development: The Continuing Struggle in Africa and the Americas (Volume II)*, Edward W. Crosby, Leroy Davis, and Anne Adams Graves, editors (Needham Heights, Mass.: Ginn Press, 1980), 37–60.
4 Quoted in *The Indiana Junior Historian*, February 1992, 2.
5 Nancy F. Cott, "What's in a Name? The Limits of 'Social Feminism': Or, Expanding the Vocabulary of Women's History," *Journal of American History* 76 (December 1989): 827; Elsa Barkley Brown, "Womanist Consciousness: Maggie Lena Walker and the Independent Order of Saint Luke," *Signs* 14 (Spring 1989): 610–633.
6 *The Indiana Junior Historian*, March 1992, 1.

7 Evelyn Brooks Higginbotham, *Righteous Discontent: The Women's Movement in the Black Baptist Church, 1880–1920* (Cambridge, Mass.: Harvard University Press, 1993) 8–9.
8 Madam C. J. Walker Collection, Box 26, F 1, Indiana Historical Society.
9 Charles Latham Jr., "Madam C. J. Walker and Company" *Traces*, Vol. 1, no. 3 (summer 1989): 28–36.

Paul Robeson: Truth and Punishment

1 In his biography Robeson himself notes, "The main charge against me has centered upon my remarks at the World Peace Conference held in Paris in 1949, and what I said on that occasion has been distorted and misquoted in such a way as to impugn my character as a loyal American citizen." Paul Robeson, *Here I Stand* (Boston: Beacon Press, 1958), 41. Marie Seton, *Paul Robeson* (London: Dennis Dobson, 1958), 196. Edwin P. Hoyt, *Paul Robeson: The American Othello* (New York: World Publishing Co., 1967), 173. See the impressive biography by Martin Bauml Duberman, *Robeson* (New York: Alfred A. Knopf, 1988); and Dorothy Butler Gilliam, *Paul Robeson, All-American* (Washington, D.C.: The New Republic Book Co., 1976).
2 Lamont Yeakey, "Robeson's Contribution to Domestic Politics and International Affairs," paper delivered at the National Conference on Paul Robeson, Purdue University, April 22, 1976.
3 Hope R. Stevens, "Paul Robeson-Democracy's Most Powerful Voice," *Freedomways*, Vol. 5, no. 3 (1965): 366.
4 Sterling Stuckey, "Cultural Philosophy of Paul Robeson," paper delivered at the National Conference on Paul Robeson, 1976. For further information on his cultural philosophy and talents as a linguist, see Sterling Stuckey, "The Cultural Philosophy of Paul Robeson," *Freedomways*, Vol. 11, no. 1 (1971): 78–90.
5 Richard M. Dalfiume, "The 'Forgotten Years' of the Negro Revolution," *Journal of American History* 55 (June 1968): 90–106.

6 Robeson, *Here I Stand*, 83.
7 Dalfiume, "The 'Forgotten Years' of the Negro Revolution," 90–106.
8 Excerpts from *Freedom*, March 1954 in *Freedomways*, Vol. 11, no. 1 (1971): 121. J. H. O'dell, "A Rock in a Weary Lan'": Paul Robeson's Leadership and 'The Movement' in the Decade before Montgomery," Ibid., 34–36.
9 J. H. O'dell, "A Rock," 34–36.
10 Excerpts from address to the National Labor Conference for Negro Rights, Chicago, June 10, 1950 in *Freedomways*, Vol. 11, no. 1 (1971): 121.
11 Excerpts from "Ho Chi Minh is Toussaint L'Ouverture of Indo-China," *Freedom*, March 1954, in *Freedomways*, Vol. 11, no. 1 (1971): 112.
12 Excerpts of a Speech given in 1953, reprinted in *Freedomways*, Vol. 11, no. 1 (1971): 119.
13 Jack Anderson, "U.S. Support Latin Dictators," Lafayette *Journal and Courier*, October 11, 1976.
14 Excerpts from address to National Labor Conference for Negro Rights. Marie Seton, *Paul Robeson*, 161–170.
15 Seton, *Paul Robeson*, 169–170, taken from speech delivered at a Madison Square Garden Rally in New York sponsored by the Council on African Affairs, June 6, 1946. Henry A. Kissinger, in a speech before the Opportunities Industrialization Centers, "The Challenges of Africa," (Philadelphia, August 31, 1976), said, "Nearly a third of the world's some 150 sovereign nations are on the continent of Africa. Africa's independence has transformed the character and scope of international institutions; their importance to the world economy is growing; the interdependence of Africa and the industrialized world is obvious." But he concluded his remarks with prophetic words: "We are determined to avoid unnecessary arms races. But when friendly and moderate nations like Kenya or Zaire make modest and responsible requests for assistance to protect themselves against belligerent neighbors possessing substantial quantities of modern Soviet weapons, we owe them our serious considerations." Robeson, *Here I Stand*, 87.
16 Quoted in Robeson, *Here I Stand*, 87.
17 Virginia Hamilton, *Paul Robeson: The Life and Times of a Free Black Man* (New York: Harper and Row, 1971), 164; Hoyt, *Paul Robeson*, 205; Seton, *Paul Robeson*, 230.
18 Robeson, *Here I Stand*, 68.
19 Ibid., 66–67.
20 Hoyt, *Paul Robeson*, 205–212; Hamilton, *Paul Robeson*, 164.
21 Hoyt, *Paul Robeson*, 212.
22 *Rockwell Kent v. John Foster Dulles, Secretary of State*, 357 U.S. 116, 2 L ed. 1204.
23 Hamilton, *Paul Robeson*, 181.

Divine Obsessions: History and Culture of Miles Davis

1 Nat Hentoff, *Miles Davis: The Columbia Years, 1955–1985*, four compact discs (New York: CBS Records, 1988).
2 Lawrence Levine, *Black Culture, Black Consciousness: Afro-American Folk Thought from Slavery to Freedom* (New York: Oxford University Press, 1977), 400-401.
3 Miles Davis, *Miles: The Autobiography* (New York: Simon & Schuster, 1989), 375.
4 Ibid., 306.

An Angle of Vision: Black Women and the Constitution, 1787–1987

1 Darlene Clark Hine, "Lifting the Veil, Shattering the Silence: Black Women's History in Slavery and Freedom," in Hine, *The State of Afro-American History*, 223–249.
2 William W. Freehling, "The Founding Fathers and Slavery," *The American Historical Review* 77 (February 1972): 81–93; Robert McColley, *Slavery and Jeffersonian Virginia* (Urbana: University of Illinois Press, 1964); Jordan, *White Over Black;* John Hope Franklin, *From Slavery to Freedom: A History of Negro Americans*, 4th edition (New York: Knopf, 1974), 89, 100; Mary Frances

Berry and John W. Blassingame, *Long Memory: The Black Experience in America* (New York: Oxford University Press, 1982). Berry and Blassingame comment that, "As long as black people labored in chains, the Declaration of Independence and Constitution symbolized the American's ability to lie to himself" (15).
3 Mary McLeod Bethune, "A Century of Progress of Negro Women," address delivered at the Chicago Women's Federation, June 30, 1933, quoted in Gerda Lerner, ed., *Black Women in America: A Documentary History* (New York: Vintage Books, 1973), 50. Also see Fannie Barrier Williams, "Club Movement Among Colored Women of America," in J. E. MacBrady, ed., *A New Negro for a New Century* (Chicago: American Publishing House, 1900), 381–383, 427–428.
4 For a thorough discussion of the debilitating proscriptions endured by free blacks, see Ira Berlin, *Slaves Without Masters: The Free Negro in the Antebellum South* (New York: Random House, 1974); Leon Litwack, *North of Slavery: The Negro in the Free States, 1790–1860* (Chicago: University of Chicago Press, 1961), 70–72; Jacqueline Jones, *Labor of Love, Labor of Sorrow: Black Women, Work, and the Family from Slavery to Freedom* (New York: Basic Books, 1985). Also see A. Leon Higginbotham, Jr., *In the Matter of Color: Race and the American Legal Process: The Colonial Period* (New York: Oxford University Press, 1978). Higginbotham asserts that "perhaps if the framers of 1776 had not declared the concept of equality in such universal terms it may have been more difficult to challenge and partially eradicate the pervasive barriers of discrimination on race and sex" (389); Leon F. Litwack, "Trouble in Mind: The Bicentennial and the Afro-American Experience," *The Journal of American History* 74 (September 1987): 315–337.
5 Arthur Zilversmit, "Quok Walker, Mumbet, and the Abolition of Slavery in Massachusetts," *The William and Mary Quarterly* 25 (October 1968): 614; Elaine MacEacheren, "Emancipation of Slavery in Massachusetts, 1770–1790," *Journal of Negro History* 55 (October 1970): 289–360; Sidney Kaplan, *The Black Presence in the Era of the American Revolution, 1770–1800* (New York: New York Graphic Society, 1973), 216; Giddings, *When and Where I Enter*, 40.
6 Maria W. Stewart, *Meditations from the Pen of Mrs. Maria W. Stewart, Negro* (Washington, D.C., 1879), reprinted in Bert James Loewenberg and Ruth Bogin, eds., *Black Women in Nineteenth-Century American Life: Their Words, Their Thoughts, Their Feelings* (University Park: Pennsylvania State University Press, 1976), 192. For an exhaustive treatment of Stewart's life and writings, see Marilyn Richardson, ed., *We Claim our Rights: The Essays and Speeches of Maria W. Stewart, America's First Black Woman Political Writer* (Bloomington: Indiana University Press, 1987); Stewart, "What if I am a Woman," quoted in Lerner, *Black Women in White America*, 562–566.
7 Stewart, "Let Us make a Mighty Effort and Rise," in Loewenberg and Bogin, *Black Women in Nineteenth Century America*, 190–191.
8 Ibid.
9 Don E. Fehrenbacker, *The Dred Scott Case: Its Significance in American Law and Politics* (New York: Oxford University Press, 1978); Walter Ehrlich, *They Have No Rights: Dred Scott's Struggle for Freedom* (Westport, Conn.: Greenwood Publishers, 1979); William M. Wiecek, "Slavery and Abolition before the United States Supreme Court, 1820–1860," *The Journal of American History* 65 (June 1978): 34–49. Wiecek observes that "Taney's grudging concession of the power of the states to make citizens of whom they please was offset by his denial that blacks might thereby become 'citizens' entitled to the privileges and immunities specified in Article IV section 2 of the Constitution and by his insistence that, upon migration, these black free-state citizens would lose their status and acquire whatever status the state they removed to might choose to confer on them" (55).

10 Dorothy Sterling, ed., *We Are Your Sisters: Black Women in the Nineteenth Century* (New York: W. W. Norton, 1984), 175.

11 "Miss Remond's First Lecture in Dublin," *Anti-slavery Advocate* 2 (April 1859), 221, reprinted in Loewenberg and Bogin, *Black Women in Nineteenth-Century American Life*, 233.

12 Ruth Bogin, "Sara Parker Remond: Black Abolitionist from Salem," *Essex Institute Historical Collections* 100 (April 1974): 120–150; Dorothy Porter, "Sarah Parker Remond, Abolitionist and Physician," *Journal of Negro History* 20 (July 1935): 187–193.

13 Willie Lee Rose, *A Documentary History of Slavery in North America* (New York: Oxford University Press, 1976), 220–222; Peter H. Wood, *Black Majority: Negroes in Colonial South Carolina from 1670 through the Stono Rebellion* (New York: Knopf, 1974), 292.

14 Quoted in Lerner, *Black Women in White America*, 35.

15 White, *Ar'n't I a Woman?*, 76. For a slightly different interpretation of female slave resistance, see Darlene Clark Hine and Kate Wittenstein, "Female Slave Resistance: The Economics of Sex," in Filomina Chioma Steady, ed., *The Black Woman Cross-Culturally*, (Cambridge, Mass.: Schenkman Publishing Company, 1981), 189–300.

16 Quoted in Lerner, *Black Women in White America*, 567.

17 Ibid., 571.

18 Ibid., 569.

19 Ibid.

20 Darlene Clark Hine, *Black Victory: The Rise and Fall of the White Primary in Texas* (Millwood, N.Y.: Kraus Thomson, 1979), 5–6.

21 Litwack, "Trouble in Mind," 316.

22 Alfreda M. Duster, editor, *Ida B. Wells, Crusade for Justice: The Autobiography of Ida B. Wells* (Chicago: University of Chicago Press, 1970), 19–20; Thomas C. Holt, "The Lonely Warrior: Ida B. Wells-Barnett and the Struggle for Black Leadership," in John Hope Franklin and August Meier, eds., *Black Leaders of the Twentieth Century* (Urbana: University of Illinois Press, 1982), 29–61. Holt aptly describes Wells-Barnett, "She was born a slave during the Civil War in 1862, reared in a politically active family during Reconstruction, and educated at schools run by northern missionaries; she came of age as the Jim Crow system evolved. She was a founder of the National Association for the Advancement of Colored People, a friend of Marcus Garvey, a social worker in Chicago's ghetto during the first wave of the great northern migration, and an activist in the initial political awakening of black northerners in the first quarter of the twentieth century. But she is best known as the champion of the turn-of-the-century anti-lynching crusade" (40).

23 Charlotte Hawkins Brown to F. P. Hobgood Jr., October 19, 1921, in Lerner, *Black Women in White America*, 376; Sadie Iola Daniel, "Charlotte Hawkins Brown," in *Women Builders*, (Washington, D.C.: The Associated Publishers, 1969), 137–167.

24 Quoted in Lerner, *Black Women in White America*, 382; Cynthia Neverdon-Morton, "The Black Woman's Struggle for Equality in the South, 1895–1925," in Sharon Harley and Rosalyn Terborg-Penn, *The Afro-American Woman: Struggles and Images* (Port Washington, N.Y.: Kennikat Press, 1978), 43–55.

25 Frances E. W. Harper, *Sketches of Southern Life* (Philadelphia: Ferguson Brothers, 1983), in Lerner, *Black Women in White America*, 249.

26 Barbara Hilkert Andolsen, *"Daughters of Jefferson, Daughters of Bootblacks": Racism and American Feminism* (Macon, Ga.: Mercer University Press, 1986), 20; Rosalyn Terborg-Penn, "Discrimination Against Afro-American Women in the Woman's Movement, 1830–1920," in Terborg-Penn and Harley, *The Afro-American Woman*, 17–27.

27 Carrie W. Clifford, "Votes for Children," *The Crisis*, August 1915, 185, quoted in Andolsen, *Daughters of Jefferson*, 62.

28 Evelyn Brooks Barnett, "Nannie Burroughs and the Education of Black Women," in Terborg-Penn and Harley,

The Afro-American Woman, 97–108; Daniel, "Nannie Helen Burroughs," *Women Builders*, 111–136; Nannie H. Burroughs, "Black Women and Reform," *The Crisis* 10, August 1915, 187; Rosalyn Terborg-Penn, "Woman Suffrage: 'First Because We Are Women and Second Because We Are Colored Women,'" *Truth: Newsletter of the Association of Black Women Historians*, April 1985, 9.

29 Steven F. Lawson, *Black Ballots: Voting Rights in the South, 1944–1969* (New York: Columbia University Press, 1976), 82.

30 Hine, "Lifting the Veil, Shattering the Silence," 244. In 1935 Bethune was appointed by President Roosevelt to the National Advisory Committee of the National Youth Administration.

31 Giddings, *When and Where I Enter*, 202; Susan M. Hartman, "Women's Organizations During World War II: The Interaction of Class, Race, and Feminism," *Woman's Being, Woman's Place: Female Identity and Vocation in American History* (Boston: G. K. Hall, 1979), 318.

32 Sara Evans, *Personal Politics: The Roots of Women's Liberation in the Civil Rights Movement and the New Left* (New York: Vintage Books, 1979). Aldon D. Morris, *The Origins of the Civil Rights Movement* (New York: Free Press, 1985) contains an excellent discussion of the role black women in initiating and sustaining grass-roots momentum in the black rights quest.

33 Hine, "Lifting the Veil, Shattering the Silence," 247; Giddings, *When and Where I Enter*, 287–294; Morris, *The Origins of the Civil Rights Movement*, 102–113.

Black Lawyers and the Twentieth-Century Struggle for Constitutional Change

1 Charles V. Hamilton quoted in Charles W. Eagles, *The Civil Rights Movement in America* (Jackson: University Press of Mississippi, 1986), 97.

2 There are noteworthy exceptions. For excellent studies of two black lawyers, see Gilbert Ware, *William Hastie: Grace Under Pressure* (New York: Oxford University Press, 1984); Genna Rae McNeil, *Groundwork: Charles Hamilton Houston and the Struggle for Civil Rights*. (Philadelphia: University of Pennsylvania Press, 1983). Also see, for discussion of local black lawyers, Robert L. Gill, "The Role of Five Negro Lawyers in the Civil Rights Struggle," *Quarterly Review of Higher Education Among Negroes* 31 (July 1963): 31–58; Irvin C. Mollison, "Negro Lawyers in Mississippi," *The Journal of Negro History* 25 (January 1930): 38–71; "Commentary: Negro Members of the Alabama Bar," *Alabama Law Review* 21 (1969): 306–331; "Virginia Section: The Negro Lawyer in Virginia: A Survey," *Virginia Law Review* 51 (1965): 521–545.

3 Kenneth S. Tollett, "Black Lawyers, Their Education, and the Black Community," *Howard Law Journal* 17 (1972): 332–333, 336, 347.

4 Philip B. Kurland, "Foreword: Equal in Origin and Equal in Title to the Legislative and Executive Branches of the Government," *Harvard Law Review* 78 (1964): 143.

5 Walter J. Leonard, "The Development of the Black Bar," *American Academy of Political and Social Science* (1973): 141.

6 J. Skelly Wright, *Amistad Symposium on Southern Civil Rights Litigation Records for the 1960s* (New Orleans: Dillard University, The Amistad Research Center, 1978), 9; Derrick A. Bell, Jr., *Race, Racism and American Law* (Boston, Little, Brown & Co., 1980), 302. Bell reminds us that many of the black protest cases were actually lost in the courts.

7 Donald L. Hallowell, "The Black Lawyer and the Human and Civil Rights Struggle," *Harvard Law School Bulletin* 22 (February, 1971): 18–21. Members of the earlier generation of black lawyers were not infrequently assaulted. On February 27, 1942, Leon A. Ransom was attacked by a former deputy sheriff in the hall of the Davidson County Courthouse in Nashville, Tennessee. *The Crisis* reported, "The attack came when Ransom walked out into the hall from the courtroom where he was sitting with Z. Alexander Looby, local NAACP attorney, on a case involving the exclusion of Negroes from a jury. . . . When the scuffle began, Negroes who would have aided Ransom were held back by a former constable (white) named Hill, who drew his gun and shouted: 'We are going to teach these northern Negroes not to come down here raising fancy court questions'" (137).

8 Burke Marshall, "The Protest Movement and the Law," *Virginia Law Review* 51 (1965): 795; Constance Baker Motley, "The Role of Law in Effecting Social Change," *The Crisis* 85 (January 1978): 24–28.

9 Maynard H. Jackson, "The Black American and the Legal Profession: A Study in Commitment," *Journal of Public Law* 20 (1971): 379.

10 Robert L. Carter, "The Black Lawyer," *The Humanist*, September/October 1969, 12.

11 Robert C. Weaver, "William Henry Hastie, 1904–1976," *The Crisis* 83 (October 1976): 267–270; Ware, *Hastie*, 142–143.

12 Carter, "The Black Lawyer," 12.

13 Leonard, "Development of the Black Bar," 140; Tollett, "Black Lawyers, Their Education, and the Black Community," 326–357; Marcia Graham Synnott, *The Half-Opened Door: Discrimination and Admissions at Harvard, Yale, and Princeton, 1900–1970* (Westport, Conn.: Greenwood Press, 1979), 47–52, 134, 174–176, 218–220; Ernest Gellhorn, "The Law Schools and the Negro," *Duke University Law Review* (1968): 1069–1097.

14 Chicago philanthropist Julius Rosenwald contributed $2500 to the campaign on the stipulation that the school raise an additional $500 from its alumni or friends. Charles Houston, A Personal Message to Friends, April 12, 1926, Julius Rosenwald Papers, Box XIX, Folder 6, University of Chicago Library, Chicago. Houston to Rosenwald, April 28, 1926; see also Houston to Judge Julian W. Mack, January 8, 1926, Rosenwald Papers, Box 19, Folder 6. Houston outlined the campaign and described what he hoped to obtain from various groups. "We are also working on a regional organization of Negro lawyers into Bar Associations, and hope to draw support for the library from that. Through such an organization or organizations we would tap most of the alumni of the law school. I want the students and alumni in particular, and the Negro business in general, to feel an ever increasing responsibility for our legal education, and to develop the habit of systematic contributions upon which we can rely for its support."

15 Ibid.

16 Genna Rae McNeil, "To Meet the Group Needs: The Transformation of Howard University School of Law, 1920–1935," in *New Perspectives in Black Educational History*, Vincent P. Franklin and James D. Anderson, editors (Boston: G. K. Hall, 1979), 156–157.

17 Charles H. Houston, Report, Status of Negro Lawyers, May 3, 1928, 10, Laura Spelman Rockefeller Memorial Fund (Hereafter LSRMF), Box 101, Folder 1018, Rockefeller Archive and Research Center, North Tarrytown, New York.

18 Ibid., 11–12.

19 William H. Hastie, "Charles Hamilton Houston, 1895–1950," *The Negro History Bulletin* 13 (June 1950): 207–208. Leonard, "Development of the Black Bar," 134–143.

20 Hastie, "Charles Hamilton Houston, 1895–1950," 208.

21 Ibid., 210.

22 Ibid., 213.

23 Charles H. Houston, "Tentative Statement Concerning Policy of NAACP in Its Program of Attack on Educational Discrimination," July 12, 1935, NAACP Administration Files, C-197, Library of Congress, Washington, D.C.

24 Houston to J. Reuben Sheeler, October 18, 1935, NAACP Legal Files, D-96.

25 Jerold Auerbach, *Unequal Justice: Lawyers and Social Change in Modern*

America (New York: Oxford University Press, 1976), 212–216.

26 Hine, *Black Victory*, 188. When Leon Ransom died in 1954, Arthur E. Spingarn observed, "While many talented lawyers became too busy with their private affairs to devote much time to public service, Dr. Ransom over the years gave brilliant and devoted attention to legal cases in the civil rights field, often with no more reward than his bare expenses and the satisfaction of having established a new frontier in civil rights law for the benefit of his people." Thurgood Marshall likewise declared, "Negro Americans, whether they know it or not, owe a great debt of gratitude to Andy Ransom and men like him who battled in the courts down a span of years to bring us to the place we now occupy in the enjoyment of our constitutional rights as citizens. In helping to build up the NAACP legal program step by step, in the skill which he gave to individual cases and to the planning of strategy, Dr. Ransom left a legacy to the whole population." *The Crisis* 59 (October 1954): 494.

27 August Meier and Elliott Rudwick, "Attorneys Black and White: A Case Study of Race Relations Within the NAACP," in *Along the Color Line: Explorations in the Black Experience*, August Meier and Elliott Rudwick, editors (Urbana: University of Illinois Press, 1976), 154.

28 Hine, *Black Victory*, 189–192.

29 Houston to Leon Ransom, Z. Alexander Looby, and Carl Cowan; to Sidney Redmond and to Thurgood Marshall, September 17, 1936; NAACP Papers Box D-96, Library of Congress, Washington, D.C.

30 News Release concerning University of Tennessee Case, 1937. Tennessee had no scholarship provisions for Negro students, so that it made no provisions for pharmaceutical instruction for Negroes either at an institution within the state or by scholarship outside the state. Memorandum from Charles Houston to Roy Wilkins, April 22, 1937, NAACP Papers, Legal Files, Box D-97. Also see A Statement Regarding the Mandamus Suit by a Negro Citizen for Admission to the School of Pharmacy of the University of Tennessee, March 21, 1937, by Z. Alexander Looby, Leon Ransom, and Charles Houston, NAACP Legal Files, D-97.

31 Office Memorandum on (William) Redmond Case by Leon A. Ransom, December 16, 1936, NAACP Legal Files, D-96; Mark V. Tushnet, *The NAACP's Legal Strategy Against Segregated Education, 1925–1950* (Chapel Hill: University of North Carolina Press, 1987), 55.

32 Memorandum of Leon Ranson on the Redmond Case, December 16, 1936, NAACP Legal Files, D-97.

33 Ibid.

34 Ibid.

35 Ibid.

36 Houston to Sidney R. Redmond, July 15, 1935, NAACP Legal Files, D-94.

37 Houston to Redmond, October 4, 1935, NAACP Legal Files, D-94.

38 Houston to Redmond, December 26, 1935, NAACP Legal Files, D-94.

39 William B. Hixson Jr., *Moorfield Story and the Abolitionist Tradition* (New York: Oxford University Press, 1972), 118–119.

40 Arnold Rose, *The Negro in America* (New York: Harper and Row, 1944), 112.

41 Lester C. Lamon, *Black Tennesseans, 1900–1930* (Knoxville: University of Tennessee Press, 1977), 9–10.

42 McNeil, *Groundwork*, 6–7.

43 Meier and Rudwick, "Attorneys Black and White," 145.

44 Ibid., 171; *Houston Informer and Texas Freeman*, July 16, 1932.

45 Fitzhugh L. Styles, *Negroes and the Law* (Boston: Christopher Publishing House, 1937), ix.; Smith, "The Black Bar Association," 660.

46 McNeil, "To Meet the Group Needs," 157.

47 Ibid., 33; Veteran Alabama black attorney Arthur D. Shores boasted that "No greater opportunity is offered anywhere in the country to raise the level of the Negro through the efforts of the Negro lawyer and be amply compensated, than here in the Deep South." "The Negro at the Bar, The South," *National Bar Journal* 4 (1944): 271.

48 Tushnet, *The NAACP's Legal Strategy*, 43–44; Charles H. Houston, "Don't Shout Too Soon," *The Crisis* 43 (March 1936): 79, 91. Also see Richard Kluger, *Simple Justice The History of Brown v. Board of Education and Black America's Struggle for Equality* (New York: Alfred A. Knopf, 1976), 346–366.

49 J. Clay Smith, "The Black Bar Association and Civil Rights," *Creighton Law Review* 15 (1962): 651–675.

50 Raymond Pace Alexander, "Foreword-Editorial: The National Bar Association—Its Aims and Purposes," *National Bar Journal* 1 (July 1941): 1–2.

51 Auerbach, *Unequal Justice*, 212.

52 Tushnet, *The NAACP's Legal Strategy*, 102.

53 The cases included, *Moore v. Dempsey*, 261 U.S. 86 (Feb. 19, 1923), the Elaine, Arkansas riot case; *Harmon v. Taylor*, 273 U.S. (1926), New Orleans residential segregation case; the two white primary cases, *Nixon v. Herndon*, 273 U.S. 536 (March 7, 1927), *Nixon v. Condon*, 286 U.S. 73 (May 2, 1932); *City of Richmond v. Dean*, 281 U.S. 704 (1930), a residential segregation case; *Brown, Ellington and Shields v. State of Mississippi*, 297 U.S. 278 (February 17, 1936), right to a fair trial free from torture to extract confessions; *Joe Hale v. Commonwealth of Kentucky*, 303 U.S. 613 (April 11, 1938), right of blacks to serve on juries. *New Negro Alliance v. Sanitary Grocery Company*, Vol. 82, No. 13 L. Ed. Adv. Opinion Supreme Ct. involved right of blacks to picket a store in their neighborhood to force employment of blacks. The picketing was done by black men and women members of the New Negro Alliance, a civic association. *Gaines v. University of Missouri* (December 18, 1938). In this momentous decision the Court ruled "By the operation of the laws of Missouri a privilege has been created for white law students which is denied to Negroes by reason of their race. The white resident is afforded legal education within the State; the Negro resident having the same qualifications is refused it there and must go outside the State to obtain it. That is a denial of the equality of legal right to the enjoyment of the privilege which the State has set up and the provision for the payment of tuition fees in another State does not remove the discrimination. *Missouri ex rel. Gaines v Canada*, 305 U.S 337 (1938), Missouri accordingly was found guilty of having violated the equal protection of the laws clause of the Fourteenth Amendment. This case was argued by Sidney Redmond who in 1941 was the president of the NBA. Tushnet, *The NAACP's Legal Strategy*, 70–77. In *Chambers v. Florida*, 309 U.S. 227 (Feb. 12, 1940), black lawyers argued against torture used to extract confessions case. Two identical ones were also argued, *Canty v. Alabama*, 309 U.S. 629 (March 11, 1940), and *White v. Texas*, 309 U.S. 631 (March 25, 1940). A series of cases involving the equalization of teachers' salaries included *School Board of the City of Norfolk, Va. v. Alston*, 85 L. Ed. 81, (Oct. 28, 1940). *Hansberry v. Lee*, 85 L. Ed. 11 (November 12, 1940), involved the use of a restrictive covenant. In a case concerning the refusal on the part of interstate carriers to give first-class accommodations to blacks traveling between states, *Congressman Arthur W. Mitchell v. The Illinois Central Railway*, the Court ruled that blacks who purchase first-class tickets may not be denied pullman berths or any of the accommodations which go with first-class tickets while riding interstate. All of these cases are discussed in Raymond Pace Alexander, "The National Bar Association—Its Aims and Purposes," *The National Bar Journal* 1 (1941): 5–14. For a discussion of major civil rights cases between 1954 and 1964, see Robert L. Gill, "The Negro in the Supreme Court, 1954–64," *The Negro History Bulletin* 28 (December 1964): 51–52, 65; 28 (January 1965): 86–88; 28 (February 1965): 117–119.

54 *Missouri ex rel. Gaines v. Canada* 305 U.S. 337 (1938); *Sipuel v. University of Oklahoma* 332 U.S. 631 (1948); *Fisher v.*

Hurst 333 U.S. 147 (1948); *Sweatt v. Painter* 339 U.S. 629 (1950); *Mclaurin v. Oklahoma State Regents* 339 U.S. 637 (1950); *Gray v. University of Tennessee* 342 U.S. 517 (1952). The "infamous" *Brown* was actually five cases: *Brown v. Board of Education of Topeka* 98 F. Supp. 797 D., Kan. 1951; *Briggs v. Elliot* 103 F. Supp. 920 E.D.S.C. 1952 from South Carolina; *Davis v. County School Board of Prince Edward County* 103 F. Supp. 337 (E.D. Va. 1952), Virginia; *Gebhart v. Belton* 33 Del. Ch. 144, 91 A. 2nd 137 (1952) from Delaware. A companion case, *Bolling v. Sharpe* 347 U.S. 397 (1954), was argued for the District of Columbia. See "The Fight for Equal Justice Under Law: Report of the Legal Department," *NAACP Annual Report, 1947*, 20–33; "It is so Ordered: Report of the Legal Department," *NAACP Annual Report, 1954*, 23–40.
55 Tushnet, *The NAACP's Legal Strategy*, 34.

The Intersection of Race, Class, and Gender in the Nursing Profession

1 A. H. Jones, ed., *Images of Nurses: Perspectives from History, Art and Literature* (Philadelphia: University of Pennsylvania, 1988), 178.
2 E. M. Rudwick, "A Brief History of Mercy-Douglass Hospital in Philadelphia," *Journal of Negro Education* 20 (1951): 52.
3 J. Kenney, Memorandum to executive council, February 4, 1909, Booker T. Washington Papers, Library of Congress.
4 J. E. Perry, *Forty Cords of Wood: Memoirs of a Medical Doctor* (Jefferson City, Mo.: Lincoln University Press, 1947), 376, 382.
5 J. Rosenwald to J.M.T. Finney Jr., September 25, 1928, Julius Rosenwald Papers, University of Chicago, Chicago, Illinois.
6 R. Fosdick, W. Rose, and J. H. Dillard, Interoffice Memo on Negro Education, October 6, 1922, General Education Board Papers, Rockefeller Archive Center, Pocantico Hills, North Tarrytown, New York.
7 A. M. Brandt, *No Magic Bullet: A Social History of Venereal Disease in the United States since 1880* (New York: Oxford University Press, 1987), 157–158.

To Heal the Race: African-American Health Care Professionals in Historical Perspective

1 L. H. Owens, *This Species of Property: Slave Life in the Old South* (New York: Oxford University Press, 1976), 31.
2 V. N. Gamble, *The Black Community Hospital: Contemporary Dilemmas in Historical Perspective* (New York: Garland Publishing, 1989).
3 W. White, *A Man Called White: The Autobiography of Walter White* (Bloomington: Indiana University Press, 1948), 135.
4 W. Young Jr., *To Be Equal* (New York: McGraw-Hill, 1964), 190.
5 Hine, *Black Women in White*.
6 E. R. Ferguson, "The Woman's Improvement Club of Indianapolis: Black Women Pioneers in Tuberculosis Work, 1903–1938," *Indiana Magazine of History* 84 (1988):237–261.
7 J. Summerville, *Educating Black Doctors: A History of Meharry Medical College* (University: University of Alabama Press, 1983).
8 C. Neverdon-Morton, *Afro-American Women of the South and the Advancement of the Race, 1895–1925* (Knoxville: University of Tennessee Press, 1989), 161–162.
9 W. M. Cobb, *The Black American in Medicine*, 1981.
10 Ibid.; Brandt, *No Magic Bullet*; Jones, *Bad Blood*.
11 Cobb, *The Black American in Medicine*.
12 A. Flexner, *Medical Education in the United States and Canada* (New York: Carnegie Foundation, 1910), 10; R. W. Logan, *Howard University: The First*

Hundred Years, 1867–1967 (New York: New York University Press, 1967), 164; Hine, *Black Women in White*, 173–192.

13 Hine, *Black Women in White*, 109.

14 Brandt, *No Magic Bullet*, 157–158; Jones, *Bad Blood*.

15 Hine, *Black Women in White*, 25–50.

16 D. H. Williams, "The Need of Hospitals and Training Schools for Colored People of the South," *National Hospital and Sanitarium Record*, 3 (1900): 3–7.

17 A. C. McClennan, Editorial, *Hospital Herald: A Journal Devoted to Hospital Work, Nurse Training, and Domestic and Public Hygiene* 1 (1898): 5.

18 C. E. Rosenberg, *The Care of Strangers: The Rise of America's Hospital System* (New York: Basic Books, 1987).

19 D. K Newman et al., *Protest, Politics, and Prosperity: Black Americans and White Institutions, 1940–75* (New York: Pantheon Books, 1978), 196.

20 Hine, *Black Women in White*, 3–25.

21 Newman, *Protest, Politics, and Prosperity*, 188.

Acknowledgments

I am empowered and sustained by the generosity and encouragement of my colleagues, friends, and family. The numerous debts incurred during the process of making this book cannot possibly be repaid, only acknowledged and appreciated. A warm and heartfelt thank-you is owed Joe W. Trotter of Carnegie Mellon University for taking the time away from his own demanding teaching and publishing schedule to read the entire manuscript and to prepare a preface that is in itself worth the price of this book. I am grateful to Ralph Carlson and Carlson Publishing, and to Ann Harakawa for the exquisite attention paid to the design and production of this book. I deeply value the insightful critiques and helpful comments that William C. Hine of South Carolina State University made on the introduction and virtually every essay. Robert L. Harris Jr. of Cornell University, Barry Gaspar of Duke University, and Gordon Stewart, Harry Reed, and Richard W. Thomas of Michigan State University made astute observations that saved me from egregious errors and strengthened my arguments. While I did not always heed their advice or follow each suggestion, this book is enriched because of their interest, support, and intellectual engagement.

Several individuals provided so much essential assistance that a mere thank-you only underscores my need for greater linguistic virtuosity. My incomparable assistant, Linda Werbish, typed the manuscript. Linda and Peggy Jeffrey, with humor and patience, helped me to stay on course. Several of my graduate students assisted in various important ways. I am eternally grateful to Jacqueline McLeod, Earnestine Jenkins, and LaTrese Adkins, and to undergraduate student Marshanda Smith for their research assistance, critiques of, and enthusiasm for, these essays. Judee Brownlee is the most wonderful neighbor one could ever hope to have. I shall never forget the hot bowls of chili she brought to me and the laughter and the caring conversations we shared in my Union Pier writing hideaway.

No acknowledgment would be complete without special words of thanks to my grandmother Fannie Venerable Thompson, sisters Barbara Ann Clark and Alma Jean Mitchell, and my daughter Robbie Davine. I am humbled by their unwavering support and love. For a friendship spanning three decades I dedicate this volume to Murry N. DePillars, executive vice president, Chicago State University. And although he never lived to see me as a professional black woman, the memory of my uncle, Willie Leon Thompson, and the beautiful music he made with his trumpet makes "peace be still."

Permission Credits

Some of the chapters of this book originally appeared elsewhere. They have been revised for publication here. We gratefully acknowledge permission to republish them. The original publication information is provided below:

"Interview with Darlene Clark Hine" by Roger Adelson, *The Historian*, Vol. 57, no. 2 (Winter 1995): 259–274.

"Ivory-Tower Reflections: A Black Woman in the Academy." A shorter version was first published as "Commentary" in Lois Banner et al., *Careers: The Uneasy Balance*, a report of the Women's Committee of the American Studies Association, 1990, 17–20.

" 'In the Kingdom of Culture': Black Women and the Intersection of Race, Gender, and Class in Black History" from Gerald Early, ed., *Lure and Loathing: Essays on Race, Identity, and the Ambivalence of Assimilation* (New York: Penguin Books, 1993), 337–351.

"Quilts and African-American Women's Cultural History" from Marsha MacDowell, ed., *African-American Quilt Making Traditions in Michigan* (East Lansing: Michigan State University Press, 1996).

"Culture, Consciousness, and Community: The Making of an African-American Women's History," The Lawrence F. Brewster Lecture in History, XIII (Greenville, N.C.: East Carolina University, 1994).

"The Making of *Black Women in America: An Historical Encyclopedia*," from Linda K. Kerber, Alice Kessler-Harris, and Kathryn

Kish Sklar, eds., *U.S. History as Women's History: New Feminist Essays* (Chapel Hill: University of North Carolina Press, 1995), 335–347.

"For Pleasure, Profit, and Power: The Sexual Exploitation of Black Women, or Anita Hill and Clarence Thomas in Historical Perspective," from Geneva Smitherman, ed., *African American Women Speak Out on Anita Hill–Clarence Thomas* (Detroit: Wayne State University Press, 1995).

"An Angle of Vision: Black Women and the Constitution, 1787–1987," *OAH Magazine of History* Vol. 3, no. 1 (1988): 7–13.

"Black Lawyers and the Twentieth-Century Struggle for Constitutional Change" from John Hope Franklin and Genna Rae McNeil, eds., *African Americans and the Living Constitution* (Washington, D.C.: Smithsonian Institution Press, 1995), 33–55.

"The Intersection of Race, Class, and Gender in the Nursing Profession," from Darwin H. Stapleton and Cathryne A. Welch, eds., *Critical Issues in American Nursing in the Twentieth Century: Perspectives and Case Studies,* Proceedings of a conference held May 20–21, 1993, at the Rockefeller Archive Center, North Tarrytown, New York.

INDEX

Adelson, Roger
 interview with Darlene Clark Hine, xxxv–lii
Adjei, Ako
 quoted, 110–111
Afric-America Female Intelligence Society
 and Maria Stewart, 133
African-American Quilt Making Traditions in Michigan, 49
"The Afro-American Tradition in Decorative Arts"
 exhibition at Cleveland Museum of Art, 50
The Afro-American Woman: Struggles and Images (Terborg-Penn and Harley, eds.), 48
Aldridge, Delores
 Black Women in America: An Historical Encyclopedia, 78
Alexander, Margaret Walker
 quoted, 7
Alexander, Raymond Pace
 collaboration with Charles H. Houston, 156
 and NAACP National Legal Committee, 157
 quoted, 166–167
Ali, Muhammad, 120
Alligood, Clarence
 killed by Joan Little, 84
American Bar Association, xxii, 178
 expulsion of William H. Lewis, 162
 racial policies of, 162–163
 refuses blacks membership, 156
American Historical Association, xxii
 conference on black history, 20
American Medical Association, xxii, 178, 190
American Nurses' Association (ANA), xxii, 25, 174, 178, 179, 190
Anderson, Jack
 quoted, 109–110
Anderson, James D., 28
Andrews, William
 and NAACP National Legal Committee, 157
Armed Forces Nurse Corps, xlv
Armstrong, Louis, 121
Ar'n't I A Woman?: Female Slaves in the Plantation South (White), 35
Asante, Kariamu Welsh
 and *Black Women in America: An Historical Encyclopedia*, 74
Association for the Study of Afro-American Life and History, 15, 27, 76–77
Association for the Study of Negro Life and History, xxii
Association of Black Women Historians, 24, 27
 and *Black Women in America: An Historical Encyclopedia*, 77

Atlanta Cotton States and International Exposition
 Booker T. Washington's speech there, 100
The Autobiography of Malcolm X, xl

Baker, Ella, 55, 144
Baldwin, James, xxx, 120
 quoted on blacks and World War II, 107
Banks, Anna De Costa, 76
 biography of, 25
 founder of Charleston Hospital and Nurse Training School, 59
Baraka, Amiri
 The Dutchman and *The Slave*, xli
Barnes, Linda, xxx
Barrett, Janie Porter, 55
Barry, Marion, 123
Bass, Charlotta A.
 vice-presidential candidacy of, 144
Bass, Jack
 The Orangeburg Massacre quoted, 3–4
Bates, Daisy, 64, 144
Beck, William, 183–184
The Bell Curve: Intelligence and Class Structure in American Life
 Carl Degler's review of, xix
Bennett, Lerone
 lecturing at Roosevelt University, xli
Berkshire Conference of Women Historians, 28
Berlin, Ira, 8
Berry, Mary Frances, 13, 28
 and *Black Women in America: An Historical Encyclopedia*, 74
Berthrong, Donald J., xliii, 29
Bethune, Mary McLeod, 57
 as black icon, xxiii
 and Daytona Normal and Industrial Institute for Negro Girls, 62
 and founding of National Council of Negro Women, 143
Bidelman, Patrick
 and Black Women in the Middle West Project, 19, 67, 95
 co-editor of *Black Women in the Middle West: A Comprehensive Research Guide, Illinois and Indiana*, xliv
Birth of the Cool (Miles Davis), 116
Bitches Brew (Miles Davis), 123
Black Culture and Black Consciousness: Afro-American Folk Thought from Slavery to Freedom (Levine), 49
Black Milwaukee: The Making of an Industrial Proletariat, 1915–45 (Trotter), viii
Black Victory: The Rise and Fall of the White Primary in Texas (Hine), xxvi, 6
 publication of, xliii

Black Women in America: An Historical Encyclopedia (Hine, Brown, Terborg-Penn), xxxi
and black women's history, 54–55
history, background, and development of, 65–80
as validating black women's history, 48–49
Black Women in the Middle West: A Comprehensive Research Guide, Illinois and Indiana (Hine and Bidelman, eds.), xliv
Black Women in the Middle West Project, xliv, 15
history of, 66–67
and Madam C.J.Walker, 95
Black Women in White: Racial Conflict and Cooperation in the Nursing Profession, 1890–1950 (Hine), xliv–xlv, 23–26, 170
Black Women in White America: A Documentary History (Lerner), xxvii, 48, 69
Blassingame, John, 8
Bontemps, Arna
co-editor of *Forever Free: Art by African American Women, 1862–1980*, 51–52
Born to Rebel (Mays), xx
Bracey, John
quoted, 7
Brandon, Betty, 28
Brandt, Allan M.
on Tuskegee syphilis study, 178, 188
Broussard, Albert S.
and *Black Women in America: An Historical Encyclopedia*, 76
Brown, Cecil, xxx
Brown, Charlotte Hawkins, 61
biography of, 62–63
The Correct Thing to Do, to Say, and to Wear, 63
railroad suit of, 140
Brown, Elsa Barkley, 28, 55
and *Black Women in America: An Historical Encyclopedia*, xxxi, 72–75, 77
quoted, 71, 101
Brown v. Board of Education, 120, 156
Brown-Guillory, Elizabeth
and *Black Women in America: An Historical Encyclopedia*, 74
Buchanan, Elwood
and Miles Davis, 116
Bunche, Ralph, xxiv
Bundles, Alelia Perry
biography of Madam C.J. Walker, 98
Burke, James Lee, xxx
Burkett, Randall K.
and *Black Women in America: An Historical Encyclopedia*, 78
Burroughs, Nannie Helen
quoted on black woman suffrage, 142
Bus Ride to Justice (Gray), xxvi
Butler, Octavia, xxx
Byrd, Rudolph, xxvii

Canny, Nicholas, xxvi
Carlson, Ralph, vii, 66, 67
and *Black Women in America: An Historical Encyclopedia*, 68–69, 72, 78–79
and Darlene Clark Hine publications, 21
publishing program of, xxxi
Carlson Publishing, Inc.
and Darlene Clark Hine, xxxi
Carnegie, Andrew, 100
Carnegie, Elizabeth
quoted, 172
Carson, Clayborne, 15
Carter, Robert L., 150
quoted on Howard Law School, 151
Celia (slave), xxv
Celia, A Slave, 35, 84
life of, 86
Charleston Hospital and Nurse Training School, 59
Chelsea House
Milestones in Black American History series, xlviii
Chicago Historical Society, 19
Chisholm, Shirley
presidential campaign of, 144
Clark Levester (father of Darlene Clark Hine), xxxvi–xxxvii
Clark, Barbara (sister of Darlene Clark Hine), vii, xxxi–xxxii
Clark, Lottie Mae (mother of Darlene Clark Hine), xxxvi–xxxvii
Clark, Mark, 124
Clark, Mary Higgins, xxx
Clark, Robbie Davine (daughter of Darlene Clark Hine), xxxix–xl
Clark, Septima Poinsette
and Southern Christian Leadership Conference voter registration, 145
Clarke, John Henrik
lecturing at Roosevelt University, xli
Cleage, Pearl, 125
Cleveland Museum of Art
"The Afro-American Tradition in Decorative Arts" exhibition, 50
Clifford, Carrie W.
quoted, 142
Clinton, Catherine
and *Black Women in America: An Historical Encyclopedia*, 74
Coal, Class and Color: Blacks in Southern West Virginia, 1915–32 (Trotter), ix
Cobb, James
and NAACP National Legal Committee, 157
Cobb, W. Montague
quoted, 185
Collins, Marva, 57
Coltrane, John, 121
Comparative Black History program, Michigan State University, xlviii–xlix, 16–17

Constitution (U.S)
  and black women, 129–145
  Fifteenth Amendment to, 39, 138–139, 150
  Fourteenth Amendment to, 138, 150, 158–159
  and James Madison, 147
  Nineteenth Amendment to and black women, 142
  quoted, 131
  Thirteenth Amendment to, 138
  Twenty-fourth Amendment to, 143
Cooke, Sam, 124
Cornwell, Patricia, xxx
Corporation for Public Broadcasting, 11
The Correct Thing to Do, to Say, and to Wear (Brown), 63
Cott, Nancy
  quoted, 100–101
Cotton States and International Exposition
  Booker T. Washington's speech there, 100
Council of African Affairs
  and Paul Robeson, 110
Cowan, Carl
  Charles H. Houston memo to about University of Tennessee desegregation case, 158
Crawford, Vicki
  co-editor of *Women in the Civil Rights Movement: Trailblazers and Torchbearers*, 55
Crisis
  Charles H. Houston's articles in, 165
Cross, Amanda, xxx

Dabney, Virginius
  quoted, 108
Darkwater: Voices from Within the Veil (Du Bois), quoted, 53
Davis, Cleota (mother of Miles Davis), 116
Davis, Francis
  and Miles Davis, 122
Davis, Gussie
  letter praising her, 59
Davis, Leroy
  quoted on Madam C.J. Walker, 97
Davis, Miles, xxviii–xxix
  article on, 115–125
Davis, Miles Dewey II (father of Miles Davis), 116
Davis, Ossie, 124
Daytona Normal and Industrial Institute for Negro Girls, 62
Degler, Carl
  review of *The Bell Curve: Intelligence and Class Structure in American Life*, xix
Delaney, Samuel, xxx
"Deliverance" (Frances Ellen Watkins poem) quoted, 141
Democratic National Convention (1964)
  and Mississippi Freedom Democratic Party, 144
Democratic National Convention (1968)
  and Darlene Clark Hine, xl

DePillars, Murry N., xl, 122
Dickerson, Earl
  and NAACP National Legal Committee, 157
Dorsey, Carolyn
  and *Black Women in America: An Historical Encyclopedia*, 78
"A Double Standard" (Harper), quoted, 84
Douglass, Frederick
  quoted, 139
Down Beat, 118
Downey, Virtea
  and Black Women in the Middle West Project, 19, 95
  and Indiana black women's history, xliii–xliv, 18
Drake, St. Clare
  lecturing at Roosevelt University, xli
Drew, Charles
  as black icon, xxiii
Dublin Ladies' Anti-Slavery Society
  Sarah Parker Remond lecture to, 135
Du Bois, W.E.B., xxiv, 40, 108, 118, 119, 121
  Darkwater: Voices from Within the Veil, 53
  graduate of Harvard University, xxii
  and *Lure and Loathing: Essays on Race, Identity, and the Ambivalence of Assimilation* (Early), xxviii
  The Souls of Black Folk, 33–34
The Dutchman (Baraka), xli

Eadie, John, 14
Early, Gerald, xxvii–xxviii
  Lure and Loathing: Essays on Race, Identity, and the Ambivalence of Assimilation, xxviii
Early, James
  support for the Black Women in the Middle West Project, 67
Eckstine, Billy
  and Miles Davis, 116
Edelman, Marion Wright, 57
Ellington, Duke, 121
Ellison, Ralph, xxx, 120
  Invisible Man, xli
Evans, Sara
  quoted on black women in the civil rights movement, 144
Evers, Medgar, 119
Eyes on the Prize, li
  Darlene Clark Hine's involvement with, 15

Fanon, Frantz
  Wretched of the Earth, xl
"feminism" and "womanism"
  Darlene Clark Hine on, l–li
Fields, Barbara, 8
Flack, Roberta, 125
Flexner, Abraham
  Report on medical education, 185–186
Fonville-Bontemps, Jacqueline
  co-editor of *Forever Free: Art by African American Women, 1862–1980*, 51–52

Ford Foundation, 7, 15, 17
　grant to Michigan State University for Comparative Black History, xlviii
Forever Free: Art by African American Women, 1862–1980 (Bontemps and Fonville-Bontemps, eds), 51–52
Franklin, John Hope, 15
　graduate of Harvard University, xxii
　lecturing at Roosevelt University, xli
　quoted, 53
Frederick, N.P.
　praised by Charles H. Houston in 1928 report on black bar, 153
Freeman, Elizabeth
　slave who sued for freedom, 132

Gaines, Ernest, xxx
Gandhi, Mahatma, 108
Garnet, Henry Highland, 107
Garrow, David, 15
　and *Black Women in America: An Historical Encyclopedia*, 78
Garvey, Marcus, 40, 104
Gaspar, David Barry
　and Comparative Black History, 17
General Education Board, 177–178, 184
Genovese, Eugene, 8
Gibbs, Phillip L., 4
Gibson, Kenneth, 120
Giddings, Paula, 55
　and *Black Women in America: An Historical Encyclopedia*, 74
　quoted on Madam C.J. Walker, 97
Gordon, Linda
　quoted, 55
Grafton, Sue, xxx
Gray, Fred D., xxviii
　Bus Ride to Justice, xxvi
　and Darlene Clark Hine, xxvi
　and the Montgomery bus boycott, xxi
Green, James Earl, 4
Grisham, John, xxx
Griswold, Erwin N.
　quoted on Charles H. Houston, 154
Grossman, James
　quoted, ix
Grovey v. Townsend, xlii
Gubert, Betty
　and *Black Women in America: An Historical Encyclopedia*, 78
Gutman, Herbert, 8

Haines Normal and Industrial Institute, 61–62
Hamer, Fannie Lou, 55, 64
　and Mississippi Freedom Democratic Party, 144
Hamilton, Charles V.
　lecturing at Roosevelt University, xli
　quoted, 147–148
Hammond, Samuel, Jr., 3
Hammonds, Evelynn
　and MIT Black Women in the Academy Conference, 21

Hampton, Fred, 124
Hampton, Henry, 15
Hampton, Isabel, 174
Hannah, John A., xlix, 13–14
Hannah (John A.) Professorship, Michigan State University, 13–15
Harding, Vincent, 15
Harley, Sharon, 28, 55
　and *Black Women in America: An Historical Encyclopedia*, 74
　editor of *The Afro-American Woman: Struggles and Images*, 48
Harper, Frances Ellen Watkins, 57
　poem "Deliverance" quoted, 141
　poem "A Double Standard" quoted, 84
Harris, Alice Kessler
　as editor of *U.S. History as Women's History*, xxvii
Harrison, Daphne Duval
　and *Black Women in America: An Historical Encyclopedia*, 74
Harvard University
　distinguished black graduates, xxii
Hastie, William Henry, xxvi, 120
　biography of, 151
　as Harvard University Law School graduate, xxii
　collaboration with Charles H. Houston, 156
　quoted on Charles H. Houston, 154
　and NAACP National Legal Committee, 157
Hatch, Orrin
　and Clarence Thomas confirmation hearings, 88–89
Hatcher, Richard, 120
Hawkins, W. Ashbie
　praised by Charles H. Houston in 1928 report on black bar, 153
Hawse, Bessie, 176
　quoted on nursing experience, 60
Hendricks, Wanda, 15
Herd, Shirley
　and Black Women in the Middle West Project, 19, 67, 95
　and Indiana black women's history, xliii–xliv, 17–18, 66
Heslip, Jesse
　quoted, 164
Higginbotham, Evelyn Brooks, 18–19, 28, 55, 101
　and *Black Women in America: An Historical Encyclopedia*, 74
　on metalanguage of race, 98
Hill, Anita
　and Clarence Thomas confirmation hearings, xxv, 83–93, *passim*
Himes, Chester, xxx, 120
Hine, Darlene Clark
　biography of, xxxv
　birth of daughter, xxxix–xl
　Black Victory: The Rise and Fall of the White Primary in Texas, xxvi, xliii, 6

Black Women in the Middle West: A Comprehensive Research Guide, Illinois and Indiana, xliv
Black Women in White: Racial Conflict and Cooperation in the Nursing Profession, 1890–1950, xliv–xlv, 23–26, 170
and Black Women in the Middle West Project, xliv
and Barbara Clark (sister), xxxi–xxxii
and Carlson Publishing, Inc., xxxi, 21
and Comparative Black History program at Michigan State University, xlviii–xlix
and Democratic National Convention (1968), xl
dissertation research, xlii–xliii
early life of, xxxvi–xxxix
and *Eyes on the Prize*, 15
favorite reading, xxx
on "feminism," l–li
and Fred D. Gray, xxvi
and John A. Hannah Professorship (Michigan State University), 13–15
Hine Sight: Black Women and the Re-Construction of American History, xviii, xlv
and Indiana black women's history, xliii–xliv
interview with, xxxv–lii
and Kent State University, xli, 4–5
and August Meier, xli, xlii
Milestones in Black American History series, xlviii
at Purdue University, xliii
and Roosevelt University education, xxxix–xli
and *Sentimental Women Need Not Apply: A History of American Nursing* (film), 15
at South Carolina State College, xli–xlii
The State of Afro-American History: Past, Present, and Future, 20
"Stop the Global Holocaust," xlv
When the Truth is Told: Black Women's Community and Culture in Indiana, 1875–1950, xlliv, 18, 66
on "womanism," l–li
Hine, William C., xlii, 29
Hine Sight: Black Women and the Re-Construction of American History (Hine), xviii, xlv
Hixson, William B., 29
Ho Chi Minh, 108
Hocutt, Thomas R.
and William Henry Hastie, 151
Holiday, Billie, xxiv
Hollis, Lynch, xli
hooks, bell
quoted, 91
Hope, Lugenia Burns, 55
Hornsby, Alton, 28
Hospital Herald
Alonzo C. McClennan article in, 189
Housewives' League of Detroit, xlv
Houston, Charles Hamilton, xxvi, 120, 150–160 *passim*
advice to Sidney Redmond, 161–162

articles in *Crisis*, 165
biography of, 150–151
as Harvard University Law School graduate, xxii
and Howard Law School, 152–153
leadership of NAACP Legal and Educational Defense Fund, Inc., 154–159
1928 report on the status of the black bar, 153–154
and *Redmond v. University of Tennessee School of Pharmacy*, 159–160
Howard University
School of Law, xxii, 151–153
School of Medicine, xxii, 174, 186, 187
Huggins, Nathan
quoted, 10
Hughes, Langston, xxiv
Hunter, Clementine, 76
Hunter, Tera, 55
Hustchins, Styles L., 163
Hyman, Harold, 29

Incidents in the Life of a Slave Girl (Jacobs), 84
Indian National Movement, 108
Indiana Historical Society, 19
International League of the Darker Peoples, 104
Invisible Man (Ellison), xli

Jacks, James T., 41–42
Jackson, Isalene (sister of Joe W. Trotter), vii
Jackson, Jesse
quoted on quilting, 47
Jackson, Maynard H.
quoted, 150
Jacobs, Harriet, xxv, 35
Incidents in the Life of a Slave Girl, 84, 85–86
Jefferson, Thomas, 131
Jenkins, Earnestine, 122
Johnson, Charles, xxx
Johnson, Ed, 164
Johnson, Michael, 8
Jones, Anne Hudson
and *Black Women in America: An Historical Encyclopedia*, 76
Jones, Jacqueline
and *Black Women in America: An Historical Encyclopedia*, 74
Jones, Rev. Jenkins Lloyd
and founding of Provident Hospital and School of Nursing (Chicago), 45
Jones, Scipio A.
praised by Charles H. Houston in 1928 report on black bar, 153
Jordan, Barbara, 145
Jordan, Winthrop, 90
Journal of Negro History, 15
Just, E.E., xxiv

Keckley, Elizabeth, 35
Kelley, Robin D.G., ix, xix, 123
Kenney, John A., 60, 176

Kent State University
 and Darlene Clark Hine, xli, 4–5
Kerber, Linda
 as editor of *U.S. History as Women's History*, xxvii
Kilson, Robin
 and MIT Black Women in the Academy Conference, 21
Kind of Blue (Miles Davis), 123
King, Coretta Scott, 64
King, Martin Luther Jr., 109, 119, 121, 122, 191
 and Fred D. Gray, xxvi
King, Rodney, 124
King, Stephen, xxx
King, Wilma, 29, 55
 and *Black Women in America: An Historical Encyclopedia*, 74, 78
Krause, Allison, 3

Lamon, Lester
 quoted, 163
Laney, Lucy Craft
 biography of, 61–62
Lawson, Steven, 29
Leadbetter, Rev. E.F., xxxviii
Leonard, Elmore, xxx
Lerner, Gerda, 28, 73
 Black Women in White America: A Documentary History, xxvii, 48, 69
Levine, Lawrence, 123
 Black Culture and Black Consciousness: Afro-American Folk Thought from Slavery to Freedom, 49
Lewis, Earl, ix, xix
 quoted on Norfolk, Virginia, x
Lewis, Samella, 51
Lewis, William H.
 expulsion from the American Bar Association, 162
The Liberator
 and Maria Stewart, 133
Little, Joan, xxv, 84–85, 88
Logan, Rayford, 39, 119
Looby, Z. Alexander
 Charles H. Houston memo to about University of Tennessee desegregation case, 158
 and NAACP National Legal Committee, 157
Lunardini, Christine, 75, 79
Lure and Loathing: Essays on Race, Identity, and the Ambivalence of Assimilation (Early), xxviii
Lynk, M. Vandehurst, 185

McClennan, Alonzo C.
 founder of Charleston Hospital and Nurse Training School, 59
 quoted, 189
McCoy, Cecil
 and William Henry Hastie, 151

McGill, S.D.
 praised by Charles H. Houston in 1928
 report on black bar, 153
McKay, Nellie
 and *Black Women in America: An Historical Encyclopedia*, 74
McLaurin, Melton A.
 quoted on Celia, 86
 Celia, A Slave, 35
McMillan, Terry, xxx
McNeil, Genna Rae
 on Charles H. Houston, 154
Madame C.J. Walker Hair Culturists Union of America
 described, 102–103
Madison, James, 148
 and United States Constitution, 147
Mahoney, Mary Eliza, 171
 biography of, 24–25
Malcolm X, xix, 119, 122, 124
 Autobiography, xl
Malone, Annie Turnbo
 and Madam C.J. Walker, 98
 Poro company of, 96
The Man Who Cried I Am (Williams), xl–xli
March on Washington Movement, 119–120
Marcus, Harold, 14, 29
Marshall, Burke
 quoted, 150
Marshall, Paule, xxx, 48
Marshall, Thurgood, xxvi, xxviii, 120, 122, 167
 and Charles H. Houston, 156, 158
Matera, Lia, xxx
Matthews, Victoria Earle, 55
Mayfield, Robert L.
 barred by Tennessee Bar Association, 163
Mays, Benjamin
 Born to Rebel, xx
Meharry Medical College, xxi–xxii, 174, 186, 187
Meier, August
 and Darlene Clark Hine, xli, xlii
 quoted on Charles H. Houston, 157
Memphis Daily Appeal
 and Ida B. Wells-Barnett, 139
Merritt, Carole
 quoted, 11
Metronome, 118
Michigan State University
 Comparative Black History program, xlviii–xlix, 16–17
 John A. Hannah Professorship, 13–15
Middleton, Delano, 3
Miles: The Autobiography, 115
Miller, Jeff, 3
Mills, C. Wright
 quoted, xiv
Milwaukee
 black community, x
Mississippi Freedom Democratic Party, 144
Missouri ex rel. Gaines v. Canada, 161–162

MIT
  and Black Women in the Academy Conference, 21
Monk, Thelonius
  and Miles Davis, 116
Montgomery bus boycott
  and Fred D. Gray, xxi
Montgomery Improvement Association
  and Fred D. Gray, xxvi
Moody, Ann, 144
Morrison, Toni, xxx, 48
Morton, Patricia
  and negative depictions of black women, 90
Moseley-Braun, Carol, 54
Mosley, Walter, xxx
Motley, Constance Baker
  first black female federal judge, 145

NAACP. *See* National Association for the Advancement of Colored People
NAACP Legal and Educational Defense Fund, Inc., 149, 154
Nabrit, James M. 167
  and Charles H. Houston, 156, 157–158
  and NAACP National Legal Committee, 157
Nash, Gary
  quoted, 10–11
Nash, Dr. Helen, 76
National Anti-Tuberculosis Association, 183
National Association for the Advancement of Colored People, xxvi, 143
  Legal and Educational Defense Fund, Inc., 149, 154
National Association of Colored Graduate Nurses, xxii, xlv, 24, 25, 179–180, 190
  activities of, 43
National Association of Colored Women, 40
National Bar Association, xxii, xxvi, 149, 162, 179
  coming of age in the 1940s, 167
  and elevation of black lawyers's esteem, 164–165
  founding of, 166
National Bar Journal, 167
National Black Nurses Association
  founding of, 180
National Council of Negro Women
  founding of, 143
National Endowment for the Arts, 10, 11
National Endowment for the Humanities, xliv, 10, 11
  and the Black Women in the Middle West Project, 66–67
National Humanities Center, 15
National Labor Conference for Negro Rights
  Paul Robeson speech quoted, 108–109
National League of Nursing Education, 17
National Medical Association, xxii, 179, 190
National Negro Business League, 101, 184
National Negro Cosmetic Manufacturers Association
  charter quoted, 104
  and Madam C.J. Walker, 103
National Negro Health Week movement
  description of, 184
Native Son (Wright), xli
Naylor, Gloria, xxx
Neeley, Barbara, xxx
Nehru, Jawaharlal, 108
Nelson, Jack
  The Orangeburg Massacre quoted, 3–4
Neverdon-Morton, Cynthia, 55
  and *Black Women in America: An Historical Encyclopedia*, 74
New England Hospital for Women and Children, 171
Newman, Richard
  and *Black Women in America: An Historical Encyclopedia*, 78
Newsom, Robert
  and Celia (slave), 86–87
Nixon, Richard, 7
Nixon v. Condon, xlii
Nixon v. Herndon, xlii
Northwest Ordinance (1787)
  quoted, 133
Nurses Associated Alumnae, 24–25

O'Connor, Sandra Day, xxvi
The Orangeburg Massacre (Bass and Nelson)
  quoted, 3–4
Osborne, Estelle Massey
  biography of, 25–26
Owens, Leslie, 8

Painter, Nell Irvin, 13, 28
  and *Black Women in America: An Historical Encyclopedia*, 74, 78
Palmer Memorial Institute
  and Charlotte Hawkins Brown, 62
Parden, Noah W., 163
Paretsky, Sara, xxx
Parker, Charlie "Yard Bird," 121
  and Miles Davis, 116
Parker, Robert B., xxx
Parks, Rosa, 64, 144
  and Fred D. Gray, xxvi
  and the Montgomery bus boycott, xxi
Patterson, James, xxx
Patterson, Orlando, 88
  quoted on Clarence Thomas hearings, 83
Patterson, Tiffany R.L.
  and *Black Women in America: An Historical Encyclopedia*, 74
Pearson, Conrad
  and William Henry Hastie, 151
Perkins, Kathy
  and *Black Women in America: An Historical Encyclopedia*, 74
Perkins, Linda
  quoted, 57–58
Perry, Dennis
  uncle of Darlene Clark Hine, xxxix
Perry, J. Edward
  quoted on nursing, 176–177

Phi Alpha Theta, lii
Plessy v. Ferguson, xlii
Powell, Adam Clayton Jr., 123
 and International League of the Darker
  Peoples, 104
Powers, Harriet
 quilts of, 51
Prosser, Gabriel, 134, 136
Provident Hospital and School of Nursing
  (Chicago)
 founding of, 44–45
Public Health Service
 and Tuskegee syphilis study, 178
Purdue University
 Darlene Clark Hine's career there, xliii

quilts
 and black women, 47–52

Raboteau, Albert, 8
Randolph, A. Philip
 March on Washington Movement, 119–120
Ransom, Freeman B.
 and Madam C.J. Walker, 101–102
Ransom, Leon A., 166, 167
 collaboration with Charles H. Houston, 156
 Charles H. Houston memo to about
  University of Tennessee desegregation case,
  158
 and NAACP National Legal Committee,
  157
 and *Redmond v. University of Tennessee School
  of Pharmacy*, 159
Redd, Lawrence
 and *Black Women in America: An Historical
  Encyclopedia*, 76
Redmond, S.D.
 praised by Charles H. Houston in 1928
  report on black bar, 153
Redmond, Sidney
 and *Missouri ex rel. Gaines v. Canada*, 161–162
Redmond, William B. II
 desegregation case of, 158–159
*Redmond v. University of Tennessee School of
 Pharmacy*, 158–159
Reed, Ismael, xxx
Reed, Linda, 28
 and *Black Women in America: An Historical
  Encyclopedia*, 74
Remond, Sarah Parker
 as anti-slavery activist, 134–135
Reverby, Susan, 28
Reymonds, Emma
 and founding of Provident Hospital and
  School of Nursing (Chicago), 45
Rhodes, Eugene Washington
 quoted, 165
Riddle, Estelle Massey
 and National Association of Colored
  Graduate Nurses, 179–180
Rivers, Eunice
 and the Tuskegee syphilis experiment, xxiii

Roark, James, 8
Robeson, Paul, xxviii, 119, 121
 article about, 105–113
Robinson, Gwendolyn Keita, 29
 and *Black Women in America: An Historical
  Encyclopedia*, 74
 biography of Madam C.J. Walker, 98
Robinson, Jackie, 119
Robinson, Jo Ann, 55, 64, 144
 and the Montgomery bus boycott, xxi
Rockefeller, John D., 100
Rockefeller Foundation, 7, 15
Rockefeller Fund, 177
Rockefeller (Laura Spelman) Memorial Fund
 financed report on the black bar, 153
Rockwell Kent v. John Foster Dulles, 112
Roosevelt, Franklin Delano
 and Executive Order 8802, 119–120
Roosevelt University
 Darlene Clark Hine as student, xxxix–xli
Rose, Lillie (Darlene Clark Hine's Sunday
  school teacher), xxxviii
Rosenberg, Charles E., 190
Rosenwald, Julius, 100
Rosenwald, Julius, Fund, 177, 179, 184
Rouse, Jacqueline, 55
 and *Black Women in America: An Historical
  Encyclopedia*, 74
 and education as priority for black women,
  57
 co-editor of *Women in the Civil Rights
  Movement: Trailblazers and Torchbearers*, 55
Rout, Leslie, 14
Rudwick, Elliott
 quoted on Charles H. Houston, 157

Sanford, John, xxx
Savitt, Todd, 8
Scheuer, Sandy, 3
Schroeder, Bill, 3
Schuyler, George S.
 quoted on Madam C.J. Walker, 96–97
Scott, Anne Firor, 28
Scott, David, 14
*Sentimental Women Need Not Apply: A History
 of American Nursing* (film)
 Darlene Clark Hine appears in, 15
Shaw, Stephanie
 and *Black Women in America: An Historical
  Encyclopedia*, 74
Shelley v. Kraemer, 156
Simpson, Alan
 and Clarence Thomas confirmation hearings,
  88–89
Sims-Wood, Janet
 and *Black Women in America: An Historical
  Encyclopedia*, 74
Sketches in Spain (Miles Davis), 123
Sklar, Kathryn Kish
 as editor of *U.S. History as Women's History*,
  xxvii
The Slave (Baraka), xli

slavery
  and black women, 35–38
Smith, Henry, 3
Smith, Jessie Carney
  distinguished publications of, xxvii
Smith v. Allwright, xlii, 120, 155
Smitherman, Geneva
  edits anthology on Clarence Thomas
    confirmation hearings, xxv
The Souls of Black Folk (Du Bois), 33–34
South Carolina State College
  Darlene Clark Hine teaches there, xli–xlii
Southern Association of Women Historians, 28
Southern Christian Leadership Conference, 149
  voter registration drive, 145
Specter, Arlen
  and Clarence Thomas confirmation hearings, 89
The State of Afro-American History: Past, Present, and Future (Hine), 20
Staupers, Mabel Keaton
  biography of, 25
  and National Association of Colored Graduate Nurses, 43, 179–180
Stettinius, Edward, 106
Steward, Susan McKinney
  biography of, 24
Stewart, Gordon, 14, 29
Stewart, Maria, 33, 57
  quoted 133–134
Stewart-Lai, Carlotta, 76
Stokes, Carl, 120
Stono Rebellion, 136
"Stop the Global Holocaust," (Hine), xlv
Story, Moorfield
  and American Bar Association racial policies, 162–163
Strickland, Arvarh
  and *Black Women in America: An Historical Encyclopedia*, 78
Stuckey, Sterling, 107
Student Nonviolent Coordinating Committee, 149

Taney, Roger B., 87
Tanner, Henry Ossawa, 121
Taylor, Susie King, 23
Tennessee, University of. *See* University of Tennessee
Tennessee Bar Association
  bars Robert L. Mayfield, 163
Terborg-Penn, Rosalyn, 28, 55
  and *The Afro-American Woman: Struggles and Images*, 48
  and *Black Women in America: An Historical Encyclopedia*, xxxi, 72–75, 77
Terrell, Mary Church
  and founding of National Council of Negro Women, 143
  "What it Means to be Colored in the Capital of the United States," 140

Third World Press, xli
Thomas, Clarence
  confirmation hearings of, xxv, 83–93, *passim*
Thompson, Fannie Venerable (grandmother of Darlene Clark Hine), xxxvi–xxxvii
Thompson, Kathleen
  and *Black Women in America: An Historical Encyclopedia*, 79
Till, Emmett, 119
Trotter, Joe W., xix
  Black Milwaukee: The Making of an Industrial Proletariat, 1915–45, viii
  Coal, Class and Color: Blacks in Southern West Virginia, 1915–32, ix
Truth, Sojourner, 23, 48, 75, 99
  and personal identity formation, 38
  quoted, 137–138
Tubman, Harriet, 23, 40, 48, 75, 99
  and personal identity formation, 38
Tureau, Alexander P.
  and NAACP National Legal Committee, 157
Turner, Bishop Henry McNeal, 107
Turner, Nat, 134, 136
Turow, Scott, xxx
Tuskegee syphilis study, xxiii, 178, 187–188
  and Fred D. Gray, xxvi
Tyson, Cicely
  and Miles Davis, 122
Tyson, Mike, 123

United States Constitution. *See* Constitution (U.S.)
Universal Negro Improvement Association, 104
University of Tennessee
  desegregation case of, 158–159

Vesey, Denmark, 134, 136
Vlach, John
  curator of the exhibition "The Afro-American Tradition in Decorative Arts," 50–51
Voting Rights Act of 1965, 143

Walden, A.T.
  praised by Charles H. Houston in 1928
  report on black bar, 153
Walker, A'Lelia (daughter of Madam C.J. Walker), 119
Walker, Alice, xxvi, xxx, 48
Walker, Charles J. (husband of Madam C.J. Walker), 96, 100
Walker, Madam C.J., ix, xxvii
  article about, 95–104
  and Black Women in the Middle West Project, 95
  reasons for success of company, 41
Walker, David, 107
Walker, Maggie Lena
  Elsa Barkley Brown on, 71
Washington, Booker T., xxvii, 40, 95, 175, 176, 183, 184, 188

speech at Atlanta Cotton States and
International Exposition, 100
and Madam C.J. Walker, 95–104, *passim*
Washington, Booker T., Sanitarium (Harlem),
25
Washington, Margaret Murray, 55
Wells-Barnett, Ida B., 40, 57, 70, 99, 119
railroad suit of, 139–140
"What it Means to be Colored in the Capital
of the United States" (Terrell), quoted, 140
Wheatley, Phillis, 33, 48, 75
*When the Truth is Told: Black Women's
Community and Culture in Indiana, 1875–
1950* (Hine), xliv, 18, 66
White, Deborah Gray, 8
and *Black Women in America: An Historical
Encyclopedia*, 74
*Ar'n't I A Woman?: Female Slaves in the
Plantation South*, 35
and negative depictions of black women, 90
quoted on female slaves, 136
White, Walter
quoted, 182
Wilkins, Roy
quoted on Charles H. Houston, 157
Williams, Daniel Hale, 174, 175, 188
and founding of Provident Hospital and
School of Nursing (Chicago), 45
quoted, 189
Williams, Fannie Barrier
and founding of Provident Hospital and
School of Nursing (Chicago), 45
Williams, Fred, 14
Williams, John A., xxx, 120
The Man Who Cried I Am, xl–xli
Williams, Lillian S., 55
and *Black Women in America: An Historical
Encyclopedia*, 74
Williams, Patricia
review of *Black Women in America: An
Historical Encyclopedia*, 54, 79

Williamson, Joel
quoted, 90
Wilson, William Julius, xix
Wilson, Woodrow
telegram to from C.J. Walker agents, 103
"womanism" and "feminism"
Darlene Clark Hine on, l–li
*Women in the Civil Rights Movement:
Trailblazers and Torchbearers* (Crawford,
Woods, Rouse, eds.), 55
Wood, Peter, 8
Woodman, Harold, xliii, 29
Woods, Barbara
co-editor of *Women in the Civil Rights
Movement: Trailblazers and Torchbearers*, 55
Woodson, Carter G.
as black icon, xxiii
graduate of Harvard University, xxii
Woodson, George H.
and National Bar Association, 166
Wretched of the Earth (Fanon), xl
Wright, Judge J. Skelly
quoted 149–150
Wright, Mary
ex-slave quoted on quilting, 51
Wright, Richard, xxx, 120
Native Son, xli
Wyer, Mary
Editor-in-Chief of *Black Women in America:
An Historical Encyclopedia*, 77, 79

Yeakey, Lamont
quoted on Paul Robeson, 106
Young, Whitney
quoted, 182–183
You're Under Arrest (Miles Davis), 124